Teaching a Methods Course in Social Work with Groups

Strengthening Group Work Education

Volume 1

A Series from the

Council on Social Work Education
and
Association for the Advancement of Social Work with Groups

Lawrence Shulman, Series Editor

Teaching a Methods Course in Social Work with Groups

Roselle Kurland and Robert Salmon

Council on Social Work Education

Alexandria, VA

About the Authors

Roselle Kurland, PhD, is a professor at the Hunter College School of Social Work, where she has chaired the group work sequence. Dr. Kurland is editor of the journal *Social Work with Groups*, a member of the board of directors of the Association for the Advancement of Social Work with Groups, and a consultant to a range of social agencies where she works with staff to enhance their skills in group work practice and to develop creative programs.

Robert Salmon, DSW, is a professor at the Hunter College School of Social Work, where he formerly served as the associate dean and the acting dean for a period of 16 years. He teaches courses in social work with groups and administration and recently received the President's Award for Excellence in Teaching. He is a consultant to a variety of organizations and is treasurer and a member of the board of directors of the Association for the Advancement of Social Work with Groups.

Drs. Kurland and Salmon have been colleagues at Hunter College for 20 years. Their collaboration began in the early 1980s when they started to write and present work together. They have co-authored a series of articles on the practice and teaching of group work and co-edited *Group Work Practice in a Troubled Society: Problems and Opportunities* (Haworth, 1995).

Copyright © 1998 by the Council on Social Work Education, Inc.

Reprinted 2005

Library of Congress Cataloging-in-Publication Data

Kurland, Roselle.
    Teaching a methods course in social work with groups / Roselle Kurland and Robert Salmon.
        p. cm. — (Strengthening group work education ; no. 1)
    Includes bibliographical references.
    ISBN 0-87293-060-2
    1. Social group work—Study and teaching—United States. 2. Social group work—United States—Methodology. I. Salmon, Robert, 1930– . II. Title. III. Series.
3. Social work with youth—Congresses. 4. Family social work—Congresses.
HV45.K83 1998
361.4'071'073—dc21   98-11283
                                      CIP

Manufactured in the United States of America.

To our teachers and students, from whom we have learned so much.

To Sheila Salmon, who always is a source of inspiration and support.

We thank Esther Rohatiner and Tatiana Kalinin for their essential help in the preparation of this book.

TABLE OF CONTENTS

SERIES INTRODUCTION
STRENGTHENING GROUP WORK EDUCATION

This book is the first in a series of three joint publications of the Council on Social Work Education and the Association for the Advancement of Social Work with Groups (AASWG). It is the result of a cooperative effort between CSWE and the AASWG Commission for Strengthening Group Work in Social Work Education. The effort began three years ago and has included the development of a network of faculty liaisons across the country who have worked on a local level holding conferences and training programs for interested faculty. Workshops have also been presented at national conferences for social work educators.

In this book, Roselle Kurland and Robert Salmon, two outstanding social group work educators, have shared their knowledge and experience by providing an excellent guide on how to develop a group work practice course. One future volume in this series will explore integrating group work content into the foundation practice course, and a second will explore integrating group work into the field work experience. Roselle and Robert have launched this important effort with their usual display of competence.

Lawrence Shulman
Chair, AASWG Commission for
Strengthening Group Work in Social Work Education
Dean, School of Social Work,
State University of New York at Buffalo

INTRODUCTION

Social group work is a very positive and optimistic way of working with people. It is truly empowering and affirming of people's strengths. In fact, the very act of forming a group is a statement of belief in people's strengths and in the contribution that each person can make to others' lives. In today's troubled world, effective group work is needed more than ever. This volume has been prepared in response to this need. It is intended to assist social work faculty in preparing students for competent practice in social work with groups.

Among the most helpful definitions of the small group as conceptualized in social work are those of Margaret Hartford (1971) and William Schwartz (1971).

Hartford defines a small group as:

> at least two people—but usually more—gathered with common purposes or like interests in a cognitive, affective, and social interchange in single or repeated encounters sufficient for the participants to form impressions of one another, creating a set of norms for their functioning together, developing goals for their collective activity, evolving a sense of cohesion so that they think of themselves and are thought of by others as an entity distinct from all other collectivities.
> ...This definition takes account of size, location, frequency of meetings, purpose for convening, and goals for group activity which emerge out of the interaction. It also contains the notion of mutual influence, the adoption of group norms, and the establishment of group cohesiveness that grows out of the members' attachment to one another and to the group-as-a-whole. (p. 26)

Schwartz's concise definition of a group captures the interrelationship between group members and the agency: "A collection of people who need each other in order to work on certain common tasks, in an agency that is hospitable to those tasks" (p. 7).

The values inherent in group work practice can be specified and transmitted. The knowledge and techniques that are the foundation of good practice in social work with groups can be explicated and taught. Effective instructors will impart these values, knowledge, and skills, sharing their excitement about the method and serving as role models of competent group work practice. In particular, instructors' knowledge of the literature and demonstration of useful group skills in teaching are effective in preparing students for practice. This book serves primarily as a resource for faculty teaching group work courses, although its materials can help faculty in related disciplines.

The authors teach in a school that requires three courses in group work for group work majors and one methods course in group work practice for students majoring in casework, community organization, or administration. The one-semester methods course covers the key subject areas taught in one academic year to group work majors. The goal of the course is to provide nonmajors with an overview of groups and their characteristics from the pre-group stage through termination. The course explores issues and themes that commonly arise during each stage of group development and the corresponding roles of the worker. In addition, it covers the roots of social group work practice, the relationship between agency function and professional values and knowledge, and the impact that cultural, institutional, and developmental factors have on group life. The course described in this book is based on the one-semester group work course that is offered. However, we have added additional content here. It is not likely that in a single semester an instructor could use all of the material that is presented in this book. Even if not used directly with students, however, the material provides the instructor with a foundation of knowledge that may be influential in his or her approach to teaching and presentations in the classroom.

Social workers work with many kinds of groups. Socialization groups, cognitive behavioral groups, therapy groups, task groups, educational groups, behavior modification groups, support groups, supervisory groups, and administrative groups are all important. Our aim is to examine the commonalities of knowledge and skills needed to work effectively with a range of groups. Starting from this foundation, students can then build the specialized knowledge and skills needed for work with a particular type of group or theoretical approach. We believe that the commonalities should be the focus of a one-semester course. To try to cover more in a single course risks creating a survey course that does not allow students to develop depth of understanding and skill. We believe this book distills the values, knowledge, and skills most crucial to beginning practice in social work with groups.

The one-semester course in group work described in this book is presented in the form of teaching units that often require more than one class period. At the end of each unit, a list of suggested readings is provided that reflects and illuminates the material covered in that unit. These are included for their potential usefulness both to the instructor and to creating student assignments. Two of the 10 appendices are presented as background material for the instructor; one covers models of group work practice, the other covers issues confronting group work. An extensive select bibliography is included in Appendix C for further reading materials for students and faculty. The remaining appendices comprise a list of suggested assignments and the handouts used in the classroom.

Teaching Approaches

The principle of *equifinality*, so important to systems theory, states that one may take a variety of paths to reach a single goal. Knowing the ultimate destination, however, is essential. Crucial to the development of a group work course is clarity in regard to its aims. Such clarity around goals allows instructors to use different methodologies and styles in a teaching course. Simply put: Clarity of ends permits diversity of means. For example, faculty may vary in the degree to which they make use of didactic methods, student records and experiences, role playing, videotapes and films, and problem solving in the classroom. But because knowing the destination is crucial, each unit in this book begins with a specification of its objectives.

The approaches to teaching that we value are demonstrated in the teaching units. Above all, we want students to think for themselves and to take responsibility for their own ideas. We try to spur students' appreciation of the complexity of the ideas, situations, and problems inherent to groups and group work. We try to challenge their thinking, especially when they arrive at solutions to problems, questions, or issues too easily, too quickly— solutions that do not account for situational complexities. We believe that knowing how to think through problems, issues, and questions is more important than knowing the answers. The classroom should be a place where students can struggle with ideas together. We ask students to challenge one another, not competitively to show how bright they are, but in a spirit of collegial cooperation. We ask them to work together in confronting real issues for which there are no easy answers. We believe this common struggle toward understanding is more effective in helping students gain competence in group work than are experiential exercises imposed upon them or examinations of the class as a group. This common struggle, which contributes to the group feeling, characterizes our own classes and is reflected in this volume.

Our approach to students is simultaneously demanding and supportive. We expect a lot from students while we foster their professional growth. As we make substantial demands of them, as we take them and their work seriously, as we hold them accountable for their learning and thinking, they begin to do the same for themselves and one another. The assignments presented here are intended to help accomplish this as they meet the goals and purpose of this course. The assignments, such as those found in Appendix D, contribute to each student's growth and development as a practitioner of social work with groups in individualized ways.

References

Hartford, Margaret E. (1971). *Groups in Social Work*. New York: Columbia University Press.

Schwartz, William. (1971). On the Use of Groups in Social Work Practice. In William Schwartz & Serapio Zalba (Eds.), *The Practice of Group Work* (pp. 3-34). New York: Columbia University Press.

Unit 1
Launching the Course

The way an instructor begins a course is particularly important. It sets the tone, creates an environment for learning, and builds expectations for what is to follow. Although a class is not a social work group, the two are similar. In this case, how the instructor conducts the first class sessions models for students how they might conduct their first group meetings. Several class meetings will be required to set the course foundation. During these initial sessions, the instructor needs to

- describe course expectations,
- provide opportunities for students to gain a sense of one another and of the instructor,
- discuss the importance, values, and unique qualities of the small group in today's world, and
- enable students to see that they all share common fears and concerns about working with groups.

This teaching unit has five objectives for students:

1. To become familiar with the expectations of the course.
2. To begin to get to know the instructor and the other students in the class.
3. To consider the values of the small group.
4. To see that having fears about working with groups is normal.
5. To understand the mutual-aid feature of group work practice.

All students enter a course such as this one with three areas of concern. First, they wonder what the course is about: what material will be covered, how it will be covered (i.e., whether it will be conducted with the class as a group), what the reading and assignments will be, and what will be asked of them, both in the class and outside it. Second, they wonder about the instructor: what she or he will be like, what classroom style will be used, and what perspectives and experiences she or he will bring to bear.

Finally, they wonder about their classmates: what they will be like and whether they will fit in with them.

It is difficult to address all three of these pressing student concerns in depth in the first class session. Students certainly want to know and may even be anxious about what the course will demand of them, especially in regard to reading and assignments. But if the instructor engages in a full discussion of this, it will occupy most of the first session, making introductions cursory and secondary in importance. On the other hand, if introductions are done first, and in a meaningful way, there may not be enough time to discuss course requirements and expectations. Given this dilemma, we suggest the following sequence. First, instructors can speak *briefly* about the purpose, organization, and expectations of the course. Next, instructors can introduce themselves, and finally they can ask the students to introduce themselves.

We suggest starting with a brief course description because this is generally students' primary concern. Also, in any new group the members welcome a chance to observe and avoid being put on the spot immediately. As the instructor describes the course, the students have a chance to sit and listen, ask questions if they wish, and become more comfortable in the new class. In regard to introductions, we suggest that the instructor speak first, because students might feel unsure of the instructor's style and expectations and would be called upon to take a difficult risk when speaking first. By following the instructor, students can match the content and style of the instructor's introduction at a time when they might be uncertain about what to say.

In describing the course to students, we emphasize the purpose, organization, and presentation of the course:

• *Course Purpose.* We view the course as having two major purposes: to increase students' appreciation of, knowledge about, and skill in social work with groups (including group work's history and value base); and to increase students' level of comfort in group work practice. Basically, our aim is to cover the commonalities of knowledge and skills social workers need to effectively use a psychosocial practice approach with a variety of groups. From this foundation, students can then build the specialized knowledge and skills needed for work that is more specific to a particular type of group or theoretical approach.

• *Course Organization and Presentation.* The stages of group development, from pre-group planning through termination, provide the organizing framework for the course. The content covers the characteristics and themes of each developmental stage, the issues likely to arise in each, and the implications for worker role and interventions in each. A range of instruction methods are used: lecture, group discussion, experiential exercises (such as role play, group problem solving, and brainstorming), examination of case material and scenarios, and videotapes. Although there are similarities between a class and a group, the emphasis is placed on learning from didactic material rather than from examining internal class processes as the primary exemplar of group development.

At this point, we refer to the course bibliography (see Appendix C), which includes the basic texts used, and we briefly describe the course assignments. We let students know that the readings and assignments will be discussed at greater length after introductions.

Introductions

Each instructor's style and predilections will determine the amount of personal information and professional experience shared with students in the introduction. Although introductory statements vary, their purpose is to help students start to gain a sense of the instructor as a person and as a teacher who has the competence to conduct the class.

It is important for instructors to include in the introduction some statements about groups, about their beliefs around teaching and learning, and about the atmosphere they want to create in the class. We include the following statements in our introductions.

• My belief is that work with groups is fun—serious work, but fun. The process of social work with groups is orderly because it is sequential. That is, all groups go through *stages* as they develop: planning, beginning, middle, and end. In each of these, specific issues arise (for example, conflict, vying for status, establishment of norms), and these issues determine the role of the social worker—that is, what you need to do.

• Many people believe that the ability to work with a group is "in your blood," that either you have it or you don't; and if you don't, it cannot be transfused. I believe, however, that work with groups requires knowledge and skills that can be learned and can be taught.

• I also believe that there are many more commonalities than differences involved in working with groups which have different populations and are in different settings. In this course, we will address a variety of types of groups in a range of settings with a range of client populations.

• In regard to my style of teaching and this class, I like to think of myself as a teacher who is simultaneously demanding and supportive. I place great value on your thinking. I believe a good teacher is someone who can make you think, stretch, and ask, examine and answer questions you did not think you could answer. I value trying to stimulate your thinking. In doing that, I hope you will come to appreciate the difficulty, complexity, pleasure, and excitement of working with groups.

• As for the class itself, it is important that we create an atmosphere of cooperation rather than competition. It's important that people *not* try to look smart, to look good. It's important that people really listen and hear and try to help one another. It's important that people be willing to share, to risk, to not be afraid to "look stupid."

After these introductory statements, we read a poem by R. D. Laing (1972, p. 56) that captures the essence of our comments about the class atmosphere.

> There is something I don't know
> that I am supposed to know.
> I don't know what it is I don't know,
> and yet am supposed to know,
> and I feel I look stupid
> if I seem both not to know it
> and not know what it is I don't know.
> Therefore I pretend I know it.
> This is nerve-wracking
> since I don't know what I must pretend to know.
> Therefore I pretend to know everything.
>
> I feel you know what I am supposed to know
> but you can't tell me what it is
> because you don't know that I don't know what it is.
>
> You may know what I don't know, but not
> that I don't know it,
> and I can't tell you. So you will have to tell me everything.

Student Introductions

In the first meeting of any group, a leader needs to provide structure and direction. This is an important principle when students are asked to introduce themselves. The manner in which an instructor has introduced himself or herself will provide a model for student introductions. At this point in the class, the instructor needs to offer students additional direction. Without structure and boundaries, students may say too much, including material that is too intimate for a first class session, or they may be perfunctory. We suggest that students use their introductions to comment on the genesis of their interest in groups, their experience as group members and/or leaders, and any special interests they may have in regard to groups. Even with this direction, however, the unexpected may occur.

For example, one semester the first student to introduce herself said movingly,

> "My name is Jane. I became interested in groups when my baby died in the hospital shortly after birth. Almost immediately I was asked to join a group dealing with loss. That group experience, I really believe, is what helped me to preserve my sanity. In fact, I have now been leading these kinds of groups in the hospital for several years. I'm in school because I want to learn to be better at leading groups. . . ." Richard, the next student, then said, "My name is Richard. I had not planned to say this, but after hearing what Jane said, I will tell you that I'm here because I joined a group after my brother committed suicide. After that I went into group therapy and it really helped me." The next student said, almost embarrassed, "My name is Ellen and I just got out of college. You all are so experienced and I've had none."

Even such an unexpected and difficult sequence of introductory statements presents teaching opportunities for the instructor. The instructor need not say much, perhaps simply acknowledge the importance of experiences which students bring to the class. The instructor also models the importance of each class member. In this instance, the instructor confirmed the power of Jane's motivation, thanked Richard for his comments, and pointed out to Ellen, through back-and-forth questioning, that her life experience had in fact included much group participation. Other class members were encouraged by the instructor to ask questions of their classmates as they made their introductions. Where appropriate, the instructor can also underscore the commonalities among the students. In so doing, the instructor models a group work skill crucial in the beginning stage.

Course Orientation

After the student introductions, the instructor can discuss the course bibliography, basic textbooks, and assignments in detail and answer students' questions about them. Our bibliography and basic texts are presented in Appendix C. The assignments that we use in our classes are in Appendix D. Certainly, alternative readings and assignments can be tailored to meet the particular needs of each class.

Group Values

The use of groups has grown immensely in the recent past, perhaps in response to the increasing depersonalization in society, the growing feelings of powerlessness, and a decreasing sense of community. After becoming familiar with the course expectations, the instructor, and one another, we ask students about the values of the small group and what groups offer their members that is unique. Their responses generally fall into the following areas:

- *Sharing.* People feel less isolated and more reassured when they find their feelings are shared by others. ("You mean I'm not the only one who feels that way? What a relief!")

- *Identification.* People can readily identify with others in the same situation. ("I feel just like you do.")

- *Peer Help.* People tend to accept help more readily from peers than from those in positions of authority. ("If it worked for you, maybe it will for me, too.")

- *Mutual Aid.* People are often able to help others who have encountered the same or similar situations, resulting in increased self-esteem for the helper. ("I faced the same problem. The way I handled it was. . . .")

- *Testing.* People can test themselves out in different roles in the group—as leaders, members, helpers, and helpees.

- *Social Exchange and Acceptance.* People are social beings who need social exchange, to be accepted, to belong, to have a place among others. The group affords such a place of exchange and acceptance.

* *Getting Things Done.* People in groups may experience power in numbers, finding that they can succeed in social action when an individual, working alone, might not succeed.

During this discussion, it is a good idea for the instructor to ask students to give examples, if they can, that illustrate the values enumerated, and to give her or his own examples. The acceptance that members find in a group is especially important to emphasize in this beginning session, for it is a quality the instructor wants to help establish in the class itself.

We read aloud an example to illustrate the acceptance that a member might feel in a group.

> A group of 11- and 12-year-old sixth-grade girls had been meeting twice a week for five months. Their worker asked them if they'd like to use some time in the group to talk about sexuality. "Oh, no," Mary responded immediately. "In school, Mrs. Thomas [their teacher] keeps a book in the back of the room and any time we wish we can look things up." The other girls in the group nodded in agreement and indicated they felt no need to discuss sex in this group. The worker was surprised, but did not pursue the subject. At the start of the next group meeting, Joann, another of the group members, said to the worker, "We've been talking and we just have one question about sex." At that point the group became quite involved in asking questions they had about sex and their own development. In the course of the discussion, the word "breast" was mentioned a number of times. Anna, a group member who had been quiet up to this point, finally spoke. "What's a breast?" she asked. The other members and the worker responded to her question seriously and without making fun of her lack of knowledge.

This example illustrates that a group can provide a place where its members can truly be themselves—not striving to look good and not being afraid that they will be rejected by their peers for saying a wrong thing. We point out that anyone who has been a member of a group in which they have been able to truly be themselves and know that they will be accepted is fortunate, and that membership in such a group is empowering for all its participants.

We also use another example of acceptance and inclusion. We ask the students to think about past classes and consider: "How many times have you raised your hand to make a comment, only to pull it down before being called upon because you had doubts about the comment and didn't want to sound stupid?" Usually class members nod and it is apparent that they identify with this situation. "In a good group," we tell them, "a member would not be fearful of making a comment that might sound stupid because even if it were, this person would know rejection would not follow." As we did after reading the poem, we emphasize here that we hope that norms of acceptance, honesty, and directness will develop in this class.

Then, to summarize this discussion of group work values, we read some quotations that reflect our thoughts about why groups develop, what needs they serve, and why they are effective.

> Man is a social animal, primarily concerned with survival and secondarily with a need to belong to others of his kind. Belonging to a group actually seems to assist in meeting the primary need of survival. . . . As in other species, the individual's survival is often dependent on the group.
>
> Isolation is a condition man does not choose. If forced to experience isolation for long periods of time during his developmental years, he would suffer severe social and psychological impairment. (Brandler & Roman, p. 2)

> Identity formation, validation of self, acceptance, support, and effective communication are necessary for human survival. How to meet those needs is learned initially through the primary group (family) and continually reinforced or changed through other significant secondary groups (peer groups). The effectiveness of meeting these needs determines the quality of an individual's life. Therefore, the group modality becomes an effective secondary societal force in developing the ability to negotiate need gratification more effectively both within the individual and between the individual and his cultural environment.
>
> What, then, is a group? Let us conceive for a moment of the group as an entity, a separate living being, a being with its own personality composed of many separate and unique parts, each part contributing to the

whole. Like the personality of a person, it is multi-faceted. It has a total personality all its own and distinct from any other. (Brandler & Roman, p. 3)

Fears about Group Work

Using this material as background, we next address the attitudes most students, and even most workers, have about group work. Generally, people approach group work with fear, and it is important that students have a chance to put their fears on the table. Doing so enables them to benefit from some of the values of the group, for they see that their fears are shared by others in the class and are then able to identify with their peers. This *I'm not the only one* phenomenon fosters a general sense of acceptance and relief. Discussing fears with a light touch helps students, who may be anxious, to begin to laugh at themselves. To encourage students to talk about their fears, we read from a past student log.

> The problem is I am extremely uncomfortable in the role of worker in a group situation. . . . I like to work with people on a one-to-one basis, behind closed doors, and without a tape recorder. Admittedly, this is a situation in which my process recording,[1] which should follow the theme of "I said, she said, I said, she said" occasionally goes more like, "I said, she said, I said, she said, I *should* have said. . . ." It's fairly obvious that at times I lack self-confidence in my abilities as a social worker, so if I screw up an interview, I don't want a big audience.

We tell students that *all* people approach group work with some fears, and that this is to be expected. Then we ask them what some of their own fears are, what they envision as the worst possible things that might happen when they imagine themselves working with a group. Students usually respond eagerly to these questions and their responses are often laced with humor.

> "Nobody will come," Lenny immediately said in response to my questions. "No, no, no, not that nobody will come. They'll come to the first meeting, but then

---

[1] Appendix E provides an outline for a group process recording.

nobody will come back to the second one," Joan jumped in. "Yes, right, nobody will come back," Bob said forcefully. "That's not what worries me," said Natalie. "What worries me is that nobody will talk." "Or one person will keep talking and I won't know how to shut him up," Glen said. "The members will get into a fight and I won't be able to stop it," Lois added. "No, no, they won't fight with each other but they'll get mad at me," Paul said. "Or nobody in the group will listen to me, the group will get out of control, I'll have to tell my supervisor about it, and she'll think I'm totally incompetent," Marie added. As the students talked, I listed their fears on the blackboard for everyone to see.

The fears that students enumerate fall generally into seven categories:

- fear that the worker will lose control of the group,
- fear that group members will exhibit excessive hostility,
- fear that members will act out,
- fear that members will be unmanageably resistant,
- fear that members will be overwhelmingly dependent upon the worker,
- fear that the group will disintegrate, and
- fear that agency staff will judge the worker to be inadequate.

All of the fears discussed and described do not need to be handled in detail at this time. That is not the aim here. Rather, we tell students that by the end of the semester they will have developed greater skill than they can now imagine to deal with the behaviors of group members that have sparked their current fears.

We also point out that many of their fears are related to the role of authority they must assume as workers with a group, and to their perceived notion that they must—and can—control and direct all that takes place in the group. Here, we emphasize that the group itself often will "rescue" the worker in difficult situations when the worker does not know what to do or say. We let students know that one of the joys of working with groups is that the worker does not have to carry the weight of the group alone, that one can "have faith in the group."

We emphasize that mutual aid, the process through which group members help one another and the total group, is unique to social group work practice and means, among other things, that the worker with a group does not have to be all-knowing or to have all the answers, that the worker can share ideas and reactions with the group honestly and directly and ask members to engage in mutual problem-solving. We let students know that mutual aid is a concept that we will examine throughout the semester whose meaning and use will grow for them throughout this course.

Readings

Brandler, Sondra, & Roman, Camille P. (1991). Introduction. In *Group Work: Skills and Strategies for Effective Interventions* (pp. 1-13). New York: Haworth.

Getzel, George, Kurland, Roselle, & Salmon, Robert. (1987). Teaching and Learning the Practice of Social Group Work: Four Curriculum Tools. In Joseph Lassner, Kathleen Powell, & Elaine Finnegan (Eds.), *Social Group Work: Competence and Values in Practice* (pp. 35-50). New York: Haworth.

Laing, R. D. (1972). *Knots.* New York: Vintage.

Northen, Helen. (1988). *Social Work with Groups* (2nd ed., pp. 1-15). New York: Columbia University Press.

Schwartz, William. (1971). On the Use of Groups in Social Work Practice. In William Schwartz & Serapio Zalba (Eds.), *The Practice of Group Work* (pp. 3-24). New York: Columbia University Press.

Shulman, Lawrence. (1992). The Group as a Mutual Aid System. *The Skills of Helping Individuals, Families, and Groups* (3rd ed., pp. 273-289). Itasca, IL: Peacock.

UNIT 2
THE EVOLUTION OF GROUP WORK

Group work is a key method of practice in social work. But the proportion of social workers with expertise in work with groups is and always has been small in relation to the proportion of social workers whose expertise and primary interest lie in one-on-one work with individuals. Initially, group workers' primary concerns and perspectives were different from those of the social workers who practiced casework. These two conditions—group work's minority status within social work and its different point of view—were central in the historical evolution of the group work method, and they continue to influence group work practice today.

In the 19th century, religious groups were central in developing social welfare agencies and the concept of charity that informed the activities of the early casework practitioners. They conveyed a moralistic attitude toward the poor, emphasizing the need for individual rehabilitation. Others, the social reformers and socialists of the time, believed that a change in the social order was needed. The early group workers were aligned with those who believed in the need for social reform rather than those upholding individual or moral transformation. Thus, the motivations of the early group workers and caseworkers differed. This divergence affected the practice methods initially adopted by group workers and caseworkers and their evolution over the decades.

In their early days, group workers were men and women who believed they could make positive differences in the lives of the people with whom they worked by helping to instigate social change. They did not identify themselves clearly as social workers at this early time. Gisela Konopka (1983) captures this early perspective:

> Group work as a method of social work is a fairly recent concept. Originally, it was conceived of as a movement, a way of democratic action, and a part of several fields of social services. Foremost among these were informal education, youth services, camping, the labor movement, settlement houses, and community centers. (p. 2)

As part of a basic course on group work, this unit introduces students to the importance of the historical evolution of the group work method. We want to help students appreciate the connection between its philosophical foundations and current group work methods. We also want students to understand that some of the original concerns and perspectives of group workers prevail today.

This teaching unit has three objectives for students:

1. To become familiar with the history of group work.
2. To understand the definition of group work that emphasizes the needs of both individuals and society, and of both individual group members and the total group.
3. To become familiar with some of the issues and controversies that confront group work today.

We begin this unit by presenting to the class important historical highlights of the group work method. Thorough discussions of the history of group work have been prepared by Gisela Konopka (1983), Ruth Middleman and Gale Goldberg Wood (1983, 1990), Scott Briar (1971), Stanley Wenocur and Michael Reisch (1989), and Charles Garvin (1997), among others, and we draw on their material extensively in presenting the following highlights.

• Around the turn of the century, a lively—even tumultuous—period of progressive reform provided rich soil for the growth of the group work method. The self-help and recreational organizations of the time, such as settlement houses, YMCAs, Jewish centers, and youth-serving agencies, were contexts for the method's conception and development. These organizations were concerned with building character, socializing immigrants and young people, establishing needed services (e.g., kindergartens and adult education), and fostering social change and social justice. Much of the work of these agencies was with European immigrants. Some have suggested that service to African Americans was very much neglected. Although these organizations were influenced by early social workers, their identification with the profession was ambivalent because they were often focused upon informal education and recreation.

• Early group work valued and encouraged social participation and social change, the democratic process, and personal growth and learning. The major work of the group-serving agencies was with "normal" individuals rather than with the "maladjusted" or "troubled." A far smaller use of group work emerged, as well, in hospitals, where the method was employed to address the needs of physically or mentally ill people. Evidence of tension between these two emphases—drawing on the strengths of community members to improve their social environments and their opportunities for interaction, and working with the ill to improve their health/mental health status—was to surface in the decades to follow and can still be found today.

• Within social work, specializations in the group work method began to develop in the 1920s. The first course in group work was taught at Western Reserve University in 1923. A group work literature began to develop, spurred by such writers as Mary Follet, a political scientist, and Eduard Lindeman, a philosopher and social reformer (see Follet, 1942, and Lindeman, 1936). Most important was the writing of Grace Coyle, a sociologist whose 1930 work *Social Process in Organized Groups* developed a conceptual framework for understanding groups. Coyle identified group components such as objectives, membership, time, space, leadership, communication, decision making, and *esprit de corps* that guided thinking about groups. Also of crucial importance was the work of educator John Dewey. His writings on collective thinking and the problem-solving process (covered in Unit 5) influenced social group work. Finally, Wilbur Newstetter, then director at Western Reserve, provided the enduring definition of group work at the 1935 National Conference of Social Work.

Before continuing our presentation of group work's historical highlights, we ask the class to focus on Newstetter's definition. Newstetter researched and wrote about the small group and its therapeutic use in furthering the "social adjustment" of those having difficulty functioning in society. His 1935 groundbreaking definition of group work has provided a foundation for other group work writers to the current day. We ask students to read Newstetter's paper, "What Is Social Group Work?" which marked the first attempt to define the method. We ask students to note, as they read more current group work writing, the influence of Newstetter's conceptualization.

Newstetter's definition is significant because it places simultaneous emphasis on individual and social objectives, a hallmark of group work practice. In discussing Newstetter's paper in class, we accent the following two passages:

> Group work may be defined as an educational process emphasizing (1) the development and social adjustment of an individual through voluntary group association; and (2) the use of this association as a means of furthering other socially desirable ends. It is concerned therefore with both individual growth and social results. Moreover, it is the combined and consistent pursuit of both these objectives, not merely one of them, that distinguishes group work as a process. (p. 291)

> Unless there is the combined and consistent pursuit of both objectives [individual growth and social ends], the efforts do not fall entirely within this concept of group work. The underlying social-philosophical assumption is that individualized growth and social ends are interwoven and interdependent; that individuals and their social environment are equally important. (pp. 296–297)

We ask students to think about social work groups with which they are currently working or have worked in the past and to articulate how those groups illustrate the dual emphasis identified by Newstetter. Often, students are well aware of the ways in which their group work efforts are geared toward the growth of individual members; class discussion also enhances their recognition and appreciation of the *social* aims of their work with groups.

Group Work and Professional Politics

The place of group workers within professional social work became an issue in the 1930s. With their major emphasis on democracy, social change, and the social community, group workers felt themselves to be a minority within social work. They had not developed a collective consciousness about themselves as social work professionals. Because casework dominated the graduate curriculum and professional practice, and because employers did not require the social work degree, group workers did not tend to get professional education. We read aloud two passages that capture the sense of the times.

> Group workers were different, often were thought of as unprofessional by the caseworkers. They worked at night, even venturing into the 'bad' neighborhoods, were out of the office more than behind the desk, and went camping with their group members. They were women who didn't wear hats and men in plaid shirts without suitcoats and neckties. They were workers who

enjoyed having a meal or a party with their people, who used activities like singing and dancing, who weren't neutral but shared their beliefs. . . . They were workers whose work may have appeared chaotic and not so controlled, who encouraged the community to vote and become active in political and current affairs, for they were concerned with action and social issues. (Middleman, 1992, p. 26)

The problem of acceptance by other social work practitioners was felt by many group workers. The scorn exhibited toward 'those workers who play with children,' 'run dances,' 'go camping,' or 'teach arts and crafts' is well remembered. In 1936 it was reported that the California Conference of Social Work seriously questioned whether group workers were social workers. Faculty members of the School of Social Service Administration of the University of Chicago minced no words in their exclusion of any study of an activity remotely connected with recreation. The general population of the country was still dominated by the 'Protestant ethic.' (Wilson, 1976, p. 25)

Group work solidified its identification and place within social work in the 1940s. Because they felt unwelcome in the caseworker-dominated American Association of Social Workers, the sole national professional organization of the time, group workers began to organize themselves. Their struggle for professional recognition led them in 1946 to establish their own professional organization, the American Association of Group Workers. The establishment of the AAGW, however, did not signal a movement to start a separate profession. In fact, the statement of one group work leader of the time, Harleigh Trecker, was representative of the predominant view of those in group work: "Group Work is a method in social work. . . not a profession. Social work is the profession" (1944, p. 4).

Also in 1946, two leading schools had established group work sequences: the New York School of Social Work (later to become the Columbia University School of Social Work) and the University of Pittsburgh School of Social Work. Many other schools followed this pattern. Of major importance in group work's identification with social work were two 1946 papers by Grace Coyle, which were published the following year. The first, "Group Work as a Method in Recreation," clearly and finally separated group work from recreation. The second, "On Becoming Profes-

sional," helped group workers develop a professional consciousness by clearly identifying group work with social work, rather
than with informal education. In 1949, the first group work text-
book was published, *Social Group Work Practice* by Gertrude Wilson and Gladys Ryland.

Therapeutic Group Work

The decade of the 1950s witnessed another important debate
among group workers, the seeds of which were planted in the
early 1900s and the fruition of which continues to this day. The
debate concerned the relative emphasis given to "traditional"
group work, which was practiced in community agencies and
emphasized social participation and problem prevention, as opposed to "therapeutic" group work, which was increasingly practiced in psychiatric and medical settings. During this decade,
Robert Vinter (1959) advocated that greater priority be given to
therapeutic group work. He described group approaches using
concepts more familiar to casework, viewing the group as a vehicle to achieve treatment goals related to the diagnoses of individual group members.

Group work's commitment to social work became clear and
irrevocable in 1955 when it joined other specialized social work
organizations to form one professional body, the National Association of Social Workers (NASW). We read to the class a passage
from Helen Harris Perlman's (1965) review of group work's evolution during the first decade of this union.

> Group work has burst the too narrow seams of its bas-
> ketball uniform and arts-and-crafts smocks; increasingly
> it appears in the contrasting symbolic garments that
> bespeak the poles of its present scope—the authority-
> cool white coats of hospital and clinical personnel and
> the play-it-cool windbreaker of the street-corner gang
> worker. . . . Group work is increasingly involved with
> the persons, places, problems and even some of the
> processes that not too long ago were assumed to "be-
> long" to case work. (p. 169)

Theoretical advances occurred in the late 1950s and 1960s
with the publication of a number of important group work textbooks and the development of several practice models (see Appendix A). Ironically, these advancements occurred simultaneously
with events that ultimately weakened group work teaching and
practice. In 1962, NASW changed its structure, eliminating orga-

nizational units based on method. As a result, group workers lost their method-specific voice in NASW. Simultaneously, the Council on Social Work Education (CSWE) decided to move toward an integrated method curriculum and adopted curriculum standards that required schools of social work to emphasize the generic in social work practice. These moves were intended to consolidate social workers under one profession and strengthen professional identification.

The idea that social workers should be able to practice more than one method skillfully, and that schools should adopt appropriate curricula, found appeal. Many respected educators and professionals, including group workers, became advocates of this viewpoint. Others, however, remained adamantly opposed. We read to the class one divergent view, expressed by Ruth Smalley (1967):

> Sufficient difference has been identified for each of the methods to suggest that a two-year process concentration in one method, class and field, would ordinarily be necessary to produce even a beginning practice skill. To attempt to prepare students in a "generic social work method" for "generic social work practice" seems. . . to ignore the complexities and the differences of the several methods and to run counter to the way learning of skill in social work practice most surely takes place. . . . All schools have the obligation. . . to prepare students with an appreciation and understanding of all methods, and a capacity for a flexible use of method, without sacrifice of depth of knowledge and skill in one. The point being made here is that what is generic to all social work method can be learned and can *best* be learned in a single method, mastered in some depth, rather than through exposure to or a more superficial experience in several. (pp. 294–295)

This became the minority view, however, and generic teaching became the mainstream. This educational shift was a disaster for group work, as teaching about group work theory and practice diminished.

Challenge and Recovery

Throughout the 1970s and to the present time, CSWE has required schools of social work to prepare students for generalist practice. As a result, many believe that students are graduating with inadequate knowledge and understanding of groups and group work practice. In a sobering research paper, Martin Birnbaum and Charles Auerbach (1994) present evidence that most graduate students never take a group work course and do not have experience working with groups in the field. Yet, as professional social workers they are likely to practice with groups. Because graduate education has practically eliminated group work as a specialized area of study, the specific beliefs, knowledge, and skills that are the hallmark of group work are rapidly disappearing from professional practice, even as group work remains an important area of practice.

Although during the last three decades CSWE has continued to emphasize the integration of direct practice methods, a group of practitioners and educators have remained committed to the development of work with groups. Concerned about the diminution of group work in the curriculum and the resulting poor quality of group work practice in the field, they felt similar to those who founded the AAGW in 1946—determined to protect and promote group work's unique values and methods. This led to two crucial events in the late 1970s. The first was the creation in 1978 of the journal *Social Work with Groups*, which focused on group work practice and theory and provided a forum for those interested in group work to share, discuss, and develop their experience and ideas. Second was the 1979 creation of the Association for the Advancement of Social Work with Groups (AASWG), an organization committed to furthering group work within the profession. The initial activity of this fledgling organization was sponsorship of a 1979 symposium on group work. In testimony to the ongoing, even passionate, interest of those committed to work with groups, more than 400 participants from around the country came together in Cleveland for this initial event. Since then, the AASWG has sponsored annual symposia bringing together social workers from around the world to explore group work's past, present, and future. Local AASWG chapters are active in geographic areas throughout this country and abroad, and AASWG has worked with national social work organizations to revitalize group work teaching and practice.[1]

---

[1] In fact, AASWG's work with CSWE has resulted in this publication and two others that will discuss group work content in generic practice courses and group work teaching in field work.

Group work's evolution is important for students to understand and appreciate because it underscores the unique points of
view that the method brought to social work practice. Knowledge of its history gives students a context within which to place
group work practice today. Many of the issues that confront
group work today reflect the method's history and evolution.
Although the limitations of time may not allow current issues to
be fully considered in class, they are identified and discussed in
Appendix B to enhance the instructor's awareness.

Readings

Berman-Rossi, Toby, & Miller, Irving. (1994). African-Americans
    and the Settlements during the Late Nineteenth and Early Twen-
    tieth Centuries. *Social Work with Groups, 17*(3), 77-95.

Birnbaum, Martin, & Auerbach, Charles. (1994). Group Work in
    Graduate Social Work Education: The Price of Neglect. *Journal of
    Social Work Education, 30,* 325-335.

Breton, Margot. (1990). Learning from Social Group Work Tradi-
    tions. *Social Work with Groups, 13*(3), 21-45.

Briar, Scott. (1971). Social Case Work and Social Group Work: His-
    torical Foundations. In Robert Morris (Ed.), *Encyclopedia of Social
    Work* (16th ed., pp. 1237-1245). New York: National Association of
    Social Workers.

Coyle, Grace. (1930). *Social Process in Organized Groups.* New York:
    Richard R. Smith.

Coyle, Grace. (1947). On Becoming a Professional. In *Group Experience
    and Democratic Values* (pp. 81-97). New York: The Woman's Press.

Coyle, Grace. (1947). Group Work as a Method in Recreation. In
    Group Experience and Democratic Values (pp. 69-80). New York: The
    Woman's Press.

Follet, Mary P. (1942). *Dynamic Administration,* collected papers, ed-
    ited by Henry Metcalf & Lyndall Urwick. New York: Harper and
    Brothers.

Garvin, Charles D. (1997). *Contemporary Group Work* (3rd ed., pp. 23-
    32). Boston: Allyn and Bacon.

Hartford, Margaret E. (1964). Social Group Work 1930–1960: The
    Search for a Definition. In *Working Papers toward a Frame of Refer-
    ence for Social Group Work* (pp. 62-79). New York: National Associa-
    tion of Social Workers.

Konopka, Gisela. (1983). *Social Group Work: A Helping Process* (3rd
    ed., pp. 1-31). Englewood Cliffs, NJ: Prentice Hall.

Lindeman, Eduard C. (1936). *Social Discovery: An Approach to the Study of Functional Groups.* New York: Republic.

Middleman, Ruth R. (1992). Group Work and the Heimlich Maneuver: Unchoking Social Work Education. In David F. Fike & Barbara Rittner (Eds.), *Working From Strengths: The Essence of Group Work* (pp. 16-35). Miami, FL: Center for Group Work Studies.

Middleman, Ruth R., & Goldberg, Gale. (1983). Social Work Practice with Groups. In Anne Minahan (Ed.), *Encyclopedia of Social Work* (18th ed., pp. 714-729). Silver Spring, MD: National Association of Social Workers.

Middleman, Ruth R., & Wood, Gale Goldberg. (1990). From Social Group Work to Social Work with Groups. *Social Work with Groups, 13*(3), 3-20.

Newstetter, W. I. (1935). What Is Social Group Work? In *Proceedings of the National Conference of Social Work* (pp. 291-299). Chicago: University of Chicago Press.

Northen, Helen. (1988). *Social Work with Groups* (2nd ed., pp. 16-45). New York: Columbia University Press.

Perlman, Helen Harris. (1965). Social Work Method: A Review of the Past Decade. *Social Work, 10*(4), 166-178.

Schwartz, William. (1969). Private Troubles and Public Issues: One Job or Two? In *Social Welfare Forum* (pp. 22-43). New York: Columbia University Press.

Smalley, Ruth. (1967). *Theory for Social Work Practice* (pp. 294-295). New York: Columbia University Press.

Trecker, Harleigh. (1944). Group Work: Frontiers and Foundations— In Wartime. *The Compass, 25*(3), 4.

Vinter, Robert D. (1959). Group Work: Perspectives and Prospects. In *Social Work with Groups 1959* (pp. 128-149). New York: National Association of Social Workers.

Wenocur, Stanley, & Reisch, Michael. (1989). *From Charity to Enterprise: The Development of American Social Work in a Market Economy* (pp. 225-269). Urbana: University of Illinois Press.

Wilson, Gertrude. (1976). From Practice to Theory: A Personalized History. In Robert W. Roberts & Helen Northen (Eds.), *Theories of Social Work with Groups* (pp. 1-44). New York: Columbia University Press.

Wilson, Gertrude, & Ryland, Gladys. (1949). *Social Group Work Practice.* Boston: Houghton-Mifflin.

Unit 3
Pre-Group Planning and Group Formation

Planning for work with a group—that is, preparation by the worker before the first group meeting—is one of the most neglected areas in group work practice. Although it is clear that cursory attention to planning and preparation is a primary factor in group problems and failures, workers often limit their pre-meeting considerations to rather superficial issues, such as meting time and place and whether to serve refreshments. Such lack of planning can result in groups that fizzle out after only a few meetings, irregular group attendance, and groups that feel largely like a waste of time to both worker and members. Group problems often lead workers to engage in undeserved self-blame and to question their ability or talent for group work practice. Thus, the price is high for neglect of the planning phase in group work.

Often workers are unable to clearly or cogently describe the purpose of their proposed group. Also, they are often unable to define the planning process—the thinking, decision making, and actions required between conceiving the idea of forming a group and holding the first group meeting. It is essential, therefore, that a course on group work practice emphasize material on pre-group planning. Presenting this content requires considerable class time, but it provides the foundation and framework for understanding groups.

This teaching unit has four objectives for students:

1. To appreciate the importance of planning in the formation of a new group.
2. To understand what areas must be considered in planning for a new group.
3. To be able to plan for and develop a new group.
4. To be able to talk with potential group members and recruit members for a group.

We begin with a statement of the importance of planning. Ideas that the instructor might incorporate into this introduction

23

can be found in Brandler and Roman (1991), chapter 5; Hartford (1971), chapters 3–6; Northen (1988), chapters 5–8; Shulman (1992), chapters 2 and 9; and Toseland and Rivas (1998), chapter 6. Instructors may also wish to consult the sample lecture at the end of this unit.

Then we do an exercise to help students understand the areas that need to be considered by a worker planning for the formation of a group. We use as a foundation for this exercise eight areas derived from a planning model developed by Roselle Kurland (1978, 1982) and explained in detail in Appendix F. The eight general areas, listed below, are not shown to students prior to the exercise, but they are used by the instructor to guide it and are provided to students following the exercise.

1. *Need.* What wants, drives, problems, issues, or areas of concern exist among those in the target population from which potential group members will be drawn?

2. *Purpose.* What ends and objectives will the group pursue collectively? What hopes, expectations, and objectives will each member have in regard to group participation?

3. *Composition.* What is the number and what are the characteristics of the members and the worker(s) who will participate in the group?

4. *Structure.* What specific arrangements need to be made to facilitate the conduct of the group, particularly regarding time and place?

5. *Content.* What means will be used to achieve the purpose for which the group is formed? What will be done in the group? How will it be done? Why will it be done?

6. *Pre-Group Contact.* How will appropriate members be secured for participation in the group that is being planned? How will they be prepared for their participation in the group?

7. *Agency Context.* What agency factors might affect the worker's actions and the group that is being formed?

8. *Social Context.* What influences in the larger social and political environments affect the delivery of service to clients, including, perhaps, the formation of new groups?

Before a worker is ready to hold the first meeting of a new group, detailed questions related to each of these eight areas need to be addressed. Moreover, the eight areas outlined above need to be considered concurrently. The relationship among them is not a linear one; rather, the eight areas are interdependent and overlap. Decisions made in regard to one area will affect decisions about the others.

For the exercise, we divide the class into four subgroups. Each subgroup can consist of four to eight students, depending on the size of the class. We ask each group to brainstorm and compile a list of everything that a worker needs to think about, make decisions about, or do between conceiving an idea for a new group and actually holding the first group meeting. The brainstorming exercise generally takes about 15 minutes.

On the board, we make eight columns, one for each of the components described above. We do not place headings at the top of the columns, but in our mind we know that each column represents one component of the planning model. Then, we ask each subgroup, in turn, to offer one item from its brainstormed list. We place each offering in the appropriate column. If the offering is the title of a component (e.g., need, purpose, composition), we place that item at the top of a column as its heading. This allows students to inductively build the planning model.

This exercise needs to be carried out in an atmosphere of fun and high spirit, which the instructor helps to create. For example, the instructor might say jokingly that each subgroup should have exactly 462 items on its list. Or the instructor can tease the class when good-natured competition develops among the subgroups as they make it known they also had an item on their list that was just mentioned by another subgroup. Or the instructor can jokingly award "two points" to the subgroup that offers an item used as a column head. As items are listed, the instructor may choose to initiate discussion about those which are especially important (e.g., group size, how issues around confidentiality can be addressed, orientation to the group).

When the items offered by the subgroups become repetitive or start to deal with minutiae, or when student interest wanes, the instructor can wrap up the exercise by asking students for any additional important items or by adding to the list any unmentioned items deemed important. Now, the handout "A Model of Planning for Social Work with Groups" (see Appendix F) is distributed to the class. There should be no expectation that each item in the eight areas of the model will be listed on the board. Of importance here is that students begin to realize and appreciate the attention that must be given to pre-group planning—attention that goes far beyond decisions about meeting time and place and whether to serve refreshments.

For students who have the opportunity to form a new group, the Planning Model will be welcomed as it presents a very practical way for them to proceed. Other students, however, will be group facilitators for already existing groups, or will be about to assume leadership of a functioning group. These students may think that the material on planning has little or no relevance for their work. They should be helped to see that this is not true.

It is especially helpful for the instructor to review the handout with the class, concentrating on the diagrams (see Appendix F). The upper diagram, for use when group composition is *not* predetermined, applies to students who are forming groups from scratch. They must first consider the component of *Need*. The lower diagram, for use when group composition *is* predetermined, applies to students who already are working with a group or will be assuming leadership of an already existing group. In such instances, the component of *Composition* should be considered first. The lower diagram provides a framework that students working with pre-existing groups can use to analyze, understand, and influence group functioning. The Planning Model is a potent vehicle for use in the understanding and analysis of all groups, new and existing.

The process of brainstorming, inductive model development, and discussion of key items and the model's diagrams should take at least one hour.

Getting Students to Plan by Themselves

The next section of this teaching unit, which flows logically from the previous discussion, gives students experience using the planning model, and allows them to absorb the material and, ultimately, to use it outside of the classroom.

We divide the class into subgroups of five to eight students. We try to group students who are working with similar populations in the field. We give each subgroup a situation that includes a specific population and issue and ask them to assume the role of social workers doing the planning for a needed group. We use examples such as the following:

- Several members of a senior center have recently had an adult child die. Social workers there believe that a group might be useful.

- Recently, several HIV-positive mothers with young children have begun to use the services of an AIDS information and treatment agency. Workers there believe that a group with a focus on parenting issues might be useful.
- Several participants in a community-based agency serving youth have parents with AIDS. Workers there believe that a group for these youngsters could be helpful.
- Several seventh graders who are new to a junior high school appear to be lonely, scared, and unable to make friends. The workers believe that a group might be useful.
- An increasing number of young adults being treated in a public mental health agency are there because of court-mandated attendance for alcohol and drug offenses. Workers there believe that a group might be useful.

These examples are only a few possibilities. The instructor can develop other situations for use in the class based upon the field experiences of the students.

We ask each subgroup to use the model to plan for the specific group they have been assigned, focusing especially on the pregroup contact components of need, purpose, and content, and the recruitment issues which are part of a pre-group contact. Subgroups should also consider how they are going to explain the purpose of the group to those they want to recruit.

Often, the subgroup discussions are very active and intense. Discussion may last for up to 45 minutes, then subgroups present their plans to the entire class for discussion. Because the populations and problems are diverse, a variety of issues can be highlighted in this process. The junior high school group, for instance, may raise the issue of how honest the worker should be with the group members regarding their difficulties. The senior center group, on the other hand, may struggle with how to talk with potential group members about their loss. The court-mandated group may grapple with the difficulties of working with involuntary group members and issues of confidentiality.

Because students often struggle with finding an effective way to recruit group members, it is important to allow them to practice doing this in class. Role play is useful here. In the role play from our courses, we assume the role of a potential group member and ask the entire class to become the social worker attempting to recruit this person for a new group. We have found that taking the role of the elderly person whose adult child has died is an especially good choice for this practice opportunity. We play the role as realistically as possible, presenting to students the genuine difficulties of recruitment. For instance, in role, we may say such things as, "What good will it do talking to others as miserable as I am? We'll just make each other more unhappy"; "It's too personal. I don't want to talk about such things with strangers"; "My life is over—it won't help."

We found that, as the potential group member first reacts negatively to the invitation to join the group, the students often become increasingly desperate to "sell" the group—even beginning to sound a bit like used car salespeople. They tend to lose their sense of humanity, forgetting to ask the elderly person how she is doing or finding out what has been most difficult for her. The instructor can move out of role periodically, pointing out the hard-sell qualities of the students' recruitment efforts and offering more useful techniques to express empathy, compassion, and concern.

By the end of the exercise, students should be able to talk with potential group members and recruit them more effectively for a new group. The instructor may choose to repeat this exercise, using different situations and asking a student to take on the potential member role. This exercise may take up to 30 minutes.

At this point, we summarize the material on pre-group planning. Such a summary can be presented in a lecture. The instructor can use his or her own experience and predilections and make use of the articles presented in the readings section at the end of this unit. We offer the following sample lecture, however, which has content that we believe is needed by students at this point. Instructors should feel free to embellish, enlarge, or change this content to suit their own teaching style.

Sample Lecture

The choice to spend all of this time on pre-group planning has been quite purposeful on my part. It is an important step conducted summarily or not at all by too many workers. It is also a primary factor in the failure of many social work groups—that is, for their premature demise or lack of relevance or effectiveness.

The components we have discussed—need, purpose, composition, structure, content, pre-group contact, agency context, and social context—also provide a framework for examining any group, either one being formed or one already running. The questions that go along with them are always relevant: "What needs is the group attempting to meet? What is its purpose? What is its composition, who are its members? What are important areas of commonality and difference among members? How is the group structured? Where, when, and for how long does it meet? What is the rationale for all of that? How is the group's structure related to its need, purpose, and composition? What is the content of the group? What takes place during group meetings? How does the content help the group to meet its needs and achieve its purpose?

Two points should be emphasized about this planning model. First, planning does not mean imposing on people. As planning is carried out and services initiated, the worker's initial ideas on any of the components may change, especially as the worker begins to better know the clients and the situation. It is important that the worker be flexible and open to changing formulations. But the possibility that increased knowledge may change conceptions does not negate the importance of developing specific ideas and making decisions during the pre-group planning stage.

Second, it is important that the worker appreciate the interrelatedness of the model's components. Decisions in one area affect the others. Also, some of the components will be very important to some groups and not to others. Recall the differences among the groups we used in our exercises. Different decisions and emphases are critical for different groups.

I will now discuss in more detail five of the model's components.

Need

A common error of workers is to formulate a need for service in their own heads and then try to impose it on potential clients without ever determining the clients' "felt" need. Assessment of need cannot be conducted without involving potential clients. For example, a student whose placement was with the Housing Authority in a low-income housing project learned that a number of families were being asked to leave the project because they had teen-age children who were in trouble with the police. To prevent difficulty in the future, she decided it would make sense to form a group of mothers of latency-age children who were having trouble in school. It sounded like a good idea. But despite a great deal of effort on her part, nobody came to the meetings. Had this student asked potential members how they viewed such a group, she would have learned that their fear of being identified by the Housing Authority as parents of "troublesome" children and, consequently, of being at risk for eviction was far greater than their need for help in dealing with their children—although they *did* want help in this area. This group should have been presented differently to potential members. Had the student been aware of the fears of the population, she would have been able to do so.

How do you go about assessing need? Above all else, you must talk to people. You should hang out and talk with potential clients. What do they want? What are their concerns? What kinds of problems or issues do they struggle with? You should also talk with people in the community (however the community is defined), and with relevant others (e.g., teachers, nurses, parents). You "tune in." You "imaginatively consider." You look at what has been done before, at what services currently exist and at what is lacking. You look for themes—things people say over and over—and for startling things. You formulate some ideas and then you talk to people again— potential clients, people in the community, workers, relevant others. Test out your tentative ideas. Do they "click?"

You cannot begin to formulate purpose without first knowing the need.

Purpose and Content

Many workers have problems formulating a clear purpose for the group. Fuzziness of purpose is illustrated in the following excerpt from a student assignment. Looking back at her first-year group experience, she wrote:

> My supervisor somehow knew that I knew how to cook and my assignment was to formulate a cooking group, drawing the participants from a pre-existing teen organization. After the third session the group fell apart. I suppose I was never exactly sure what the purpose of the group was supposed to be. My supervisor kept stressing how I was supposed to use the group as a vehicle for expression, to verbalize conflicts that came up and issues that occurred in the girls' daily experiences. I never quite knew how to use the group for this purpose. It was clear to me the girls saw it as nothing more than a cooking group, which was what it was supposed to be. . .or was it?

This excerpt also illustrates another common error regarding purpose: Practitioners frequently form a group with a stated purpose that is, in reality, secondary in importance to the worker's real (hidden) purpose, which goes unstated. The worker's hidden purpose usually is something like: "Clients' honest expression of feel-ings about what really is of concern in their inner lives." When such disparity exists between the stated and the hidden purpose, the social worker violates the value of respect for the client. For a worker to state—and for the members to understand—one purpose, and then for the worker to pursue another purpose, is a highly manipulative act that often results in clients being labeled as "resis-tant" or "not ready." There is a principle involved here: *If you can-not say it to clients, you have no right to do it.*

Another common error is for the purpose to be stated in such general terms that it is virtually meaningless. For example, to say that a group is a "rap group" really indicates little about the group's purpose. It merely indicates that the group will engage in talking. Similarly, words like *therapy, socialization,* and *support* are gen-eral terms that do not really indicate a group's purpose.

Another common error is to confuse purpose and content. When asked about the purpose of their group, practitioners often respond by describing instead the group's content. For example, they will say: "The purpose of the group is to help members talk about...." The *ends* toward which such talking is directed defines the group's purpose. But that is the group's content (what the group will *do*), not its purpose. Content is the *means* toward achieving the group's purpose. To identify the group's purpose, workers should ask: "To-ward what *ends* will this group work?"

Thus, clarity of purpose exists when

- the purpose of the group can be stated clearly and concisely by both clients and the worker,
- the stated purpose is the same for both clients and the worker, even if they might express it in different words,
- the purpose is specific enough to provide direction and implica-tions for group content, and
- the purpose is specific enough so that both clients and the worker will know when it has been achieved.

Composition

To describe a group merely as "heterogeneous" or "homoge-neous" is neither useful nor accurate. Groups cannot be described simply in one word. Instead, the worker should identify the dimen-sions along which a group is homogeneous and heterogeneous, and identify the important areas of commonality and difference among group members.

Pre-Group Contact

In speaking with potential group members, it is important to be direct. Workers often believe that saying difficult or unpleasant things to potential members will scare them off or insult them. Quite the contrary is true, however. The worker should choose words with care. Avoid being roundabout. When the worker is direct, potential members usually will feel a tremendous sense of relief. This response arises from their sense that the worker is someone who understands what they need and what they are experiencing, and that the worker is proposing a group that really can address their needs.

It was not until the 1980s that pre-group planning began to appear in the group work literature as a serious practice issue. In the last 10 years it has been embraced by many group work authors, and their discussion has been conceptually strong and vigorous. However, despite this encouraging fact, pre-group planning continues to be a neglected area in direct practice.

Why is that so? First, social workers place great emphasis on client self-determination. Perhaps planning is viewed as client manipulation and, hence, as a negation of this important social work principle. Quite the opposite is true, however. Pre-group planning does not diminish the opportunity for client self-determination, it enhances it. The increased clarity about the group that results from careful planning increases the client's ability to make an informed decision about group participation. It removes the possibility of client manipulation and increases the opportunity for client self-determination.

A second reason that planning is neglected in practice may be social work's traditional emphasis on action. Often, social workers have equated effectiveness of helping with hands-on client activities. Quantity became important—how many meetings, how many people—and quality became secondary. Workers seem to believe, "As long as 10 people were there and they talked a lot, it was good, and I did something." In this light, planning can seem like a passive activity, at least outwardly so. In their haste to get busy and do something, social workers often cut short the planning process or leave it out altogether.

In addition to better service for clients and more successful groups, thorough and thoughtful pre-group planning has two benefits that might not be immediately obvious. First, planning increases the worker's self-confidence. Workers who know what they are doing, and why, will feel more sure of themselves. They will do a better job. They will be able to listen better to clients, to respond, and to be flexible. Second, planning helps workers—almost forces them—to obtain a much better idea of individual group members, their environments, their contexts, their backgrounds, their communities, their cultures, their attitudes and points of view, and their concerns. Workers become immersed in a process that leads to in-depth understanding of the group members and their views of their worlds. Such understanding on the part of workers is crucial to good group work practice.

Readings

Brager, George. (1960). Goal Formation: An Organizational Perspective. *Social Work with Groups 1960* (pp. 22-36). New York: National Association of Social Workers.

Brandler, Sondra, & Roman, Camille P. (1991). *Group Work: Skills and Strategies for Effective Interventions* (pp. 104-124). New York: Haworth.

Brown, Leonard N. (1991). *Groups for Growth and Change* (pp. 143-160). New York: Longman.

Davis, Larry E. (1979). Racial Composition of Groups. *Social Work*, 24(3), 208-213.

Ephross, Paul H., & Vassil, Thomas V. (1988). *Groups That Work: Structure and Process* (pp. 56-74). New York: Columbia University Press.

Garvin, Charles D. (1997). *Contemporary Group Work* (3rd ed., pp. 50-75). Boston: Allyn and Bacon.

Gitterman, Alex. (1994). Developing a New Group Service: Strategies and Skills. In Alex Gitterman & Lawrence Shulman (Eds.), *Mutual Aid Groups, Vulnerable Populations, and the Life Cycle* (2nd ed., pp. 59-80). New York: Columbia University Press.

Hartford, Margaret E. (1971). *Groups in Social Work* (pp. 63-192). New York: Columbia University Press.

Henry, Sue. (1992). *Group Skills in Social Work: A Four-Dimensional Approach* (2nd ed., pp. 43-69). Pacific Grove, CA: Brooks/Cole.

Kurland, Roselle. (1978). Planning: The Neglected Component of Group Development. *Social Work with Groups*, 1(2), 173-178.

Kurland, Roselle. (1982). *Group Formation: A Guide to the Development of Successful Groups*. New York: United Neighborhood Centers of America.

Lowy, Louis. (1973). Goal Formulation in Social Work with Groups. In Saul Bernstein (Ed.), *Further Explorations in Group Work* (pp. 116-144). Boston: Milford House.

Malekoff, Andrew. (1997). *Group Work with Adolescents: Principles and Practice* (pp. 53-80). New York: Guilford.

Meadow, Diane Ammund. (1981). The Preparatory Interview. *Social Work with Groups, 4*(3/4), pp. 135-144.

Northen, Helen. (1988). *Social Work with Groups* (2nd ed., pp. 98-184). New York: Columbia University Press.

Schmidt, Julianna T. (1969). The Use of Purpose in Casework Practice. *Social Work, 14*(1), 77-84.

Shalinsky, William. (1969). Group Composition as an Element of Social Group Work Practice. *Social Service Review, 43*(1), 42-49.

Shulman, Lawrence. (1992). *The Skills of Helping Individuals, Families, and Groups* (3rd ed., pp. 53-78, 241-314). Itasca, IL: Peacock.

Steinberg, Dominique Moyse. (1997). *The Mutual-Aid Approach to Working with Groups: Helping People Help Each Other* (pp. 43-62). Northvale, NJ: Jason Aronson.

Toseland, Ronald W., & Rivas, Robert F. (1998). *An Introduction to Group Work Practice* (3rd ed., pp. 145-172). New York: MacMillan.

Unit 4
Beginnings

As they mature, groups progress through a series of developmental stages. Knowledge of these stages is important because it informs the worker's understanding of member behavior and has important implications for intervention.

The 1965 work on group developmental stages by Garland, Jones, and Kolodny was important to group work. The authors conceptualized five group stages—pre-affiliation, power and control, intimacy, differentiation, and separation (Garland, Jones, & Kolodny, 1973). Since that time, other group work authors have examined group life using developmental stages. Although they vary in the number of stages they posit as a group moves from planning to termination—depending on how narrowly or broadly they describe the characteristics of each stage—group work authors generally agree on the basic concepts inherent in a group's progression.

Stages of group development are presented linearly. However, as in most stage theories of development, the reality is that each stage is not discrete—that is, a group may demonstrate simultaneously characteristics of more than one stage. Similarly, a worker can expect to see back-and-forth movement between stages. A worker may identify in a group characteristics of the middle stage of development and then, at the next meeting, be surprised to see evidence of the beginning stage all over again. Also, the longevity of a particular stage will vary among groups. In some groups, for instance, the beginning stage may be short-lived while in others it may take considerable time. Despite this lack of discrete linear advancement in foreseeable time increments, almost all groups will progress through a series of definable and predictable stages.

In our group work classes, we use four group developmental stages as an organizing framework: planning, beginning, middle, and ending. We ask students to look at the characteristics and themes of each stage, the issues likely to arise in each, and the implications for worker role and interventions based on the worker's understanding of the stages.

The beginning stage of a group is especially important because it provides the foundation for what will follow. It is common for members to enter a new group with mixed emotions—excitement and hope about the group's potential benefit combined with fear and dread that the group will be a negative experience. They may also be concerned that they, personally, will not measure up to their own and others' expectations.

During the beginning stage members are oriented to the group; norms of behavior get established; a common purpose begins to be defined; and commonalities among group members are recognized. The role of the worker is central at this time. Because members are often ambivalent and perhaps fearful about a new group experience, the worker must actively provide structure, direction, and guidance. Students find this difficult. They tend to be reluctant to provide the structure and direction that the group and its members need, because they are uncomfortable in a role of authority. They want the group to "belong" to its members and do not want to impose upon the group. They tend to see the provision of direction and structure as intrusive and synonymous with overly controlling leadership. As a result, their tendency is toward passivity rather than toward the active facilitating role which groups require in the beginning stage.

This unit will describe how an instructor can teach about the beginning stage of group development and the worker's role and functions. The unit has three objectives for students:

1. To become familiar with group characteristics, member needs, and worker roles in the beginning stage of group development.
2. To develop practice skills for use with groups in the beginning stage.
3. To be able to skillfully and purposefully intervene with groups in the beginning stage.

Group Needs and Worker Roles

We begin by asking students to consider a first meeting of a new group. We ask them to describe how group members might feel and behave. Usually we ask the class to discuss this in relation to the populations with which they might be working, taking into account members' race, ethnicity, culture, age, and developmental status. For instance, we ask them how a group of elderly people might feel and act as they prepare to come to the first meeting of a new group. We ask them to compare this to how a group of teen-agers might feel and act. As students reply, we list their responses on the board in two columns under the headings "Feelings" and "Behavior." Listing their responses enables students to see that, although the two groups have common feelings, they vary in behavior according to group members' characteristics and backgrounds.

We pose the following situation to students:

> Suppose you were meeting with a new group of parents who did not know one another. You arrive at the meeting room 10 minutes before the first meeting is set to begin. A few group members are already in the room. What do you see? What do you hear?

Students respond with a variety of observations. They note that members may be sitting doing nothing, spread out and unconnected from others in the room, that some may be reading agency brochures, one or two may be standing at the window gazing out. Generally, they describe the members as waiting silently. Other students will note that the group members may talk politely and formally with one another. When asked about the likely content of those conversations, students respond that new members probably talk about acceptable and non-risky subjects, such as the weather, the terrible public transportation system, or when the meeting is supposed to start.

Depending on the students' responses, the instructor can add to the discussion from personal experience: an elderly woman sits next to the door in an upright, tense position with her coat buttoned to her neck; a teenager arrives only to immediately announce from the doorway that she may have to leave the meeting early because she has to pick up her brother; a 10-year-old needs to leave the room for frequent drinks of water.

We ask students what these types of behavior indicate. A discussion ensues of how difficult it is for group members to enter a new situation, how their ambivalent and approach/avoidance feelings can affect their initial actions. The member who sits near the door with her coat on and the teenager who may have to leave early are both giving themselves an "out"—either symbolically or literally indicating that if they do not like what takes place in this first group meeting, they are quite ready to flee. We point out that such behavior is understandable in a new situation. To bring the point home, we ask students to reflect on and discuss their own behavior and feelings when faced with a new and uncomfortable situation.

By drawing responses from the students, we help them, inductively, to come to an understanding of what needs to happen at this point in the life of the group. Members need to be helped to feel comfortable, to feel welcomed, to believe that they can succeed in this new group. In a situation similar to students in the first class session of this course (see Unit 1), they need to get a beginning sense of the purpose of this group, how the group will operate, what the group leader is like, and who the other group members are.

Given these needs, we ask students to consider what the worker should do in this early stage of group development. Here we want to emphasize the role of the worker in providing needed structure, direction, and guidance.

Some negative examples of beginning group process help students see the importance of understanding and being responsive to members' beginning needs and the powerful impact of the worker's role in this stage. In recounting examples such as the following, we draw from our own experience and from workers we have observed.

• Without even introducing herself, a worker begins the first meeting by saying: "Let's start by getting to know each other a bit." Then, turning to the first person on her left, she smilingly commands, "Why don't you begin by telling us something about yourself." Members seem immediately uncomfortable, each apparently struggling with how much to say and what not to say in introducing themselves.

• Without sharing any of her own thoughts about the group, a worker immediately asks general, open-ended questions such as: "What do you see as the purpose of this group?" "What do you hope to get from this group?" "What made you come to this group?" Members find these very difficult to answer and, as a result, seem to feel inept and as having somehow already failed.

• A worker gets into a tussle with a member who has her coat on. He says, "Mary, don't you want to take your coat off? It's hot in the room." When Mary responds that she's fine, the worker continues, "Oh, no, Mary. It's so warm in here. Please take your coat off. You'll be much more comfortable."

These negative examples allow the class to then consider what *should* be done in the beginning stage. An open-ended statement such as "tell us about yourself" leaves group members floundering at a point when they are already feeling nervous. As the instructor modeled in the first session of this course (see Unit 1), the worker needs to provide structure for the members' introductions by suggesting areas that they might include. In addition, if the worker makes the first introduction, she or he provides a model that members can follow. At this point in the life of the group, members look to the worker for direction, structure, and help at a difficult time.

Similarly, open-ended questions such as "What do you see as the purpose of this group?" place members in an uncomfortable position at a time when they are already feeling vulnerable. Members often do not know or cannot yet put into words their conceptions of the group's purpose. Here again, they need the worker's help. The worker's initiating a discussion of group purpose by describing how and why the group came about will help orient members and give them a sense of the commonalities that have brought them together. In addition, the worker's sharing some personal views on the group's possibilities and objectives enables members to begin to articulate some of their ideas on the purpose of the group and the ways it might address some of their needs. Here, too, the worker takes an active role to provide direction and guidance.

Insisting that a member take her coat off also increases the anxiety and discomfort group members may feel in the beginning stage. It insensitively violates the need that members have to keep their distance, to remain uncommitted, to give themselves an "out." We point out to the class that, once the member begins to feel comfortable in the group, the coat will come off quite naturally.

Usually, the discussion of the beginning stage is active and animated. Class members are able to draw upon their own life experiences in a range of beginning situations to inform their understanding of what this stage is like for group members. To summarize all that has been said, we distribute a handout, "Stages of Group Development—Beginning" (see Appendix G), which we then review with the class. Given the extensive discussion that has taken place, the material on the handout is seen as logical to them and representative of many of the ideas they expressed.

As the class reviews the handout, the instructor can highlight important areas that may not have been considered. One of these areas entails emphasizing commonalities among the group members in the beginning stage. Such commonalities form the foundation for group cohesiveness as the group evolves.

In the first session, the worker may point out commonalities among the members as they introduce themselves. In class, the instructor can remind students that this was done during the first class session with them, as well. It is important to make clear that commonalities can be found in the details of everyday life, such as likes and dislikes (in food, movies, clothing, etc.), interests (in sports, cooking, reading, etc.), or descriptive characteristics (birth order, grade in school, marital status, etc.). Commonalities can also be found in the major issues or difficulties that brought the members to the group (whether loss, illness, addiction, loneliness, or others).

Another area that may not have been discussed fully is norms and the way they are established in the beginning stage. Group norms are the standards of behavior that members accept for the group. The instructor needs to emphasize that, in the beginning stage of group development, the worker is central and active in modeling acceptable behaviors for the group. How the worker listens to group members, how she or he communicates respect for each member's contribution, the care taken to involve all members—these will set the tone for members' expected behavior toward one another.

Group Practice Skills

Next, we turn to the second objective of this unit: helping students to develop practice skills for use with groups in the beginning stage. To accomplish this objective, we define, describe, and demonstrate selected skills and then ask students, in a class exercise, to practice using these skills so that they begin to "own" them.

We define skill as a specific action or intervention that accomplishes a purpose and is based on knowledge and understanding. Skills are more than techniques alone. Students must know not only how to intervene, but also when and why to intervene in particular ways. In other words, their actions should be purposeful and informed.

Because students often do not know how or why to intervene, the material on skills is welcomed enthusiastically and with a sense of relief. Often, students view the worker's role and actions as an impenetrable mystery, a kind of mystique that leaves them feeling ignorant, unprepared, and left out. Discovering that group work practice involves masterable skills provides them with hope that they can become competent workers.

Ruth Middleman and Gale Goldberg Wood (1990) have elo-
quently described the range of skills used by social work practitioners. Their book *Skills for Direct Practice in Social Work* pays
special attention to skills needed for working with groups. From
the skills they delineate, we describe and demonstrate eight that
we believe workers are most likely to need and use in the beginning stage of a group.

- *Scanning:* to take in the whole group with one's eyes;
- *Selecting communication patterns purposefully:* to make a judgment about a communication format that is consistent with
  the group's needs and set it in motion;
- *Verbalizing norms:* to let the group know what actions are
  acceptable and unacceptable as one begins to establish standards of expected behavior;
- *Referring to purpose:* to state the reasons that clients and worker
  have come together;
- *Reaching for information:* to ask a member for facts, opinions,
  impressions, or judgments that increase knowledge of a situation or event;
- *Building on strengths:* to point out and focus on all that a
  member knows and can do;
- *Reaching for a feeling link:* to ask others to connect with a
  feeling that has been expressed;
- *Inviting full participation:* to ask nonparticipants to speak by
  looking at them or verbally seeking their comments.

Having introduced these skills, we next provide an opportunity for the class to practice using them with the aim of having
students adopt them as part of their helping repertoire. We do
this via an in-class exercise. We divide the class into subgroups of
seven or eight and present to them a school-based situation with
which they are quite familiar. Because we want them to focus on
skill development rather than the content of the exercise, we use
a situation for which they have background knowledge and will
be able to readily express their own views, rather than one for
which they would have to assume unfamiliar perspectives or
experiences. This exercise is intended to enhance students' comfort and reduce their fear of taking risks as they try to use the
above skills.

We distribute the following situation description:

> Students have been expressing a number of concerns about curriculum—there are too many required courses and not enough electives, not enough courses have cultural-specific content, some course content and some professors seem outdated and not relevant, students don't have enough say about choice of professors, etc. Student government has decided to form a curriculum committee to explore these and to identify any specific changes students wish to recommend to administration. A sign-up sheet is posted for students wishing to be on the curriculum committee. Twenty students sign up and 8 are elected by a vote of all students. The student who got the most votes is designated as the curriculum committee chair. This is the first meeting of the committee.

Then we distribute to each subgroup slips of paper, each containing a short description of a character we want a subgroup member to assume. We note that these role assignments will be rotated, so that each student will have the opportunity to practice a variety of skills. The characterizations distributed to students are as follows:

- You have been elected to chair this committee.
- You live some distance away and drive to school. The meeting was called for 3:00 p.m., and because you are worried about hitting rush-hour traffic on the way home, you want the meeting to end by 4:15 p.m. at the latest. You keep looking at your watch.
- You talk a lot and believe it is especially unfair that there are so few electives in the curriculum, particularly in the area of cultural diversity.
- You have strong opinions, and one is that a social policy course is especially a waste of time and irrelevant to practice today.
- You are a "harmonizer" and do not like conflict. When disagreements or differences of opinion arise, you try to smooth them over and be a peacemaker.
- You say very little and have difficulty expressing your opinion in a group, but you wanted to be on this committee because you think it is important that students have a choice of professors rather than be assigned class sections with no input.

Depending on the number of students in each subgroup, some slips of paper might say "Just be yourself," or some students can be assigned to observe the chair's use of the skills in practice.

After the students briefly play out their assignments, the instructor stops the action and subgroup members are asked to briefly discuss the chair's attempts to implement any or all of the eight skills. The student in the chair's role should be encouraged to comment upon her or his own efforts to use these skills. Then students are asked to pass their slips of paper to the right, giving each a chance to assume a new role. This approach allows each student to play a range of characters and allows most to employ the skills in the role of chair. Post-rotation discussions can be brief or held off until two or three rotations have taken place. In addition, the instructor might want to make some observations and lead a general discussion with the entire class at the end of this exercise.

Students tend to participate in this exercise with liveliness and humor. The quick rotation of roles adds to a spirited context in which no student is on the spot for very long, and all students exhibit support of one another's efforts to be skillful. Also, students find practicing the skills from Middleman and Wood's book exciting, because it starts to dispel the seeming mystery that surrounds practice interventions. We find that once the material has been introduced, students tend to read the rest of the book avidly.

Group Interventions

Finally, we turn to the third objective of this unit: helping students to skillfully and purposefully intervene with groups in the beginning stage. To accomplish this we use role play. However, before students participate in this role play, we introduce them to the essential third element of successful social work with groups—the agency in which the group will meet. William Schwartz (1971) defined a client group as "a collection of people who need each other in order to work on certain common tasks in an agency hospitable to those tasks" (p. 7). This description of a client group, concise yet profound, adds the agency's stake to the work of the group.

We want students to understand that they are not working in a vacuum, but rather that they are representatives of the agencies in which they have their field placements. Agencies have societal tasks, functions, and purposes, and their workers have a responsibility to help carry these out. Thus, students need to understand that they are not independent practitioners who can do whatever they wish, but that the role of the agency for which they work influences the kinds of groups they form and lead.

They must try to bring together the agency's functions and the group members' needs through purposeful group intervention.

Referring to the class exercise on group formation (see Unit 3), we explain that we have selected for the role play one of the hypothetical groups the class has previously discussed—a group in a community-based agency for 8- to 12-year-olds who have a parent with AIDS. We distribute a handout describing the characteristics of each group member (see below) and initiate a discussion of what might occur in the first meeting of this group. This discussion usually focuses on three areas: group members testing the worker; the worker sharing personal information; and the worker and group members discussing the group's purpose.

Group Role Play

The following are short descriptions of five children, each of whom has a parent with AIDS. They are all members of a group based in a youth-serving agency. The purpose of the group is to increase members' understanding of AIDS and their ability to cope with their parent's illness.

Lester: African-American, age 12, loud, outspoken, bossy, doesn't have many friends; has one sister, age 10, also in group, whom he takes care of and is close with; mother has AIDS but is functioning well; she's told children but minimizes it, tells them not to worry; father does not live at home and Lester sees him only sporadically.

Diane: African-American, age 10 (Lester's sister), quiet, does very well in school, reads a lot; doesn't talk much but she's worried about her mother and how things will be if her mother gets real sick.

Roberta: White, age 12, smart, talkative, articulate, only child; father died of AIDS when she was 8, now mother has just been diagnosed HIV-positive; took her mother's diagnosis quite badly because she remembers father's death; is worried about what will happen if her mother dies, too, but hasn't talked about this much except to one staff member at the agency.

Anna: Dominican, age 10; father has AIDS and is quite ill; mother tries to protect Anna, but doesn't like to talk about AIDS with her; has 3 brothers (ages 21–25) who also protect her; she knows her father has AIDS but doesn't understand much about what that means.

Michael: African-American, age 12, a loner; has one good friend who is about to move away and he's upset about that; only child, does not see his father; mother has AIDS and has made arrangements for Michael to live with her sister when she dies; Michael knows this but does not like his aunt, whom he views as strict; he also doesn't like his cousins (aunt's children) and does not want to live with them.

Testing the Worker

The following vignette provides an example of a typical discussion of testing in the beginning stage that might evolve as students consider the characteristics of the group members we have presented.

I asked the class, "How would you handle it if Lester arrived with a Walkman in his ear?" Joan said, "I'd want to be democratic. I'd ask the other members if it bothered them that Lester's wearing his Walkman." "Right, good idea," Mitch said, "ask the group." "We don't mind, it doesn't bother us if Lester has his Walkman," I said, taking on the voice of group members. Class members smiled in recognition of that likely response. "Why might you get that response?" I asked. "No one wants to confront Lester," John said. "No one wants to risk being unpopular," Lew said, "or go against one's peer." "So how would you handle it?" I asked again. "I'd tell him he must remove it," Melody said. "Yeah, but what if he wouldn't? Then what would you do?" Priscilla asked. "I'd insist," said Melody. "And then. . .what if he still didn't?" Priscilla continued. "It sounds as if we're getting into a power struggle—something adolescents are especially familiar with," I said. "I think it's a mistake to do that. If you get into a power struggle with Lester, he'll most likely feel he cannot afford to lose that struggle in front of his peers and you put yourself in an untenable position as a leader." Melody asked, "So what should we do? How should we respond?"

Such an interchange provides useful teaching opportunities for the instructor. Students can be helped to understand that all group members will initially test the worker, often in ways consistent with their age or other characteristics. Students need not fear using the authority of their role as group leader in a firm, consistent, and fair manner. In this example, the worker needs to ask Lester to remove his Walkman *because in this group everyone needs to be able to listen to one another.* " In other words, the worker needs to share with the group the *reasons* for such demands, making it clear that they are connected to the group's purpose rather than an arbitrary exercise of authority. In doing so, the worker begins to establish group norms.

Sharing Personal Information

In the beginning stage, group members are likely to ask the worker personal questions. Preparation for the role play also allows students to explore how they might respond to such questions. Another class vignette illustrates this concern.

"What if in the beginning of the group one of the members asks me whether I have AIDS? What should I say?" Maria asked. I assured the class that Maria's question was an apt one, that if members didn't ask you that in the first meeting, they'd get around to the question later, or at least wonder about it. "Any thoughts on how you would respond?" I asked the class. "Think it through out loud." "If I said, 'No, I don't have AIDS,' they'd think I wouldn't know what it was like," Josh said. "But you can't lie to them and say you have it when you don't," Manny said. "But what if you have HIV?" Joanne said. "Do you tell them that?" "You have to be honest," Anita said. "Yeah, but I don't have to share my personal business with the group if I consider it too private," Paul said.

Students tend to become intensely involved in the discussion of how to respond to personal questions. It is a concern felt by all who lead groups. Students tend to have much uncertainty, and therefore discomfort, about sharing personal information with the group. How much should the worker say in the beginning stage, even when members do not ask? How should the worker respond to the inevitable personal or even intrusive questions? Although there are no absolute answers to these questions, there are some important principles that should inform the worker's decisions about sharing personal information.

First, the worker's response needs to be guided by an assessment of the ways in which her or his response will affect the life of the group. Giving too much personal information may detract from the group's purpose by focusing attention on the worker rather than on the group's task and process. The group's needs must take precedence, despite any desire by the worker to prove herself or himself through personal revelations.

Second, the worker should feel free to share what could be useful to the group within the boundaries of privacy and personal comfort. Students need to understand that there is a range of comfort levels for sharing personal information. A worker has the right to decline to respond to a personal question when not comfortable with the content. In doing so, the worker provides a model for group members who have a similar right not to respond in the group.

Finally, when workers are asked "intrusive" questions, *how* they respond is often more important than *what* they choose to share. Group members are concerned about how the worker accepts their questions, regardless of the actual response. The members will try to determine through their questions the kind of person the worker is and the type of authority she or he represents.

Discussing the Group's Purpose

The third area of preparation for the role play revolves around ways to engage the group members in discussing the group's purpose. We emphasize to the class that they need to know in advance what they will say to the group about their vision for the group, their hopes for group accomplishments, and their reasons for, and the agency's interests in, bringing the group members together. We refer back to earlier class discussions about the need for the worker to provide direction in these early group discussions of purpose.

Role Play

After the preparatory discussion, we set up the class for the role play. Because this is the first time we role play a client group in the class, we want to ensure that everyone participates and that no one feels that their participation is being observed and critiqued by others. Therefore, we divide the class into subgroups of six and ask each subgroup to decide who will play which role, including that of the worker. We indicate that we may rotate role assignments. We instruct the class not to consider their own gender, age, or race in assigning roles. We also let them know that, because this is a learning experience, anyone in the group can stop the role play and ask that the group discuss what is occurring—including the person who is playing the worker if she or he is unsure of what to say. This guideline is intended to increase all students' comfort level and especially that of the student in the worker role.

As students engage in the role play, we circulate among the groups, listening, asking questions, redirecting, and making suggestions, as appropriate. Periodically, we may stop the action and initiate brief discussion with the entire class of common issues we have observed.

At the end of the role play, which usually lasts 20—30 minutes, we bring the class together for discussion. We begin by asking those who played the role of worker to comment on their own experience, what they found difficult, what surprised them, what they think they did particularly well or poorly. Giving the students in the worker role the opportunity to critique their own performances first creates a class environment of support and diminishes the competitiveness that can surface when students begin by criticizing their peers. The self-criticism of the students in the worker role creates an empathic response from the others in the class.

We bring this unit to a close by sharing our impressions of the students' work in the role play. We point out to them what they did well—for example, listening to one another, using beginning-stage skills, incorporating understanding of members' needs, supporting one another's efforts, taking risks, encouraging member participation, and providing direction and structure. We also point out what they did not do very well—for example, trying to achieve their own agendas by imposing their plans on the group, rather than using the comments and contributions of the group members as they occur; not helping members see the commonalities they share; discussing group purpose in a superficial and perfunctory way (seeming almost relieved to be done with it so they can move on to "real" issues); having difficulty drawing out the ideas, feelings, and concerns of the group members; and staying with the discussion of purpose.

We reassure the class that the areas with which they had difficulty are not easy ones, and that struggling with them is to be expected at this stage in their learning. We want them to recognize and appreciate all that they have come to comprehend about the beginning stage of group development and the worker's role during that stage. We let them know that we value the understanding and the skill they have achieved.

Readings

Brandler, Sondra, & Roman, Camille P. (1991). *Group Work: Skills and Strategies for Effective Interventions* (pp. 14-36). New York: Haworth.

Brown, Leonard N. (1991). *Groups for Growth and Change* (pp. 161-188). New York: Longman.

Garland, James, Jones, Hubert, & Kolodny, Ralph. (1973). A Model for Stages of Development in Social Work Groups. In Saul Bernstein (Ed.), *Explorations in Group Work* (pp. 17-71). Boston: Milford House.

Garvin, Charles D. (1997). *Contemporary Group Work* (pp. 76-98). Boston: Allyn and Bacon.

Glassman, Urania, & Kates, Len. (1990). *Group Work: A Humanistic Approach* (pp. 73-104). Newbury Park, CA: Sage.

Hartford, Margaret E. (1971). *Groups in Social Work* (pp. 63-94). New York: Columbia University Press.

Henry, Sue. (1992). *Group Skills in Social Work: A Four-Dimensional Approach* (2nd ed., pp. 70-126). Pacific Grove, CA: Brooks/Cole.

Malekoff, Andrew. (1997). *Group Work with Adolescents: Principles and Practice* (pp. 81-101). New York: Guilford.

Middleman, Ruth R., & Wood, Gale Goldberg. (1990). *Skills for Direct Practice in Social Work* (pp. 91-154). New York: Columbia University Press.

Northen, Helen. (1988). *Social Work with Groups* (2nd ed., pp. 185-221). New York: Columbia University Press.

Schwartz, William. (1971). On the Use of Groups in Social Work Practice. In William Schwartz & Serapio Zalba (Eds.), *The Practice of Group Work* (pp. 3-24). New York: Columbia University Press.

Shulman, Lawrence. (1992). *The Skills of Helping Individuals, Families and Groups* (3rd ed., pp. 79-102, 315-400). Itasca, IL: Peacock.

Steinberg, Dominique Moyse. (1997). *The Mutual-Aid Approach to Working with Groups: Helping People Help Each Other* (pp. 63-78). Northvale, NJ: Jason Aronson.

Toseland, Ronald W., & Rivas, Robert F. (1998). *An Introduction to Group Work Practice* (3rd ed., pp. 173-232). Boston: Allyn and Bacon.

UNIT 5
THE PROBLEM-SOLVING PROCESS IN GROUP WORK PRACTICE

Problem solving is a process central to social group work practice. It is used throughout the life of a group to resolve issues around how the group will be conducted and how problematic behavior of group members will be addressed. Effective group practice demands that workers fully understand and appreciate how to help a group engage in the problem-solving process.

This teaching unit has four objectives for students:

1. To become familiar with the problem-solving process of John Dewey.
2. To understand the problem-solving process in use with a group.
3. To become familiar with the common mistakes made by workers in using the problem-solving process with a group.
4. To be able to skillfully apply the problem-solving process in a group.

John Dewey's Approach

The term "problem-solving process" is widely used by social work practitioners, but it is often poorly understood and misapplied. Many practitioners do not know the genesis of the term, nor do they know the steps in the process. The problem-solving process comes from the work of John Dewey, a progressive educator who in 1910 identified a series of steps that provided a model for reaching decision and action. According to Northen (1988), "Problem-solving emphasizes a process of reflective thinking used for coping with questions and difficulties. It integrates feelings with rational thought processes and takes into account both conscious and unconscious elements" (p. 47).

In beginning this unit, we stress the centrality of the problem-solving process in group work practice and how it is used throughout the group's life to address a range of issues, both group and individual. We tell the class that the primary aim of this discussion is for students to see what the problem-solving process actu-

51

ally looks like in a group. We let the class know of its origins in the work of John Dewey.

Because the word "problem" has a negative connotation for many and because we want the class to assume a broad view of its meaning, we underscore the importance of students' seeing the word "problem" as synonymous with the word "issue." We emphasize that the process we are about to discuss is one that they will use frequently each time an issue arises in the ongoing activities and interchanges that take place in the life of the group.

We then distribute a handout summarizing the five steps in Dewey's method, as presented in his language (see Appendix H). We read each step in the handout to the class and then translate his language to more relevant terms for students—terms that more clearly reflect the importance of exploring issues in this process.

• Dewey's Step 1: There occurs "an indeterminate situation," a situation in which there is some rupture, great or small, to the smooth on-flowing of life's affairs.

• Dewey's Step 2: There then occurs a refinement of the difficulty into a more particular problematic form; steps are taken by the individual (group) to diagnose the situation, to see more precisely what the problem is.

• Dewey's Step 3: The individual (group) sets out in search of every conceivable potential solution to the problem; the imagination is permitted to run free; any guess, any hunch, any intuition is admissible.

• Dewey's Step 4: Project these possible solutions in the mind so as to consider the consequences each would be likely to lead to. We think through what would happen if we adopted one or another plan of action.

• Dewey's Step 5: Testing. In actual experience or in imagination, do the conjectured consequences actually occur? Test out each solution individually, act on each proposal *as if* it were the answer. Act out the solutions so as to experience the consequences to which they lead. Then evaluate and judge, reach a "conclusion."

We rephrase Dewey's five steps in the following manner and list them on the board.

1. Something is up, the worker has a sense that there is a problem/issue.
2. The problem/issue is identified.

3. The problem/issue is explored.
4. Possible "solutions" are identified.
5. A "solution" is selected, tried out, and evaluated.

Analyzing Three Records

We then distribute to the class the first of three student records involving group problem solving (see p. 54). We ask a volunteer to read the record aloud while everyone listens and follows along. Having someone read it aloud, rather than asking everyone to read it silently by themselves, brings the record to life, gives it immediacy, and makes it more real for the class.

We pose two questions to the class intended to spark an analysis and evaluation of the problem-solving process evidenced in the record: What problem or issue is this group attempting to address? What is the problem with the problem-solving process in this record?

Because students tend to want to jump in and deal with the personal issues presented by the group members rather than examine the quality of the problem-solving process that has occurred, it is important to ask these two questions separately.

> "What problem or issue is this group is attempting to address?" I asked. "How the group is going to handle eating in the group," Angelina responded. "Right," I said. "Now, what is the problem with the problem-solving process in this record?" "Nobody seems willing to talk about the problem, to impose on the others," Gerald said. "That may be true," I responded. "But that is not what we are looking at here. We're focusing on the problem with the problem-solving process." Zachary then said, "The leaders are doing a lot of the talking." Again I said, "That may be true, but remember, we're focusing on the problem with the problem-solving process. Look at the steps we've listed on the board." The class was silent. Pointing to Step 1 on the board, I asked, "Do you think the worker had a sense that there was a problem/issue in the group?" There was a chorus of agreement from the class. Pointing to Step 2, I continued, "Was the issue identified?" Some class members said "yes," others said "no" and still others said nothing. "Some think it was," I said. "Identify exactly where in the record the issue was identified." Max read from

Record # 1

Setting: Day treatment center for the chronic mentally ill

Members: May, Theresa, Diane, Robert, Mike, Ellie, Inez, Mary, Earl, Olivia

Leaders: Jenny (student supervisor), Susan (social work student)

The group began with Earl pointing out to Olivia that she always eats in the group even though the agency has a rule that you're not supposed to eat in the group. Olivia said it was very hard to stop eating, that she gets nervous and needs to eat.

I said that there is a rule of no eating but it's often not enforced. Jenny (supervisor) asked how everybody feels about eating in the group. May laughed and said she has to eat. Diane said she didn't care, but if she did she wouldn't ask somebody to not eat because of her.

I asked Diane why. She said she didn't like to bother anybody. Inez said eating in the group definitely bothers her because when people eat they're so busy chewing they don't say anything. But, she added, she wouldn't ask somebody not to eat because of her, either; she didn't want to impose on the others. Robert said he's on a diet and watching someone else eat is hard for him, but it wouldn't be fair for him to tell other people what to do.

I asked how other members felt about what Inez, Diane, and Robert were saying. Mary said she wouldn't ask anyone to not eat. Earl said he didn't understand why anyone needed to eat while the group was going on. Jenny said it looked like there was a group concern here—some people are bothered by the eating but feel uncomfortable speaking up about it. Inez reiterated she didn't like to impose on others. Jenny suggested that the eaters, in a way, were imposing on the others. Silence.

I suggested that those who didn't like it when people ate in the group had a right to speak up if they were bothered. Inez, Mary, Diane, and Robert shook their heads "no" and waved their hands as if to dismiss the trend of the conversation. Jenny suggested there might be ways to limit the eating in the group so that it wouldn't be bothersome. She suggested maybe the group should start out with refreshments. No one responded.

I said perhaps we should take a food break about halfway through the meeting. Inez said no, that would interrupt what was going on in the group. Many other members agreed with her. *I said if we took a break, we'd all be eating together.* Olivia said she needs to eat *while* the meeting's going on. Jenny said maybe what we should do is make it a rule that no one can eat things that smell a lot or that are crunchy and make a lot of noise when you chew them. No one responded.

Group members agreed to not prohibit eating or enforce the rule of no eating in the group. Jenny said she hoped group members would try to state their opinion or speak up when/if something is bothering them, and that this was the place to do it.

the record, "Jenny said it looked like there was a group concern here—some people are bothered by the eating but feel uncomfortable speaking up about it." Jackie immediately said, "Yes, but is the problem how to handle eating in the group or is the real problem that the members aren't assertive and won't speak up?" "Ah," I said. "That's not so clear here. The problem really isn't clearly identified." Pointing to Step 3 on the board, I continued, "Is the problem/issue explored?"

With the aim of helping the students "see" the problem-solving process in the group, we continue to look at each step of the process to gauge how it is or is not reflected in the first record. The teaching point most important in reviewing this record is that the workers jump prematurely to possible solutions—begin with refreshments, take an eating break, eat only certain kinds of foods—without ever *exploring* the issue with the group (Step 3). With a touch of humor, we label this record as being the "all solutions–no problem" brand of group work.

We then move to the second record in the sequence (see pp. 56–58). As we did with the first record, we distribute it to the class and ask for another volunteer to read it aloud as everyone follows along.

Once again, we initiate discussion of the record by posing the two questions: What is the problem or issue in this group? What is the problem with the problem-solving process? Students iden-

Record #2

Setting: Community mental health clinic
Members: Karen, Linda, Liz, Judy, Pat
Worker: Bruce (social work student)

February 1
Karen: "My daughter had this really terrible experience with my ex-husband and I'm not sure how to deal with it. I'm so upset...[she continues—at length]...and I'm really overwhelmed."

Bruce: *"Let's hear some responses or sharing in regard to what you've been saying from the other people."*

Linda [immediately beginning]: "Well, I know what your daughter went through. My father used to really beat me up but I couldn't talk to my mother about it like you and your daughter and...."

Karen [interrupting]: "It was really hard talking to my daughter...[she talks on anxiously]."

Bruce [interrupting]: *"Karen, let's finish hearing what Linda has to say. Perhaps you can get an idea of how your daughter felt by listening."*

Karen looks embarrassed, but quietly listens.

Linda: "I really couldn't talk with my mother and...[after a lengthy monologue she stops]."

After a silence Karen picks it up. She says a few sentences.

Bruce: *"Let's hear from some of the people who haven't spoken yet."*

Nobody responds.

Bruce: *"Liz, could you identify with anything that was said?"*

Liz begins to speak.

February 8
Linda: "I saw my ex-boyfriend at school today and it was really painful..." [she continues for about 5 minutes].

Silence.

Judy: "Yeah, when I ran into my ex-husband it was hard." [She gets quiet, deferring back to Linda.]

Bruce: *"Judy, could you say more about it?"*

Judy: "Well, I was really upset. It felt so awkward."

Bruce: *"It is a hard situation."*

Judy: "Yes, you don't know what to do. It brings up a lot of memories."

Silence.

Karen: "Yeah, the memories are painful."

Bruce: *"It seems as though Judy had more to say. Let's have her finish."*

Judy: "It was really painful to see him."

Silence.

Bruce: *"Has anyone else had similar experiences?"*

Karen: "I had it every time my husband came to pick up the kids."

Bruce: *"Yes, that must be difficult. Pat, can you share something with us?"*

Pat begins to share.

February 15
Bruce: *"I would like to bring something up with the group. Some people have mentioned to me that there isn't always enough time for them to talk. Sometimes many people have pressing concerns and we only have an hour and a half. I wonder if the group has ideas to deal with this problem."*

Linda: "You are saying that for my benefit because I told you the other day."

Bruce: *"You and other people who have mentioned it to me."*

Karen: "Well, I know I talked a lot when my daughter got in trouble but maybe the person who needs it most...."

Bruce: *"How could we determine that?"*

Pat: "We could ask everyone, go around."

Liz: "Why don't you just pick?"

Bruce: *"Well, I might on occasion, Liz. So Pat mentioned going around. How so?"*

Liz: "Well, just ask who wants to talk or each person says a little."

Bruce: *"Judy, what do you think about that?"*

Judy: "There's no way. The one who's most upset should talk."

Karen: "Well, we'll just ask who wants to talk at the beginning."

Bruce: *"How will we help people who have trouble speaking up?"*

Liz: "I'm not sure, we'll ask around. I think we got a good idea now."

Pat: "Yeah, we get the idea."

Bruce: *"OK. We'll discuss it again and see how it is working out."*

Silence.

Judy: "Well, my husband came home from Ecuador...."

tify the issue as time management. Again, we refer, one by one, to the steps listed on the board and ask students whether they see evidence of that step having been covered in the record.

Students are more adept at seeing the problem-solving steps in this record. They realize that a vague sense of an issue is present in the first two meetings and that the worker identified the problem/issue on February 15 when he says: "I would like to bring something up with the group. Some people have mentioned to me that there isn't always enough time for them to talk. Sometimes many people have pressing concerns and we only have an hour and a half." But then, we point out, in the very same intervention, the worker skips the problem exploration step and moves immediately to asking for "solutions." He says, "I wonder if the group has ideas to deal with this problem." Thus, without exploring the reasons that time management may be difficult, the group offers a variety of possible "solutions"—the person who needs it most should talk, the group should take turns and go around, the worker should pick the speaker, each person should say a little, the group should start with the person who's most upset. We point out that although this record is similar to the first in its focus on "solutions" without exploration, it does evince a clearer identification of the problem. Thus, rather than labeling this record "all solutions–no problem," as we did the first, we label it "mostly all solutions–a tiny bit of problem."

We then distribute the third record in the sequence and ask for a volunteer reader (see pp. 60-62).

Class discussion of this record begins by our repeating the two questions: What is the group struggling with? What is the problem with the problem-solving process? Rather quickly, the students identify the group issue as how the boys handle anger with one another. We point out that the problem-solving process in this case can be used to address issues regarding group conduct, as was true in the first two records, as well as individual behavior, as is true in this record.

We once again refer to each step of the problem-solving process listed on the board as we help students evaluate the problem-solving process in this record. Students identify two occasions of clear problem identification. The first is toward the end of the February 21 meeting when the social work student said to the group, "When you guys get mad at each other or at the activity, what you very often do is take it out on each other." The second occasion comes at the end of the February 28 meeting when the psychology intern said: "What happens, guys, is that it all goes in a circle. Darrell gets angry and bothers George; George gets angry and bothers Clyde; Clyde gets angry and bothers Mr. Fuller; Mr. Fuller gets angry and bothers Darrell, and on and on." The group members' ability to understand the problem is indicated when Darrell, following this statement, laughs and says, "I know what you mean."

Unlike the first two records, this record shows evidence of problem exploration. We point out to the class that, over the weeks, the workers ask questions, make observations, and ask group members to think about the problem. Sometimes students— especially those who have not worked with children—think that these workers are talking too much and receiving inadequate verbal response from the group members. If they raise this, we point out that the group members are being very responsive to the workers, who, by articulating what they see, are helping the members to recognize and understand what is going on among them.

The teaching point in this record is the absence of attention to "solutions." It is almost as if the workers expect that if the group members recognize the problem, they will be able to solve it by changing their behaviors on their own. But if problem solving is to be effective, the workers must engage the group in discussion and test out solutions. Thus, rather than "all solutions—no problem" or "almost all solutions—a tiny bit of problem," we label this record "all problem—no solutions."

Record #3

Setting: Mental health clinic

Members: Darrell, Clyde, George, Keith

Leaders: Ken (social work student), Robert (psychology intern)

February 21

The domino game began with all members and both workers participating. Midway through the first game, Darrell realized that he was losing the game and became visibly upset, pounding his feet on the floor and yelling loudly. George, who was sitting opposite from Darrell, was stacking his dominoes one on top of the other. Darrell looked at this, and proceeded to take a deep breath and blew down George's dominoes. George got very angry. I observed tension in his face, but he did not say anything. A few minutes passed and George turned to Clyde and took off Clyde's hat.

After the interactions among Darrell, George, and Clyde, the game ended and it was time to clean up. All members cleaned cooperatively. Ten minutes remained until the end of the meeting. I asked all the members to come back to the table and be seated. They all complied. Robert then stated: "You know, something was going on between all of you during the domino game today." Darrell and George responded with laughter. I asked George if he knew what had happened. George stopped laughing and a serious look came over his face. After several moments of silence, George said, "I got mad." I asked George if he remembered when he got mad, and he stated, "Darrell blew down my dominoes." Robert stated: "Yes, and Darrell was mad, too, when he did that." As time was running out, I said, *"When you guys get mad at each other or at the activity, what you very often do is take it out on each other. Sometimes you're real mean to one another. Let's all think about that and we'll discuss this again next week."* The session ended and the boys proceeded calmly to the elevators.

February 28

All four boys were present and on time for the group meeting. Everyone took seats around the table where snacks were served. After several minutes, Robert asked: "Do you guys remember what we were talking about at the end of our last session?" There was no response, and George, Darrell, and Keith started playing with the milk container. After several minutes of just silently observing, I said: *"I've noticed that when you guys have something difficult to talk about, you start doing other things like playing with the milk container."* George perked up in his seat and responded, "Last week we talked about getting mad." Robert responded: "That's right, George; we talked about getting mad and how sometimes when you guys are angry, you take it out on each other." Darrell, not looking at either Robert or myself, asked, "What do you mean?" I stated: *"Well, last week when we were playing dominoes, you got angry and I think you were angry with yourself. But instead of saying that you were angry or trying to improve your game, you reached out and made George angry, and then George reached out and made Clyde angry."* Darrell was silent for a few moments and then Robert added: "What happens, guys, is that it all goes in a circle. Darrell gets angry and bothers George; George gets angry and bothers Clyde; Clyde gets angry and bothers Mr. Fuller; Mr. Fuller gets angry and bothers Darrell, and on and on." Darrell laughed and said, "I know what you mean."

March 6
All four group members were present. After 15 minutes of discussion, the group chose card-playing as an activity. They established a set of rules and dealt out chips and cards for the game of 21. Keith and I were winning most of the hands. At one point, Darrell was dealt a series of cards which totaled over 21. He leaned back in his chair and then fell forward, pounding his fist on the table. The force of his punch caused George's chips to fall on the floor. George looked visibly upset, but did not speak. Robert stated: "Darrell, I think you just made George angry." There was no response. I asked George how he was feeling. There was no response. Several silent minutes went by while the game continued. In the middle of a hand, George said, "I don't want to play anymore." George then sat silently for several minutes as the game proceeded. I looked at George and said, *"You look pretty angry."* George did not respond, but reached out to knock over Keith's chips. I then stated loudly, *"George, it's happening again; you got angry with Darrell, and now you're going to make Keith angry."* George withdrew his hands from the chips

and sat silently. In a little while, Robert stated to Darrell and George, "I can understand that you guys get annoyed and frustrated with the game sometimes, but I can't understand why you take it out on each other, especially when you like each other so much." Nobody said anything until Darrell and George glanced at each other across the table and both broke out into smiles. I looked at both of them and asked, *"Do you guys know what you just did?"* They both looked up and asked, "What—what did we do?" I replied, *"You just apologized to each other."* Darrell looked at George, then laughed, and they both slapped each other's hands.

Summarizing Key Points

After we have covered the three-record sequence with the class, we distill the following key points from the exercise.

• Often, as shown in the first two records, workers jump to solutions prematurely. This pattern is much more frequent than that exhibited in the third record where the workers thoroughly explored the problem, but reached for no solutions.

• Workers tend to be more comfortable addressing solutions than problems. Perhaps this is because they want to reduce their own anxiety and increase their sense of accomplishment. Exploring an issue involves uncertainty, and a worker may fear that conflict will erupt. Solutions are more specific and less scary.

• Inadequate problem exploration results in premature solutions that are almost always ineffective. Because such solutions are not rooted in an understanding of the issue, they do not address underlying causes and will not work. Effective solutions become possible and evolve from the understanding that group members gain from identifying and exploring group issues.

• Exploring an issue involves asking members to remain engaged with that issue—what it looks like, what leads to its occurrence, why it takes place—and to resist their own tendency to move too quickly to solutions. As one student aptly exclaimed in the class, "So what you're really saying, then, is that we need to 'stay in the mess.'"

At the end of this unit we suggest that students review their process recordings and identify times when they moved to solutions prematurely. We recommend that they ask themselves what they might have said to help the group (or individual client) explore an issue in more depth. We have found that many students do this analysis and find it very helpful.

This unit is one of the most important for students. Their understanding of the problem-solving process is reflected throughout the rest of the course. Students adopt the language of the unit and will say aloud, when they look at their practice, "Uh-oh, I jumped to solutions. I needed to stay with the problem longer." The quality of their practice deepens as a result of their understanding and belief in the importance of exploration. We, too, refer back to this session as the rest of the course proceeds, for the problem-solving process is a foundation for the units that follow.

Readings

Compton, Beulah R., & Galaway, Burt. (1994). *Social Work Processes* (5th ed., pp. 43-84). Pacific Grove, CA: Brooks/Cole.

Dewey, John. (1910). *How We Think*. Boston: Heath.

Malekoff, Andrew. (1997). *Group Work with Adolescents* (pp. 119-145). New York: Guilford.

Morris, Van Cleve, & Pai, Young. (1976). *Philosophy and the American School* (pp. 149-152). Boston: Houghton Mifflin.

Northen, Helen. (1988). *Social Work with Groups* (2nd ed., pp. 47-49). New York: Columbia University Press.

Somers, Mary Louise. (1976). Problem-Solving in Small Groups. In Robert W. Roberts & Helen Northen (Eds.), *Theories of Social Work with Groups* (pp. 331-367). New York: Columbia University Press.

Toseland, Ronald W., & Rivas, Robert F. (1998). *An Introduction to Group Work Practice* (3rd ed., pp. 314-328). Boston: Allyn and Bacon.

Unit 6
Middles

When members have been oriented to the group, norms of behavior established, a common initial purpose defined, and some commonalities among group members recognized, the group enters its middle stage. Specific behavioral characteristics in this complex stage will vary from group to group. In particular, the worker's role in the middle stage changes to one that is less central and that maximizes the leadership and mutual aid of group members.

This short unit aims to provide a brief orientation to this stage of group development. Two of its central features—member roles, and conflict and difference—are addressed in more detail in the units that follow. The objectives of this teaching unit for students are two:

1. To become familiar with the characteristics, member needs, and worker's role in the middle stage of group development.
2. To become familiar with practice skills that are used with groups in the middle stage.

We begin by distributing and reviewing with the class a handout, "Stages of Group Development—Middle" (see Appendix I). In discussing the salient features of the middle stage, we emphasize several points:

• By the middle stage of group development, members have become more themselves—more natural and less concerned about the impression they make on others in the group. They now play a much more active role in the group and engage in mutual aid. The worker's role is less central and more concerned now with encouraging and improving member participation and communication. The worker actively shares observations about what is taking place in the group—sometimes confronting the group or an individual group member—and often relies on group members to address those perceptions.

• The purpose of the group also continues to be defined and redefined in relation to individual members' needs. However, the discussion of purpose that takes place in the group now has greater depth and realism and is qualitatively different than it was in beginnings. Members now have a clearer sense of the possibilities of this group, and of what they might gain from their participation in it. Their investment in the group grows and cohesiveness among members as a group develops.

• Group members have gained a greater sense of one another. Different characteristics and behaviors emerge, and as a result members come to expect others to act in particular ways. Members take on and assign to each other specific roles in the group. Some members become more powerful and influential and have greater status than others. Subgroups often form.

• Differences among members assume increasing importance as members become more willing to express honest opinions and points of view, regardless of the popularity and acceptance that such expressions may bring. Thus, conflict can become frequent and should be expected in this stage. Workers will have to help group members address such conflict constructively.

We have noticed that students in our classes who are working with groups in the field often view the total group as an entity to the exclusion of the individual group members. To help them maintain a dual vision on both the total group and the individual group members, we suggest that for use in their own groups they develop a "thumbnail sketch" of each member of their group, jotting down all that they know concerning each member—descriptive and behavioral characteristics, his or her relationship to others in the group, the ways in which the worker believes each member can benefit from the group. Developing such sketches highlights for students and inexperienced workers the uniqueness of each individual so that this person's importance in the collectivity is not ignored.

We also point out to the class that the handout on the middle stage is set up in the same format as the one they received for beginnings (see Appendix G) and the one that they will receive for endings (see Appendix J). If they wish to view the progression over time along any one dimension (e.g., where the members are, what needs to happen, or the role of the worker), they can read down a column from beginning to middle to ending. Using the handouts in this way provides specificity and completeness in each of the three areas.

As we did in Unit 4, "Beginnings," we identify for students some skills that we believe workers are most likely to need and use in the middle stage of group development. These skills are selected from Middleman and Wood's book, *Skills for Direct Practice in Social Work* (1990).

- *Reaching for consensus:* to check to see if most members agree with how things are going;
- *Reaching for difference:* to help group members see things from various angles so that a range of viewpoints and possibilities are entertained;
- *Confronting situations:* to involve relevant members in an open exchange of information and affect about a problem or issue as each person perceives it;
- *Reaching for feelings:* to invite members to describe the emotions they are experiencing;
- *Amplifying subtle messages:* to call attention to unnoticed communicative behavior (e.g., words, tone of voice, facial expressions) by commenting on it to others in the group rather than to the particular person;
- *Reporting own feelings:* to describe one's in-the-moment emotional experience when such self-disclosure is likely to be useful in shedding light on others' feelings or the situation;
- *Reaching for information:* to ask the members for facts, opinions, impressions, or judgments that increase knowledge of a situation or event;
- *Giving feedback:* to repeat the essence of what members have said and to ask if the meaning received was, in fact, the intended meaning;
- *Checking out inferences:* to ask if a certain thought, hunch, or interpretation is valid for members in a particular situation;
- *Giving information:* to offer the group facts, opinions, or ideas that may increase their knowledge of a situation or event.

The introduction of these skills is different now from their presentation in Unit 4. At this point, students are familiar with the practice skills and with the content of the Middleman and Wood book, for they have been using material from this book in their practice in the field, both with groups and individuals. Therefore, the instructor need not spend significant class time introducing the skills that are used frequently in the middle stage, nor is it necessary to engage the class in an exercise as part of this unit.

Rather, the instructor may briefly describe these skills and then choose to demonstrate one or two that seem more difficult for students to grasp and use. The skill of amplifying subtle messages is one with which students seem to have a difficult time. The following record illustrates one way an instructor can pique students' understanding of this issue.

> I scanned the room and said to the class, "Joan looks as if she is ready for a break—right now!" After a brief pause, I asked the class, "Which skill did I just use?" Denise said, with emphasis, "Amplifying subtle messages!" Flora interjected, quickly and with feeling, "I tried using that skill in my group and I don't like it. It puts the person on the spot, it makes them defensive." "Tell us how you used the skill," I said. "Well, one time in my group there was a member who was yawning a lot and I said to him, "Harry, you keep yawning." He got annoyed and became very defensive and I backed off. "But that's not how you use that skill," Ishmael said immediately. "You said it directly to the person, but you need to say it to the group." I agreed with Ishmael and pointed out that speaking to the *group* rather than commenting directly to Harry is the opposite of putting him on the spot, that this is a skill you use when you have a sense that someone in the group *wants* to and *is* saying something through his or her nonverbal behavior. Making an observation to the group about that person's behavior invites the group to recognize and encourage the individual to contribute. Turning to the class, I then observed, "It looks as if Denise is bursting with something she wants to say." There were smiles and laughs and John said, "Yeah, Denise, let's hear it." Denise smiled and said, "I use it all the time...."

After the demonstration and discussion of skills, we tell the class that member roles and conflict and differences, two areas that are central to the middle stage of group development, will be addressed in the class sessions that follow.

Readings

Brandler, Sondra, & Roman, Camille P. (1991). *Group Work: Skills and Strategies for Effective Interventions* (pp. 37-74). New York: Haworth.

Brown, Leonard N. (1991). *Groups for Growth and Change* (pp. 47-64). New York: Longman.

Garland, James, Jones, Hubert, & Kolodny, Ralph. (1973). A Model for Stages of Development in Social Work Groups. In Saul Bernstein (Ed.), *Explorations in Group Work* (pp. 17-71). Boston: Milford House.

Garvin, Charles D. (1997). *Contemporary Group Work* (3rd ed., pp. 99-137). Boston: Allyn and Bacon.

Hartford, Margaret E. (1971). *Groups in Social Work* (pp. 193-275). New York: Columbia University Press.

Henry, Sue. (1992). *Group Skills in Social Work: A Four-Dimensional Approach* (2nd ed., pp. 127-191). Pacific Grove, CA: Brooks/Cole.

Middleman, Ruth R., & Wood, Gale Goldberg. (1990). *Skills for Direct Practice in Social Work* (pp. 91-154). New York: Columbia University Press.

Northen, Helen. (1988). *Social Work with Groups* (pp. 222-297). New York: Columbia University Press.

Schiller, Linda Yael. (1995). Stages of Development in Women's Groups: A Relational Model. In Roselle Kurland & Robert Salmon (Eds.), *Group Work Practice in a Troubled Society: Problems and Opportunities* (pp. 117-138). New York: Haworth.

Shulman, Lawrence. (1992). *The Skills of Helping Individuals, Families and Groups* (pp. 103-172, 401-572). Itasca, IL: Peacock.

Toseland, Ronald W., & Rivas, Robert F. (1998). *An Introduction to Group Work Practice* (3rd ed., pp. 233-362). Boston: Allyn and Bacon.

Unit 7
Group Roles

Member roles often demand a great deal of the worker's and the members' attention in the group's middle stage. As group members interact and become more comfortable with one another, they develop expectations about their own behavior and the behavior of other group members. They often place themselves, or are placed by other group members, into expected behavior patterns usually determined by an individual's status in the group.

These member roles become differentiated in the middle stage as expectations about what is to be done and by whom become clearer. Each member can carry out many roles, which evolve through interactions with other members and with the social worker.

Generally, roles can be characterized as constructive or destructive, and we suggest differentiating them with four categories:

- Roles that contribute positively to the group's ability to achieve its purpose, such as the information seeker, the initiator, and the elaborator.
- Roles that contribute positively to the social and emotional needs of the group, such as the encourager, the harmonizer, and the welcomer.
- Roles that disrupt the group's achievement of its purpose, such as the monopolizer, the help-rejecting complainer, the intellectualizer.
- Roles that negatively affect the social and emotional needs of the group, such as the bully, the scapegoat, and the gossip.

This unit describes a range of teaching methods that emphasize the reciprocal nature of group roles and ways students can intervene to address the existence of problematic group roles. To this end, the unit has four objectives for students:

1. To understand that member roles contribute to and detract from group purpose, and that roles that meet the emotional needs of one particular member may be unhelpful to the total group.

2. To understand the reciprocity of roles—that *both* the individual in a role and the total group create and maintain member roles in the group.

3. To appreciate the importance of promoting flexibility in roles so that members can try out and experience many ways of contributing to the group and relating to others.

4. To know when and how to intervene when a group member has assumed, or been placed in, a role that is potentially destructive.

We introduce member roles in class with humor by distributing a list of roles taken from Milton Berger's *Working with People Called Patients* (1977). The list (see Figure 1) is an amusing characterization of a wide range of possible roles.

As students review the list, we ask them to keep in mind groups with which they have worked and groups in which they have been members, including teams, boards, committees, and other informal or recreational groups. Usually, students respond with laughter and signs of recognition as they read the list and identify group members they have known. We ask students to describe to the class the behavior of particular persons in a group who aptly fit one of the roles from Berger's list. We then bring up the four categories of constructive and destructive roles and ask students to identify Berger's roles, or roles from their own experience with a group, within each of the four categories. We might also add other roles that students may not have mentioned but that occur frequently in social work groups.

We emphasize the importance of promoting flexibility in member roles and trying to keep group members from being locked permanently into particular roles. Often in groups, patterns of behavior will become stabilized in such a way that the group will expect a member to behave in a particular way regularly. To lock someone into a role means that the group members will not allow that person to behave in different ways than they have come to expect, even when that member may wish to do so. A good example is the person who becomes the group clown. In the beginning stage of the group, the clown is welcomed because she or he brings about laughter and releases tension at times of anxiety in the group. But what happens as the group moves along and the clown wishes to become serious? Often her or his attempts to be serious are disappointing to the other group members whose expectations are that the clown will always be funny. For the clown, however, these attempts to behave seriously may represent a posi-

Figure 1. Berger's List of Potential Group Roles

Jester	The Judge	Prima Donna
Referee–Umpire	Overprotective	Frail Tyrant
Catalyst	Mama	Teacher's Pet
Don Juan	Kill-Joy	Prosecutor
Cockteaser	Egghead	Seducer
The Idiot	The Baiter	Guardhouse
Injustice Collector	The Doctor's	Lawyer
The Abused Type	Assistant	The Scapegoat
Missionary	Martyr	Rejection Collector
Crisis Creator	Ombudsman–	The Saint
Story Teller	Guardian	Fashion Plate
Clock-Watcher	Negativistic Clique	Innocent
Whiner	Creator	Advice Seeker
Leader of Opposition	Help-Rejecting	Runt of the Litter
Nit Picker	Complainer	Strong Silent Type
Planner	Flirt	Compulsive Helper
Self-Righteous Critic	Sophisticate	Can't Say No
Expert	Cockroach	Manipulator
Provocateur	Troublemaker	Competitor
Fragile Baby	Magician	Ostrich
General	Charmer	Fair One
Intellectual	Iconoclast	Pollyanna
Virtuously Honest	Victim	Castrator
Sadist	Vindicator	Guilt Provoker

Adapted from Milton Berger, *Working with People Called Patients*, (1977, p. 106).

tive change in behavior. One of the opportunities that group membership often presents is that it gives members a chance to test our different ways of behaving. To lock a member into a particular role is to eliminate that opportunity of membership. In addition, rigid role expectations deprive the group of the new contributions that individual members may be able to make. The worker needs to help the members not stereotype one another.

To further illustrate the importance of flexibility in roles and the different interventions that a practitioner can use, according to the group's stage of development, we focus on the monopolizer. Here is an example of a class interaction:

I asked the class, "How would you handle it if in the first session of a group, you had a monopolizer who jumped in to answer every question you asked and who went on and on nonstop in his or her responses? What are some of the things you would do?" Paulette said immediately, "I wouldn't call on that person." Jasmine added, "I wouldn't look at that person. I'd avoid eye contact." Luis said, "I'd ask if someone else in the group has anything to say." "I'd interrupt that person, try to politely cut him off," Josselyn added.

"OK, all of those are good suggestions," I responded. "How would you characterize the interventions you've suggested? What are you trying to do?"

"I want the monopolizer to stop talking so much, but I don't want to embarrass him," Margaret said. "Yes," I said, "What you're really trying to do is *indirectly* give the monopolizer the message that his or her behavior is inappropriate. By not calling on the person, by looking away, by inviting others to speak up, you hope the monopolizer realizes that he or she needs to not talk so much. Sometimes this helps to change the monopolizer's behavior.

"But suppose the group goes on and it's now the seventh session and the same monopolizer is still monopolizing," I continued. "Only now whenever he speaks other group members roll their eyes and shift in their seats and clearly are quite irritated. Now what would you do?" The class was silent.

"I tried everything I knew to do and nothing worked," James said. "I don't know what else to do except more of the same. Maybe eventually he'd get the message." "I'd figure out something else to try—maybe I'd ask him to meet with me individually after the group," Rosalind said. "But if you do that, you're taking a problem-solving opportunity away from the group," I say. The class could see that, but had no suggestions for how to intervene successfully.

The example of the monopolizer at different stages of the group's development generates a number of teaching points.

• Often, behavior that is welcomed by the group, and even by the worker in the beginning, becomes problematic if it persists into the middle stage and interferes with the group's progress. In the beginning, for instance, the group's members and social worker are relieved to have someone speaking, even if that person is monopolizing; they might even give this person positive feedback. As the group continues, however, and other members want to speak up, the monopolizer's behavior becomes disruptive and is viewed negatively. A similar dynamic of welcome in the beginning followed by increasing disapproval and resentment as the group develops can be found in a variety of other roles, as well.

• The stage of a group's development profoundly influences the worker's choice of interventions to address roles in a group. In the beginning stage, a worker might use a range of indirect techniques. The worker is more active in the beginning and would not ask group members to take the risk of commenting directly on the behavior of one of their peers. In the middle stage, however, indirect methods are unlikely to be effective, and it is fair to expect group members to comment on the behaviors of others in the group.

• Roles are reciprocal. An individual member's role behavior both conditions and is conditioned by the ways in which the group expects or reacts to such behavior. It is important to realize that there is an interaction between individual and group needs in the creation and maintenance of role behavior.

• The worker's attention often goes toward the person in the problematic role, and attention to the part that the other group members play in placing or keeping that person in the difficult role is frequently neglected. In the example, it is true that the monopolizer is taking over, but it is equally true that others in the group allow that person to take the role.

• Use of the problem-solving process (see Unit 5) is central to addressing problematic role behavior in a group's middle stage.

Problem-Solving Interventions

To illustrate dysfunctional role behavior in the middle stage of a group, we focus on the role of the scapegoat, although we emphasize that interventions directed toward the scapegoat are applicable to *any* problematic role in a group's middle stage. We begin by describing and defining the dynamics of scapegoating. The genesis of the term scapegoat is a biblical one, going back to an ancient Hebrew ritual of atonement when the chief priest of a village would symbolically lay the sins of the people on the back of a goat and then cast the goat into the wilderness, thereby cleansing and ridding the people of their sins. Shulman's (1992) definition of a scapegoat is also particularly helpful: "a member of a group who is attacked, verbally or physically, by other members who project onto the member their own negative feelings about themselves. The scapegoat role is often interactive in nature with the scapegoat fulfilling a functional role in the group" (p. 486). In short, in a small group the person who is scapegoated represents the qualities, and becomes a symbol of tendencies or characteristics, that other members do not like in themselves.

To illustrate the look and feel of a group scapegoat, we read to the class the case example of 10-year-old Amy, who is in a group concerned with future careers (see p. 77).

With the portrait of Amy we demonstrate that in a face-to-face group the scapegoat acts to evoke the behavior of the others. This is different from the systematic oppression of an entire people that can occur in larger society, where those being scapegoated (e.g., African Americans, gays and lesbians, and/or Jews) have the role imposed upon them and have not "volunteered" for it. When working with a group in which there is a scapegoat, it is important that the worker identify the behavior of the scapegoat that elicits the actions of others. The scapegoat's evocative behavior, however, does not diminish the fact that other group members' behavior can be quite cruel and attacking toward this person. This can be distressing for the worker, who is not immune to the strong emotions that such cruel behavior stirs up. Garland and Kolodny (1973, p. 55) describe it well: "The group worker confronted with scapegoating in the midst of interaction often finds himself caught up in a welter of primitive feelings, punitive and pitying, and assailed by morbid reflections on the unfairness of fate which leaves one weak and others strong."

To stimulate examination of worker intervention with a problematic role in a group's middle stage, we distribute the case example (shown on pp. 78–80) of Gladys, a 13-year-old in an after-school group who is a scapegoat. We ask class members to take on the roles of the group members by reading them aloud while the instructor reads the narrative parts. After the reading, we ask the class for reactions. Specifically, we ask them what Gladys does to make group members scapegoat her and why her behavior is infuriating and provocative to both her peers and the worker. Students easily recognize both points.

Case Example—Amy

I first noticed that Amy was setting herself up for criticism from her peers during a session on November 13th. The group had been divided into three subgroups of three. The "game" called for each group to make up a commercial to "sell" each individual's best quality. The purpose of the game was to help the girls to begin to think about what kinds of things they had special talents or interests in (e.g., cooking, math, sense of humor). A note at the end of my process record for that day says:

> "Amy seemed unable to gauge the appropriateness of some of her behavior. That is, although it was understood that no one was Barbra Streisand. . . no one took their individual act too seriously. Amy, on the other hand, in a very serious manner sang a complete song in the worst voice imaginable. . . rather as if she were standing alone in her bedroom in the middle of a daydream."

During the other sessions, I had noticed that Amy's affect seemed heightened and exaggerated. She would act very excited, especially when she was actually included in a given activity by the group members. She would literally assault the group members—not viciously, but rather as an overly affectionate relative whose bear hug ruptures your spleen and who, when you mention that their right hush puppy has mashed your five left toes, graciously springs backwards only to jar the coffee table, thereby spilling over the crystal bowl that held 529 M&M's.

Often Amy behaved in such a manner as to become the brunt of jokes in the group. She said and did things for a laugh, but the text of those comments and actions was truly lacking a sense of humor. Sense in this case refers to the perception of, or feel for, what actually is humorous—Amy lacked the *sense* in sense of humor. Her humor elicited from the group the kind of response that closet comedians have decided to avoid and that active jokesters hope to avoid. Amy acted out a fantasy insecurity that most people don't want to be exposed to at any level. Further, Amy's attempts to gain attention were so obsequious and self-debasing that we all felt completely uncomfortable. Amy's unfortunate knack was her ability to remind everybody just how silly and sad we can all be when we're trying too hard to gain acceptance from others.

Case Example–Gladys

Gladys is 13 years old, approximately 5′ 10″ tall, slightly overweight, well groomed, wears glasses, and is generally attractive. Her present school performance level is classified as "promotion in doubt." Gladys's statements about herself are usually in contradiction to the truth, with sarcastic exaggerations of her faults or imperfections as she sees them. At the first group meeting, Gladys's introductory statements and her manner of laughing *with* those who are laughing *at* her set the stage for her to be the scapegoat.

10/30
"I'm kinda fat, oh, I said that already, I must be senile too." As Gladys was talking, she stopped to watch Yolanda smirking at her. She continued, trying to talk daintily and pronounce her words precisely to the amusement of Joanne and Yolanda.

Gladys's actions do not match her size and stature. Her movements are inappropriate, which gives an outward appearance of awkwardness and imbalance. For example, rather than sit in a regular-sized chair, Gladys chose a child's size chair to sit in during group sessions.

Gladys's hair style is more appropriate for a 9- or 10-year-old. She wears several barrettes at a time with her hair in numerous braids. Despite her mature physical appearance, Gladys is very passive and backs down from any confrontation with her peers. The fact that someone so large can be intimidated by smaller members in the group acts as a vehicle for members to play with Gladys while actually ridiculing her.

After Joanne and Yolanda introduced themselves and expressed their likes and dislikes, Joanne instructed Gladys to speak next.

"My name is Gladys, I'm not too tall." Yolanda interrupted by laughing out loud. *"You had your turn to speak already, Yolanda," I said.* Gladys continued, "I have black hair, I wear glasses, I'm kinda fat." Yolanda and Joanne laughed in unison. Yolanda said, "Kinda fat? You're real fat!" Gladys joined in with the laughter.

Gladys continued to tell us which school she goes to, what class she's in, her teacher's name, what she looks like, etc. Yolanda rudely interjected, "What size shoes you wear?" Gladys answered, "Nine and a half." Yolanda yelled, "You got big feet!" As she continued to laugh, Gladys laughed, too, and said, "I can't help it if I have big feet."

Joanne and Yolanda kept on laughing. *"Why do you both find Gladys so comical? What's so funny?" I asked.* There was quiet for just a minute. "So—Gladys is laughing too," said Yolanda. *"But you're not laughing with her, you're laughing at her. There is a difference," I said.*

11/13

After giving up on playing pool, Gladys took notice of the Ping-Pong table, as Yolanda continued to play pool by herself.

I asked Gladys if she knew how to play Ping-Pong. She said she didn't know how. *I explained the game to her and suggested that we could help her to learn to play by practicing hitting the ball back and forth.* Gladys started, saying, "I'm not going to be any good at this." *I told her, "You won't really know until you try."*

When she missed the ball she would sarcastically say, "Boy, dummy, that was really a great shot! Did you see that fantastic shot I just made? I bet you can't play as bad as me, Mrs. Gray." *"To be good at anything usually takes practice, Gladys. Give it a chance," I said.*

Even though I kept telling Gladys, *"Keep your eye on the ball. . . . If at first you don't succeed. . . . Take your time. . . ,"* Gladys seemed to delight in failure. She didn't really try to successfully hit the ball. I found myself getting somewhat angry at her self-defeating attitude. After a while I got tired trying to convince her that she could learn to play. As Yolanda joined in the game of Ping-Pong, she started to make fun of Gladys every time she missed the ball. "I'm so stupid, I can't even hit this little ball," said Gladys. "You are stupid. If you don't hit it better we're not going to let you play," Yolanda said.

I pointed out to them that not everyone is good at doing everything, and that sometimes new things take a little time to master. We continued to play for a few minutes more. *I then suggested that we stop playing while the game was still fun.*

Yolanda said, "She makes me sick. Just because she can't play we have to stop." *"If you get as angry as you did, it's not a game anymore," I said.* There was a pause. *"Why did you get so angry,*

Yolanda?" I asked. "'Cause she can't even hit the ball with her big stupid self." Gladys answered, too, "I told you I didn't know how to play." Yolanda sucked her teeth and rolled her eyes at Gladys.

"Do you know what you did that made Yolanda angry, Gladys?" I asked. "Yeah, she's mad because I don't know how to play, that's why, but that's too bad. . . ." Gladys looked intently at Yolanda, trying to evoke a response. There was complete silence as the hostility grew.

"Gladys, I think that it's more what you don't do that makes Yolanda angry at you," I said. "You gave up before you even had a chance to learn." There was a pause. Gladys didn't answer. *"It seemed to me that you had already decided that you couldn't learn how to play, therefore you didn't."* Gladys very calmly replied, "I'm just not very good at sports." *"I feel you can be good at anything you want to be good at," I told her.* "Forget her!" Yolanda said as she waved her hand.

We stay with the Gladys example to teach students how to intervene, continuing with another vignette that challenges them to consider the role of the worker:

It's now the middle of January. The group has grown and been meeting regularly. Gladys comes to you individually and says that starting next week she won't be coming to the group any more. You ask her, "How come?" and she says, "Because this group never does anything good." You've noticed that Gladys has continued to be scapegoated by the group, including by the new members. They make fun of her dress and of her comments. No one wants to sit next to her during the meetings. She is the last chosen for teams, and then grudgingly so. On the other hand, you've also noticed that Gladys makes only a halfhearted attempt in group games and then passively responds when members become annoyed with her lack of effort. You also remember one time in particular when Gladys brought a bag of potato chips to the group and ate them all without offering any to the other members even though it was clear that they wanted some.

With this additional information, we engage students in a role play by asking them to collectively play the part of the worker while the instructor becomes Gladys. We begin by repeating: "You are the worker, I am Gladys. Talk to me." Usually there is a brief silence and then class members jump in, as in the following record.

"I'd tell Gladys I feel bad that she wants to leave," Mei Chan said. "I'm Gladys, talk to me," I insisted. "Oh, OK, Gladys, I feel sorry that you want to leave. I hope you'll change your mind," Mei Chan repeated. "I already asked my mother and she said that starting next week I didn't have to come to the group anymore," I (in role) said. "Don't you like the group?" Frank asked. "No, the group doesn't do anything good," I (Gladys) responded. "What kinds of things do you like to do?" Frank continued. "I like arts and crafts and all the group does is sports," I (Gladys) said. "Would you stay if we did arts and crafts sometimes?" Frank asked. "The other kids aren't going to want to do arts and crafts. They only like sports," I said. Frank seemed deflated. Sonia gave it a try: "Gladys, I'm sure the girls would miss you if you left." "No, they wouldn't," I quickly said. "They wouldn't care. They'd be glad if I left." Sonia smiled ruefully. "Why do you think they'd be glad?" Eric tried. "Because nobody likes me," I said. "Why do you think they don't like you?" Eric continued. "I don't know," I shrugged. "They're just mean." "Do you think you do anything to make them not like you?" Eric went on. "No, I'm nice to them," I responded. "They're just mean." Eric seemed stymied. "Gladys, have other kids ever been mean to you?" Lizette picked up. "Yes, I was in a group last year at the Center and the kids in that group were also nasty," I said. "What happened in that group?" Lizette continued. "I just stopped going," I said. Lizette and others in the class seemed to not know how to pick up on this.

The above excerpt is realistic. Students frequently react to Gladys with sympathy and concern, but they drown her in a myriad of questions, offer false reassurance, and look for a way to quickly fix the problem (e.g., the group will do more arts and crafts). As we pointed out in Unit 5, students tend to look for an immediate solution, which to them means keeping Gladys in the group. Seldom do they react with clear and explicit *statements* that incorporate what they have observed about behavior they have seen in the group. They seem to fear hurting Gladys if they tell her directly that they realize she has been having a difficult time in the group and that she plays a part in causing the difficulty.

In the discussion that follows the role play, we emphasize the importance of using observations and making direct statements. We find that many students believe that as social workers they are not supposed to make statements, lest they impose their views upon the client, and that they are only supposed to ask questions. We believe it is important to disabuse them of this notion and to emphasize that it is essential for them to make statements based upon their informed observations. The worker's informed observations are crucial to the group, which we convey in a light-hearted manner by saying, "Don't ask a question when you know the answer! And don't ask a question when what you really want to do is make a statement!" The class discussion about Gladys continues:

> I pointed out to the class that Lizette seemed to be on a good track, that when a person is scapegoated in one group, chances are they are having difficulty in other groups and situations. "But I didn't know what to say then," Lizette said. "You had an awful lot of background information and observations about what was going on in the group, but none of you used that information or those observations," I said to the class. "If you had been direct and said to Gladys that you realized that she was having a hard time in the group, I think Gladys would have been quite interested in hearing your observations. After all, she knows she's struggling," I added.
>
> "Yes, but I don't want to hurt Gladys. If I said that, I'm afraid I'd make her feel worse," Mei Chan said. "But you wouldn't be telling her anything she didn't already know," Eric said. "In fact, being direct with Gladys and letting her know that you know she's having a hard time might well come as a relief to her," I said, "especially if you indicate that you think there's hope for the situation and express the belief that it can be helped by talking about it in and with the group." I then asked the class what they would need to do before they'd be ready to raise the situation with the group.

By engaging the students in a group role play about scapegoating, we set the stage for the following teaching points:

• Roles are reciprocal. One needs to conceptualize this situation as having two "sides." On the one hand, there are group members who find Gladys's behavior unbearable and whose actions toward her are cruel as they place her in the scapegoat's role. On the other hand, there is Gladys, who through her behavior provokes the group in their dislike of her, but who is the recipient of abuse from the other group members. What is crucial is that the worker not take a side, but be seen by all members as able to be fair to both sides simultaneously.

• Gladys is distressed about what is taking place in the group and elsewhere in her life, in the past and present. She wants to change her situation, for otherwise she would not have announced to the worker her intention to discontinue. Nevertheless, she may say "it doesn't matter" or "I don't care." The worker needs to not accept such statements at face value and needs to challenge them. Despite her protests, Gladys, as all people, cares about the pain caused by rejection from others. She may need support from the worker to address in the group what is taking place; it will not be easy for her. The worker can provide such support in the group by physically sitting next to Gladys and/or by limiting the other members if they become overzealous in their criticism. By doing this, the worker is not necessarily taking Gladys's side, but is offering support that Gladys needs in a situation that may be difficult for her.

• The worker needs to be aware of two dangers here. First, there is the inclination toward what Shulman (1967) calls "pre-emptive intervention," the tendency to be overprotective in the face of the cruel behavior toward her. Second, there is the propensity to identify with the feelings of the group toward Gladys. The worker is not immune to the feelings that Gladys's behavior provokes.

• When the situation is discussed in the group meeting, the worker needs to help each side express its point of view about what has been happening. Gladys needs to hear from the group what she does that they do not like. The group needs to hear from Gladys how much pain she feels as a result of their actions toward her. When each side begins to develop empathy for the other, the destructive equilibrium that supported the scapegoating will begin to be disturbed and change can then follow.

• Change in the situation will occur if the group engages in the problem-solving process discussed in Unit 5. When each side begins to really communicate, there is a strong likelihood that the worker will want to rush to solutions out of the desire to bring closure to a difficult situation (e.g., "OK, Gladys will try harder at sports and share her potato chips, and the group will not call her names and will participate in some arts and crafts activities"). The worker needs to guard against a move toward a premature "quick fix." Thorough exploration and discussion of the situation are necessary here, and the worker needs to help the group stay with such exploration.

• Students are fearful that when the scapegoating situation is raised directly with the group, the members will become uncontrollable verbally and will be hurtful toward Gladys. But, as workers, they need to be helped to see that they have more control over such an eventuality than they might think. If some members react with destructiveness toward Gladys, the worker can stop the action and tell the group that honest expression of feelings is acceptable in this discussion, but expression that is purposely hurtful is not. Again, limiting destructive behavior does not mean the worker is taking a side.

• Students are generally fearful of using confrontation. They see it as synonymous with demolishing a person. Instead, they need to learn that confrontation is designed not to demolish someone, but to help a person or a group stop and think about what is taking place. To cause that to happen, the worker presents personal observations about what is occurring. In fact, even if Gladys had not come to the worker outside the group, the worker could take the initiative and raise the issue of scapegoating. The worker can always feel free to make observations to the group about things that occur. In confronting the group or one of its members, the worker can be direct and supportive at the same time. Northen's (1988) phrase "confrontation with an arm around the shoulder" captures the idea that directness used with empathy can help an individual or group hear and face the reality of what may be a difficult and painful situation.

• Because roles are reciprocal, in this situation solutions will be, as well. After thorough exploration, the worker needs to actively engage the group in looking at possible solutions—actions each side will take to try to change the situation. It is important here to caution the students that miracles are unlikely, and that it is unrealistic to expect instant and effective change as a result of discussion in a single meeting. The group can return to the problem-solving process around the issue of scapegoating as often as needed.

Following the discussion of the teaching points, we involve the class in a role play of the group meeting in which the scapegoating of Gladys is discussed. We suggest either of two options here for the instructor: to do several subgroup role plays simultaneously involving all class members, or to do one role play with most of the class members observing. The first option has the advantage of actively involving all students, the second allows the instructor to stop the action periodically to make comments, offer suggestions, and lead the total class in discussion of key points. The instructor can either assign the roles or ask for volunteers. Students can also shift roles at appropriate intervals. Having the group perform a role play following the extensive discussion helps the teaching content of this unit come alive.

At the end of the role play, we remind students that we have used the scapegoat role as an exemplar of all problematic group roles. In fact, the principles that have been discussed apply equally to the ways in which a worker in the middle stage needs to address with the group the behavior involved in any difficult role—be it a monopolizer, a help-rejecting complainer, a gossip, etc.

We have found that students are reluctant to make observations to the group about what they see taking place. We view the sharing of observations as a continuous process and a crucial worker intervention throughout the life of a group. Therefore, we emphasize the importance of workers offering their observations to the group for its examination. When observations are made, the worker needs to be prepared to share the reasons for them, that is, the events that caused the worker to speak up. Students need to be helped to see such statements/observations as essential. They provide both opportunity and direction for the group's ongoing work.

Finally, we emphasize that work on roles brings together two basic themes that are a foundation of group work practice: the stages of group development and the problem-solving process. Knowledge and understanding of the group's developmental stage affects how the worker involves the group in a problem-solving process concerning group member roles. The ways in which stages and problem-solving come together will continue to be in evidence in subsequent discussion of conflict and difference.

Readings

Berger, Milton. (1995). *Working with People Called Patients* (p. 106). New York: Brunner-Mazel.

Colman, Arthur D. (1995). *Up from Scapegoating: Awakening Consciousness in Groups*. Wilmette, IL: Chiron.

Douglas, Tom. (1995). *Scapegoats: Transferring Blame*. London: Routledge.

Garland, James, & Kolodny, Ralph. (1973). Characteristics and Resolutions of Scapegoating. In Saul Bernstein (Ed.), *Further Explorations in Group Work* (pp. 55-74). Boston: Milford House.

Malekoff, Andrew. (1997). *Group Work with Adolescents: Principles and Practice* (pp. 291-306). New York: Guilford.

Northen, Helen. (1988). *Social Work with Groups* (2nd ed., pp. 240-250, 279-282). New York: Columbia University Press.

Shulman, Lawrence. (1967). Scapegoats, Group Workers, and Preemptive Intervention. *Social Work*, 12(2), 37-43.

Shulman, Lawrence. (1992). The Skills of Helping Individuals, Families and Groups (3rd ed., pp. 439-486). Itasca, IL: Peacock.

Unit 8
Dealing with Conflict and Difference

Conflicts and differences can arise throughout the life of a group. In the beginning stage (see Unit 4), the worker strives to help group members focus on their commonalities rather than their differences with the aim of establishing a supportive foundation. In the middle stage, however, the expression of conflict/difference is critical because it provides group members with the stimulation they need to examine their own experiences, situations, and points of view. Thus, in the group's middle stage, the worker strives to help group members examine issues of conflict and difference as they arise.

Conflict here is defined as the expression of disagreement among group members where there is difference—in ideas, opinions, beliefs, values, experiences, feelings, backgrounds, characteristics, approaches, or behavior. Such expression is likely to take place as members become increasingly sure of themselves and comfortable in the group. They become more willing to express their experiences, feelings, and opinions, and more willing to risk exposure of their ideas. As they are more comfortable in the group, such expressions are not as threatening as in the group's beginnings. Over time, group members become more honest and forthright as they worry less about establishing their place in the group.

In this unit we describe a range of teaching methods to help students view conflict as an inevitable, essential, and enriching aspect of group life. The objectives for students are five:

1. To understand the connection between conflict and difference.

2. To understand different ways that conflict can be resolved, emphasizing consensus as a goal.

3. To understand that resolving differences frequently is the work of the group, even the most important work a group will do, and to appreciate that the worker's role is to help the group resolve, rather than avoid, conflict.

4. To be able to address conflict in a group, especially through use of the problem-solving process, and to be able to help a group explore differences.
5. To be able to use skills that are effective in addressing conflict.

Students' Fears of Conflict

Students often fear the expression of conflict in the group. They do not see conflict as a natural part of relationships within the group, and instead view it as negative, threatening, an interruption, something to be disposed of and handled with dispatch so the group can return to its work. They worry that conflict will get out of control and destroy the group. They are afraid that they will be seen as inadequate and unable to handle conflict when it surfaces. As a result, they often attempt to avoid it, suppress it, or take responsibility to solve it on their own.

Because of their fears about conflict, when differences arise in a group students often ignore the problem-solving process (see Unit 5) and jump prematurely to "solve" the problem. They omit the problem identification and exploration steps of the process.

In beginning the discussion of conflict with the class, we emphasize its importance and convey the idea that fearfulness about conflict is expectable and common among group workers. We highlight the belief that conflict can be an important opportunity for the group to examine differences. Such examination can lead to revitalization and greater cohesion for the total group as well as growth and new perspectives for group members. Addressing and resolving conflict/difference frequently *is* the most important work that a group will do.

Before engaging the class in specific conflict situations, we make a number of teaching points:

• Confrontation often occurs when there is conflict in the group around an issue with which the group is grappling and/or around the behavior of an individual group member. Although students fear confrontation because they view it as aggressive and destructive, the intent of confrontation is not to attack or demolish. When used by the worker as an intervention, confrontation helps the group, or an individual group member, face their differences and their behavior directly. Confrontation interrupts the group process and asks members to stop and look at what is taking place.

• Confrontation need not be harsh. The worker can confront the group or an individual member directly but with gentleness, empathy, and civility. The previously mentioned phrase cited by Northen (1988), "confrontation with an arm around the shoulder" (from Overton and Tinker, 1957), aptly captures its effective use by the worker. In other words, confrontation can be simultaneously direct and supportive.

• A key factor in dealing with conflict is respect for difference. To encourage such respect among group members, the worker needs to convey five essential beliefs:

1. Differences among group members can be positive because they can contribute to the richness of the group by stimulating members' thinking and feelings;
2. Differences need to be respected and appreciated by group members;
3. Looking at differences, rather than sweeping them under the rug, is important;
4. Disagreeing with a person does not connote dislike of that person;
5. The group will be able to resolve differences, and conflict will not tear the group apart.

• Conflict can be resolved in three ways (Follet, 1942, as cited in Bernstein, 1973). One way is through *domination,* in which one side is victorious over the other(s). This is exemplified by voting and a majority-rules approach. Domination is not an effective way of resolving difference because there always are losers. Another way is through *compromise,* where each side gives a little in order to obtain agreement. Compromise is more effective than domination, but no side will be totally satisfied with the resolution. The third and most effective way of resolving conflict is through *integration.* Here, a new solution is reached and respected that includes the views of all "sides." Thus, there is true and effective conflict resolution.

Following this discussion, we involve students in a series of situations in which difference generates conflict. We form subgroups of six to eight students and present conflictual group situations arising from four kinds of difference: difference of opinion among the group members; difference of opinion between the worker and the group members; descriptive difference between the worker and the group members; and descriptive difference among the group members.

Each situation in the series poses a dilemma for the group leader, and we ask the students to address in their subgroups how the situation might be handled. We suggest that they might choose to use role play informally in their small groups to try out alternative interventions that evolve from their discussion.

Difference of Opinion among Group Members

The first situation we present concerns difference of opinion among the group members.

> You are a social worker at a community mental health clinic working with a group of parents whose children were referred because their behavior at school was problematic. The group has been meeting for seven weeks and attendance has been quite regular. Mrs. M. has been very vocal and a monopolizer in the group. She tends to tell the other members what they should do when their children misbehave. She is critical of and judgmental about the other members' actions as parents. Furthermore, Mrs. M. has maintained that she really doesn't belong in this group because her son is just a "bad apple," that she's done the best she can with him but that nothing is going to work.
>
> At this meeting, Mrs. P., who up to now has actively listened but said little in the group, recounts an incident with her son. She caught him stealing money from her purse. "I sat him down and started to talk with him about what he'd done." At that point, Mrs. M. interrupts: "Sat him down? Talked? That's stupid! You should have just smacked him." Visibly upset, with her voice quivering, Mrs. P. stands up and says, "I've had it with her [motioning to Mrs. M.]. She thinks she knows everything and I'm sick of it. If she stays in this group, I'm leaving."
>
> You are the social worker. What would you do? What exactly would you say at this point in the process? What are the practice issues?

After an initial moment of alarmed silence, the subgroups enter into animated discussions, which can take about 15 minutes. Usually, the subgroups discuss a range of interventions. To gain a sense of the students' thinking, the instructor can move from group to group, not participating but simply listening. Then, the instructor brings the class together to discuss how each group decided to handle the situation. We try to relate the subgroups' responses to three main areas.

First, the worker's interventions are related to the stage of the group's development. Though initially panicked by a group member threatening to leave, the students usually realize that Mrs. P. is unlikely to carry out her threat. They realize that she has likely become invested in the group and its work, since the group has been meeting for a substantial period of time and attendance has been regular. Students therefore recognize that the group most likely is in the middle stage (see Unit 6). This means, we stress, that the worker can expect a response from other group members and does not have to jump in immediately to urge Mrs. P. to stay. Such encouragement can be expected to come from group members and, in fact, may be more effective if it does.

Students' concerns that the group will disintegrate as a result of the conflict are similarly unfounded because of the group's stage of development. In the middle stage, group members have become more willing to share of themselves—their experiences, opinions, and feelings. The group has become cohesive, that is, it is seen as a place where members can really discuss and work on problems—exchange, argue, confront, try out, share. The value for members of having such a place means that group members will not allow this conflict to cause the group to fall apart. It also means that the worker need not overreact, for he or she can have faith in the group and rely on group members to get involved in responding to this threat to the group's hard-earned equilibrium.

Second, we emphasize that the problem-solving process, with its emphasis on the importance of exploration (see Unit 5), is highly relevant here. In the immediacy of the crisis inherent to the situation we have presented, students often want to prematurely solve the problem. They may suggest that they themselves should urge Mrs. P. to remain, or they may suggest that group members be encouraged to urge Mrs. P. to stay. Under the stress of the situation, students often forget altogether the steps in the problem-solving process, and they may move to solutions prematurely because they are fearful of taking time to explore what is taking place in the group. Such exploration is highly possible because in the middle stage group members are able to communicate better with one another and to support and/or question the behavior of their peers. We emphasize to students that their role as workers is to facilitate exploration of the situation by the group members, rather than to solve the problem themselves or even to ask the group members to immediately find a solution.

Third, differences in the group, in both participatory style and in opinions, provide an important opportunity for the members of this group and can be discussed directly and openly. The worker needs to help the group acknowledge and examine issues of both group process (e.g., Mrs. M.'s monopolization and domination, the role of the other group members in permitting her manner of participation, and Mrs. P.'s threat to leave the group) and group content (e.g., different views held by the group members in relation to ways of handling their children's behavior). The conflict and the differences here are *group* issues, not merely disagreements between Mrs. M. and Mrs. P. alone, and as such they must be addressed by the total group. This crisis provides an opportunity for the group both to enhance its cohesiveness and to consider the content—their different views about parenting—that gave rise to the need for their participation in a group such as this.

Difference of Opinion between Worker and Group Members

Next, we present to students a situation concerning differences of opinion between the worker and group members. The situation in which clients express a point of view that the worker finds unacceptable is particularly challenging for students, because they are often unsure about how to respond professionally. We present the following practice vignette:

The Potato Grater

A group of single mothers was discussing the difficulties of setting limits and disciplining their children. One of the mothers said that when her son was bad she made him kneel down with his knees on a hardwood floor and stay there for an hour. If he was especially bad, she made him kneel with a potato grater under his knees. "That's what my mother did with me when I was a child and it worked," she said. "Nowadays you really have to show your kids who is the boss." All the other group members nodded in agreement. "You've got to be firm," one added. "Show that you're in control," said another.

Such an example, in which group members seem to agree on a point of view that the worker finds difficult to accept, is one that students find difficult. Some workers are so appalled at the clients' views that they are silent. But for the worker to say nothing implies acceptance of the clients' statements. Others want to immediately jump in and use the authority of their position to reject or challenge the clients' views. But to quickly disagree with or immediately challenge the clients' statements may result in the clients' withdrawal into silence or superficial agreement, along with a concomitant feeling that this worker does not really understand and that in this group what one strongly believes cannot be expressed. Students need to understand that the worker's aim is to help the clients explore the issue and their thinking and feelings about it, as the following class discussion demonstrates.

"Suppose you were the worker in this group," I said. "What would you do?" With a tinge of anger, Carolyn said, "This woman is abusive. I'd be required to report her." "Oh, no, that's not abuse," Mary said. "Nothing would happen if you reported her anyway," Gary said, "and it would be better for you to work with her than to report her." Juan added, "Work with her! I couldn't work with her when she's so cruel to her kid."

At this point, I stopped the discussion because I wanted the class to focus on the worker's role in handling viewpoints that she or he might find different rather than on whether the situation was one that would be defined legally as child abuse. "Wait a minute," I said. "This was a group with which I actually worked. I had come to know the mothers well. I knew the mother who said she used the potato grater. And while personally I thought this act was a harsh way of disciplining her child, I also knew that this was not an abusive mother. Reporting her never entered my mind. The issue here that I really want us to look at is how to handle a situation such as this when group members are expressing a view with which you, the worker, disagree."[1]

"I'd tell the group that I disagree with such harsh punishment, that I don't think it works," Adrian said. "Well, it worked for me," Lucienne said. "When I was growing up, my mother didn't use a potato grater, but

---

[1] The issue of mandated reporting, especially when it concerns the use of excessive corporal punishment, is a murky area. Uncertainty about when to report causes considerable anxiety. It is generally acknowledged that a worker must use reasonable professional judgment in determining when to make a report. For further discussion, see Levine & Doueck (1995) and Myers (1992).

she would make me and my brother kneel down on uncooked rice when we'd done something really bad. That kind of punishment is widely used in my culture. It's been used for generations throughout the Caribbean." "But it's so cruel," Don said. "Maybe we think it's cruel," responded Vic, "but these mothers don't. And for them, control and being firm is done so their kids don't get in trouble." "But I don't agree that that's the best way to discipline kids in our society," Louise said. "And if I were the worker with this group, I'd want to challenge them, at least make them look at the effectiveness of that kind of discipline," she added.

Following the class discussion, we make a number of teaching points:

• Rather than immediately reject the thinking and feelings of the group members, which may be the student's first impulse (especially if the student finds the client's views distasteful), the worker needs to encourage group members to say more about their thinking, about what has contributed to it, about where they are coming from. In short, students need to realize that it is important to take the time to understand the clients' points of view.

• If the members feel that the worker has listened to and heard them, that the worker has empathy for them and for their thinking and situations, then the worker is in a much better position to challenge their views. Such a challenge is a confrontation that aims to help the group members stop and think about the views that they are expressing. Knowing that the worker understands and has taken the time to learn about their views leaves group members more open to the worker's challenge to them.

• Greater understanding of the clients' points of view may bring greater acceptance of that viewpoint. The student needs to be open to that possibility. Often, clients' views may be shaped by values and experiences rooted in culture, race, ethnicity, and class that are different from those of the worker. It is essential that students be sensitive to and appreciative of the clients' backgrounds and open to the ways in which these shape beliefs and actions. Barbara Solomon comments on this in her book, *Black Empowerment* (1976), when she describes characteristics of the nonracist practitioner:

> The practitioner should possess the ability to perceive in any behavior. . . alternative explanations for that

behavior, particularly those alternatives which the self might most strongly reject as false. . . . It is tempting and easy to seize that generalization which best fits our own predilections without adequate appraisal of the alternatives; as a consequence, practitioners far too often select and utilize an extremely limited and stereotypic set of generalizations about black clients and their problems. (pp. 301–302)

• After exploring the clients' thinking and feelings, the worker might continue to disagree with the view that group members are expressing. If so, then the worker can express this disagreement directly. It is important, however, that this expression does not close off discussion, that it is nonjudgmental, and that it invites even more in-depth exploration of the issue. The worker's words, tone of voice, and body posture can be used to invite such exploration. Phrases such as "it seems to me that. . ." or "you may disagree, but I think that. . ." or "let me present a different point of view. . ." help to free the members to express their own views even if they differ from those expressed by the worker.

• The students need to understand that the worker's aim is not to impose a particular point of view on the clients. That would be impossible. Rather, the art of practice here includes the worker's ability to express her or his own viewpoint in a way that does not impose it, but instead encourages group members to look more closely at their own thinking and feelings. The worker's expression of a point of view, if done skillfully, can help group members explore their own points of view. To thoughtfully challenge the clients to explore their views is an important part of group work that does not intrude on the clients' right to self-determination.

To further emphasize these teaching points, we present another vignette that illustrates a situation in which there is difference of opinion between the worker and the group members. We ask students to discuss this vignette in their small subgroups and identify the issues and describe what they would do if they were the worker.

The SRO Bathrooms
Social work staff of a single-room occupancy (SRO) hotel that housed single adults who had been homeless determined that a priority for the building, which had been open for eight months, was to try to create a sense of community among the tenants. To do so, monthly floor meetings were held, each led by a social worker.

At the first meeting of the second-floor tenants, they complained about strangers who did not live in the building using their floor's bathrooms and kitchen. "Do you ever ask them who they are," the social worker asked, "or report them to the guard downstairs?" "Oh, no!" was the immediate and unanimous response. "The best thing to do is to do and say nothing. Who knows who the people are? You could really get in trouble by challenging them or reporting them. Who knows what they might do to you then!" All the tenants agreed that the only thing to do was to do nothing, to keep quiet, and put up with it.

After a brief small-group discussion, we consider the situation presented in the vignette with the entire class. At first, the students may view the situations described in "The SRO Bathrooms" and "The Potato Grater" as very different. The client membership differs markedly by age and situation, and the presenting problems and group types and purposes are not related. As the discussion unfolds, however, the instructor can help the students see that the practice issues are the same. Here, too, the worker differs with the point of view being expressed by the group members. Here, too, the worker needs first to listen to the tenants and understand their point of view and what has contributed to it. Many of these members were so relieved to have permanent housing that they were extremely fearful to voice a complaint about anything that took place at the residence, lest they jeopardize their resident status. Furthermore, their fears of retaliation were realistic. The worker needs to understand their situation and appreciate their fears before beginning to challenge their beliefs and expressing an alternative viewpoint. To be silent and not disagree at all will convey a sense that nothing can be done about the situation.

As in "The Potato Grater," the worker in "The SRO Bathrooms" wants to intervene by encouraging group members to reflect on the beliefs they are expressing. The teaching points already described are equally applicable to both practice vignettes and, in fact, to any situation in which there is difference of opinion between worker and members.

Descriptive Difference between Worker and Group Members

The third type of difference that we address with the class is that of descriptive difference between the worker and the group

members. Students often fear that group members will call attention to descriptive differences that exist between the student and
the members, whether such differences are based on race, age,
marital/parental status, religion, sexual orientation, socioeconomic status, health condition, or other factors. We begin by
distributing a student's case record (see pp. 98–101) in which the
elderly members of a literature discussion group in a senior center question whether the student, a man in his late 20s, can understand and be of help to them. The first comment in the record
crystallizes for many students the kind of confrontation by a
group member that they most dread: a statement that questions
the worker's ability to be helpful because of the presence of significant descriptive differences between the worker and group
members. In this record, age difference is the point of conflict. In
using the record, we ask several students to read the parts of the
group members aloud while we take the part of the worker.

After the record has been read aloud, we ask students how
they think the worker did. Although students' analyses of a record
tend to be critical, even overly so, students often agree that the
worker in this record handled the confrontation well. At times he
became a bit defensive, but it seems as if he caught himself in that
tendency and backed off from such an inclination. Although it is
not easy to be told by members so directly, as this worker was,
that one cannot understand, he invited exploration of the issue,
even when some members of the group wanted to sweep it under
the rug. The important teaching point in this record is that the
worker did not shy away from examining descriptive differences;
instead he facilitated the exploration.

We use discussion of this record to then help the class look at
difference in race between worker and group members.

> "What if the difference in the record we just dis-
> cussed were race rather than age," I said. "If you were
> the worker, would race be harder for you to address
> than age?" "Absolutely," Millie said. Many other class
> members nodded strongly in agreement. "How come?"
> I asked. "Why do you think race is harder to talk about
> than difference based on age?" There was silence for a
> moment. "Race is difficult to talk about," Clarice said.
> "Yes, in our society it's a charged issue," Sheila agreed.
>
> "I'm always afraid to talk about race in my groups,"
> Jill said, "maybe because I'm afraid I'll be opening up
> Pandora's box." I said, "What is it that you will be

Case Record – Descriptive Differences

3/1 (Tenth Session)

Ralph: There's no way a young person like yourself could really understand or help somebody my age. Not that there's anything wrong with that. I mean, how could you?

Hilde: Oh no, I don't think that's true at all. Richard is very helpful. [Others voice agreement.]

Worker: *Hold on a second. This is actually something I've often thought about. How do you think I'm unable to help you, Ralph?*

Ralph: Well, it's like this. It's not that I don't think you're doing a great job here, because you really run the group very well. It's just that I'm 86 years old. I have physical problems that I never dreamed of when I was your age, and there's no reason I should have thought about that kind of thing. And why should you? I'm the sum of 57 years more life than you are. Now that certainly doesn't mean I know more or I'm any better. It just means I've had that many more experiences.

Ella: But I don't see it that way. I think that anyone who wants to can understand another person. You don't have to walk through fire to talk to someone who has.

Hilde: I have so many dear friends who are younger people. They keep me young with their ideas and their energy.

Worker: *But do you feel like they can relate to you? Can they understand you as an older person?*

Hilde: Why should they be able to? Why should they want to?

Ralph: That's just it. There's no reason they should want to. It's not that we are uninteresting people, but when you're young the world is your oyster. You have ideas and goals that are etched in stone. . . you're ready to tackle the world, and that's how it should be. But when you are our age, you're not so sure about things anymore. You realize you don't have all the answers you thought you did.

Worker: *But you see, I do want to understand you, and I believe I can. Not everything about you, maybe not even that much, but something. I think there's a common ground, where we can talk to each other—have a give and take. You're 86, I'm 29. But we are both men trying to find something meaningful and satisfying in life.*

Hilde: I think that's right—a common ground. I like that very much.

Ralph: Yes, that may be very true.

Worker: [Laughing.] It may be, but I don't think you believe it.

Ralph: Well, no. I mean to some extent, but it's like this. When I'm sitting in the doctor's office or even just walking along the street and I see someone my own age or in somewhat similar dismal health, we exchange a knowing glance and in that look there is an understanding that you just can't talk about.

Worker: [Silence.]

Gretta: I think what Ralph is saying is true. . . but you can go too far with it.

Worker: What do you mean, too far?

Gretta: I mean when you start to let it bring you down. I believe there are valuable things you can get out of a relationship with any intelligent person.

Mollie: Intelligence isn't the only criterion. There's also sensitivity and the ability to empathize.

Gretta: I include that as part of intelligence.

Worker: Wait a minute! Let's stick with this issue of whether or not a younger person can be helpful to an older person, other than helping them cross the street. . . . Ralph, I definitely relate to what you're saying about a certain connection to people who you're in the same boat with. But what kind of connection do you think you and I can make?

Ralph: Well, that's a good question. Let me think about that one.

Hilde: I would rather be with a younger person and forget about my age than sit around and sigh with someone my own age.

Worker: But can anybody ever really forget about their age?

Mollie: I think not.

Hilde: But you needn't dwell on it!

Ella: Well, look, it's there whether you think about it or not.

Worker: *I want to ask the group the question I just asked of Ralph—what kind of connection can you as an older person have with me, a young man?*

Mollie: In what sense do you mean the word connection?

Worker: *Good question. I mean, in what way do you think the age difference between you and I comes into play in our relationship?*

Ada: Everyone is a different person with different experiences. I don't think anyone here is the same, and we can all learn from one another.

[Group silence.]

Worker: *Ralph, I feel like very little of this is getting through to you.*

Ralph: Hmm. . . I can't quite put my finger on it. Maybe I'm just resentful of your youth.

Worker: *Hmm!*

Ralph: I was once a good-looking young man myself, you know.

Gretta: Now you're a good-looking old man.

[Laughter.]

Ralph: Youth is so sure of itself. So unteetering in its attitudes.

Worker: *You know, Ralph—you have some of the same myths about youth that I had about aging. I certainly don't feel that sure of myself or unteetering.*

Ralph: Well, you should!

Worker: *Why?*

Ralph: That's one of the joys of being young!

Nica: When I was a young girl I didn't know anything, but I was so happy. . . . [She goes on to tell a story of young love, how she and her husband lived in poverty in Paris.]

3/8 (Eleventh Session)

Hilde: You know, Ralph, last week I was thinking about what you said about young people and I had an experience I

	want to tell you about. . . . [She spoke of how she went to see her ophthalmologist, a 33-year-old woman. Hilde has often said how much she likes this person. It happened that at this appointment the usually stoic Hilde was talking about how her failing vision was so depressing to her. The doctor then chastised her for such talk and gave an annoyingly superficial pep talk. Hilde was dismayed by the doctor's lack of understanding and said that Ralph was right, younger people can't really understand the aged.]
Worker:	*Wait a second! I'm guilty without a trial! I would say your doctor showed a real lack of empathy, but she is just one person.*
Ralph:	No, that's really the way it is. There's certain things a younger person just can't understand. He hasn't had to deal with them, and rightfully so.
Worker:	*I believe that's true to a certain extent, but couldn't your eye doctor have waited a minute, thought about what you said, and not just fed you aphorisms about when the going gets tough, the tough get going.*
Ella:	Yes, she could have. I've known some young people who were very understanding.
Mollie:	Charles Dickens was certainly a young man who wrote quite perceptively about older people.
Ralph:	Yes, he wrote about them. But it was all conjecture. You see, it just had to be.
Worker:	*Of course, that's true, but you see, I don't believe you have to have cancer to help someone who does or be a thief to work with criminals. If I can help you be more comfortable with yourself or to see something about yourself that you're not aware of, or to stimulate discussions that have some meaning or interest for you, then I think I'm helping.*
Ralph:	Well yes, I would agree with that. I just think that there are limits to how far you can empathize.
Worker:	*Um-hmm.*

letting out of the box? What is the issue?" "Well, there's so much feeling around race," Jill responded. "If I raise it in the group, I don't know where it's going to go and I'm afraid I'll be told I don't understand what it is to be African American or Latina because I am white. And then what do I do?" Bill added, "Maybe the group will tell me I can't understand because I'm white. Also, I worry that I may say or do something that is considered insensitive or biased or racist and I'm not. [Pause.] I know that sounds defensive. I hear it myself."

"But with all that stuff going on, there's no way to avoid discussing race," Harry said. "If members feel you don't understand because of your race, that's got to be talked about because if those feelings are there they will get in the way of the group." Charles said, "Listen, it's not just a black–white issue. I'm from the Caribbean and the members of my group are all African American. I've gotten called on my accent and my attitudes. I'm uneasy about talking about race, too. A lot of time I think the group members think I can't understand them." "But, wait a minute," Millie exclaimed, "that's not so different from what happened to the worker in the age record!"

Following the class discussion, we make a number of teaching points regarding descriptive differences between a worker and group members:

• An effective worker is someone who is comfortable with herself or himself and not defensive about descriptive characteristics and the experiences and situations that flow from such characteristics.

• A worker has a responsibility to learn as much as possible about the experiences and situations of the group members with whom she or he is working, and to try to understand their experiences and situations as fully as possible, even without having lived them personally.

• It is not productive for workers to pretend to be what they are not. Such pretending can take two opposite forms. On the one hand, there is the *ingenue* who pleadingly entreats the group to help teach her or him about themselves. On the other hand, there is the *hipster* who comes across as if she or he is one of them, speaks their lingo, and knows it all. The assumption of either role on the part of the worker is unfair to the group members, damages the worker's effectiveness, and diminishes what the worker has to offer.

• All class members will work with groups whose members have significant descriptive differences. Racial difference may be particularly difficult for students to discuss freely. Other areas of difference—sexual orientation, for example—may also be especially difficult. However, the practice principles that apply to discussion of these differences are not unique in any way. They hold true uniformly, whether the difference is one that the student approaches with ease or with trepidation. Racial differences *can* be talked about. They are not taboo. They are not set apart or in a different category from other differences. Consideration of racial difference/conflict can and often needs to be put on the table for consideration.

To enable the class to grapple with difference in race between worker and members, we ask them to discuss in their subgroups the following practice vignette. We also suggest that they might want to use role play in their small groups to try out various responses.

Is Race an Issue?

You are co-leading a group of single mothers. All the group members, as well as your co-leader, are black. You are the only white person in the room. At the fourth meeting of the group, the mothers are talking about incidents that their children have encountered at school. Many of them talk about situations in which they believe their children were treated unfairly by school personnel. Race is never mentioned. However, you get the sense that the parents are talking about white school personnel and that they are leaving race out of their descriptions because of your presence. What would you do and say?

After the subgroups meet for 10–15 minutes, we bring the class together to present their responses. Based on the content we have covered in the course so far, each subgroup will likely understand that the worker needs to raise concerns directly with the group that members might be avoiding mention of race in their descriptions because the co-leader is white.

Student descriptions of how the worker can do this may vary. They might say the worker can ask the group directly whether this is the case. (For example, "I wonder whether the teachers you are describing are white and whether you are not mentioning that because I am white.") Or they might respond that the worker should state that she senses this is so. (For example, "I get the sense that you are talking about white teachers and that you are not saying that because I am white.")

The vignette provides an opportunity for the instructor to reiterate that racial difference between worker and members *can* be talked about openly. It also enables the instructor to get the class to consider the timing of such an intervention. In the vignette, the worker's sense or question about whether race was a factor in the incidents the mothers were describing was a very real one. It arose quite naturally from the content of what members were saying. The worker did not bring up racial difference in a way that was artificial or unnecessary, or out of a false sense that she was obliged to do so. Rather, in this situation the need to raise the question of racial difference was real, and its avoidance would have undermined the work of the group.

Descriptive Difference among Group Members

The fourth and final difference that we address with the class concerns descriptive difference among group members. Our discussion builds upon the work that the class has already done in considering conflict/difference. We begin by presenting a situation that a student raised in class in a previous course.

Some Girls Don't Talk

Working with 10th-grade girls in a pregnancy prevention group in a local high school, a student reported a problem of some group members talking a great deal and others saying almost nothing. "How can I get the quiet ones to talk more and the monopolizers to talk less?" she asked in class. "I've tried calling on the quiet ones, but all I get back is one-word answers, so that doesn't work." Questions from class members uncovered the fact that all the silent members in the group were Latina, while those who were verbally active in the group were African American. With help from other students and the instructor, the student then acknowledged that there seemed to be tensions between the African-American and Latina group members, that there was a sense of uneasiness in the group, that racial and cultural differences might be contributing to the variation in the participation of the group members, and that the student leader, who was white, was afraid to raise this directly in the group.

We ask the class what they think might have contributed to this student's fears. Class members generally are able to identify that the student might be afraid that raising such differences could result in group members becoming explosive and ultimately lead to the group's destruction. Or the student might have been fearful that racial and/or cultural differences would be unresolvable. The student might have been uncomfortable with her own racial attitudes and fear that open discussion of racial and cultural difference in the group would result in her being seen as racist by the group members.

We refer back to the class discussion of racial difference between worker and group members. We point out that just as such difference between worker and members can and needs to be discussed, so, too, can racial and cultural difference among group members be addressed openly. In fact, whenever a worker senses that racial or cultural tensions exist among group members, he or she needs to raise that with the group. We reiterate that the same principles that apply to dealing with any kind of difference or conflict in a group apply equally to racial and cultural differences among members. Because of the extensive discussion that has already taken place of racial difference between worker and members, the students are quick to grasp similarities here and to realize that discussion of racial and cultural difference among group members cannot be taboo.

We ask the class to suggest how this student might have broached the difference in participation between the Latina and African-American group members. While the specifics of the suggested interventions may vary, the important point is that this student could and should share directly with the group her perception that participation in the group varied by race/culture. The student's sharing such a perception would ideally result in a discussion that could help them understand one another's point of view and style of interaction.

In the vignettes we use to illustrate the four kinds of conflict and difference, we want students to come away with an understanding that direct discussion of conflict/difference in the group is crucial. Such discussion improves understanding, expands perspectives, and enriches group life. It results in the strengthening of relationships among group members and between the worker and group members. Avoidance of such discussion interferes with the group's work and makes it impossible for the group to achieve its purpose.

Skills for Addressing Conflict and Difference

To assist students in their effort to address conflict and difference in their work with groups, we identify skills they can use. We discuss extensively skills for coping with conflict that are described by Middleman and Wood in *Skills for Direct Practice in Social Work* (1990, pp. 164–171).

• *Confronting Situations.* To confront a situation is to make a civil presentation of descriptive information—to work through differences and arrive at a solution. Don't shout or argue. Rather, confront a situation (i.e., "*We* have a problem").

• *Validating angry feelings.* Anger responds best to recognition and validation, to statements that acknowledge the anger and indicates that it is justified.

• *Focusing on facts.* When confronting situations or information that evokes anger, the worker needs to reduce the anger so joint problem solving can take place. When confronted by an angry person, the worker needs to focus on facts rather than validate the anger.

• *Converting arguments into comparisons.* Arguments are rarely productive. Therefore, it is a good idea for the worker to reinterpret the different sides of an argument as differences of opinion about the way to accomplish an end or a goal and to present options for rational consideration.

• *Proposing superordinate goals.* Superordinate goals are large, important, urgent, and basic. They are those to which all parties can subscribe and which can encompass and take precedence over partisan interests.

We read aloud to the class the practice vignettes from Middleman and Wood that illustrate each of the five skills, and ask the students to describe similar practice situations they have encountered where these skills would be applicable. Our intent is to help the students become aware of the specific intent of these skills so they can then use them purposefully in situations of conflict.

Readings

Bernstein, Saul. (1973). Conflict and Group Work. In *Explorations in Group Work* (pp. 72-106). Boston: Milford House.

Brown, Allan, & Mistry, Tara. (1994). Group Work with 'Mixed Membership' Groups: Issues of Race and Gender. *Social Work with Groups*, 17(3), 5-21.

Cowger, Charles D. (1979). Conflict and Conflict Management in Working with Groups. *Social Work with Groups*, 2(4), 309-320.

Follet, Mary P. (1942). *Dynamic Administration*, collected papers, edited by Henry Metcalf & Lyndall Urwick. New York: Harper and Brothers.

Glassman, Urania, & Kates, Len. (1990). *Group Work: A Humanistic Approach* (pp. 169-192). Newbury Park, CA: Sage.

Henry, Sue. (1992). *Group Skills in Social Work: A Four-Dimensional Approach* (2nd ed., pp. 127-159). Pacific Grove, CA: Brooks/Cole.

Kurland, Roselle, & Salmon, Robert. (1992). Self-Determination: Its Use and Misuse in Group Work Practice and Social Work Education. In David F. Fike & Barbara Rittner (Eds.), *Working from Strengths: The Essence of Group Work* (pp. 105-121). Miami, FL: Center for Group Work Studies.

Kurland, Roselle, & Salmon, Robert. (1993). Not Just One of the Gang: Group Workers and Their Roles as an Authority. *Social Work with Groups*, 16(1/2), 153-167.

Levine, Murray, & Doueck, Howard J. (1995). *The Impact of Mandated Reporting on the Therapeutic Process* (pp. 46-49). Thousand Oaks, CA: Sage.

Malekoff, Andrew. (1997). Prejudice Reduction, Intergroup Relations, and Group Identity. In *Group Work with Adolescents: Principles and Practice* (pp. 189-214). New York: Guilford.

Middleman, Ruth, & Wood, Gale Goldberg. (1990). Skills for Coping with Conflict. In *Skills for Direct Practice in Social Work* (pp. 164-171). New York: Columbia University Press.

Mondros, Jacqueline, Woodrow, Richard, & Weinstein, Lois. (1992). The Use of Groups to Manage Conflict. *Social Work with Groups*, 15(4), 43-58.

Northen, Helen. (1988). *Social Work with Groups* (2nd ed., pp. 250-254). New York: Columbia University Press.

Myers, John E. B. (1992). *Legal Issues in Child Abuse and Neglect* (pp. 102-103). Newbury Park, CA: Sage.

Overton, Alice, & Tinker, Katherine. (1957). *Casework Notebook*. St. Paul, MN: Greater St. Paul Community Chests and Councils.

Schopler, Janice H., Galinsky, Maeda J., Davis, Larry E., & Despard, Mathieu. (1996). The RAP Model: Assessing a Framework for Leading Multiracial Groups. *Social Work with Groups, 19*(3/4), 21-29.

Solomon, Barbara Bryant. (1976). Characteristics of the Nonracist Practitioner. In *Black Empowerment: Social Work in Oppressed Communities* (pp. 299-313). New York: Columbia University Press.

Steinberg, Dominique Moyse. (1993). Some Findings from a Study on the Impact of Group Work Education on Social Work Practitioners' Work with Groups. *Social Work with Groups, 16*(3), 23-39.

Unit 9
The Use of Program and Activity

The use of activity has been an integral part of group work practice from the beginning. Its use, however, has been controversial within the social work profession. Many social work practitioners accorded status and prestige to discussion and discussion groups, and denigrated participation in activity as mere recreation that had nothing to do with *real* social work. A resurgence of the use of program and activity in group work has come about today as, increasingly, social group workers have become convinced of the many benefits that participation in activity can have for members of groups.

The aim of a basic course on group work practice cannot be to turn out program/activity "specialists." Instead, the intent of this unit is to show students the vast potential that activity has to expand the quality of group work practice.

The objectives of this teaching unit for students are four:

1. To understand the history and use of program and activity in group work.
2. To appreciate the value and importance of program and activity.
3. To understand the purposeful use of program and activity with different age groups and according to the needs of groups at different stages of development.
4. To become more open to the possibility of using program and activity in a group.

History

We begin this unit by presenting a brief history of the place of program and activity in group work's development and some of the issues involved in using activity in social work with groups. Interestingly, the historical debates around the place of activity in group work practice reflect its early ambivalence about whether it saw itself as a method within the social work profession or whether it was a part of the recreation and progressive education movements (see Unit 2). A comprehensive description of the place of activity in group work has been developed by Ruth Middleman in her landmark volume *The Non-verbal Method in Working with Groups* (1982, originally published 1968), and we draw upon her work in the following teaching points.

• From early on, in settlement houses, youth-serving organizations (e.g., Boy and Girl Scouts, Camp Fire Girls, Boys' and Girls' Clubs), and religious organizations (e.g., YMCA, YWCA, Jewish Centers), program was used with groups to educate immigrants, provide opportunities for recreation and the use of leisure time, and foster democracy, Christian values, and Jewish identity. Such program clearly emphasized the *content* of group work—what the group actually did—rather than the relationships between members.

• Controversy about the use of activity in group work practice began to arise in the 1930s as group work's identity in social work came to be debated. Group work and recreation or informal education were erroneously seen by many as synonymous; group work's stress on content rather than on persons had an adverse effect on acceptance of the method in social work. Activity and the emphasis on *doing* had less status than the *talking* that was the domain of problem-centered casework, the dominant social work methodology of the time. Desire to become part of social work, and fear that group work's use of activity placed it outside the profession, led group workers to begin to deemphasize activity. The early thinking which presumed a dichotomy between talking and doing continues to fuel debates today.

• As group work moved toward a closer identification with social work, the connection among activity, individual group members, and their interactions again became more appreciated and accented. In a 1946 address at the National Conference of Social Work, Grace Coyle stressed that the dichotomy between activity and relationships among group members was a false one. We read her statement directly to the class:

> Social group work arose out of an increasing awareness that in the recreation–education activities which went on in groups there were obviously two dimensions— activity, including games, discussions, hikes, or artistic

enterprise, on the one hand, and, on the other, the interplay of personalities that creates the group process. To concentrate on one without recognizing and dealing with the other is like playing the piano with one hand only. Program and relationships are inextricably intertwined. Social group work method developed as we began to see that the understanding and the use of the human relations involved were as important as the understanding and use of various types of program. (Coyle, 1946, pp. 202-203)

• Another milestone in the exposition of program content was the 1949 publication of *Social Group Work Practice*, by Gertrude Wilson and Gladys Ryland. This timely volume included an extensive "Analysis of Program Media" and emphasized the values inherent in play and games. The book was the first to explicate the importance of nonverbal content. It did not, however, discuss how group workers could relate the content of group work to the particular purposes of social work—the connection between what the worker did and why. Such discussion of the relationship between group work theory and the use of program content followed in group work writing of the next two decades. (See, for example, Harleigh Trecker, *Social Group Work—Principles and Practice*, 1955; Gisela Konopka, *Social Group Work: A Helping Process*, 1963; Robert Vinter, "Program Activities: An Analysis of their Effects on Participant Behavior," in *Readings in Group Work Practice*, 1967; Ruth Middleman, *The Non-verbal Method in Working with Groups*, 1982; Lawrence Shulman, "'Program' in Group Work: Another Look," in William Schwartz and Serapio Zalba, Eds., *The Practice of Group Work*, 1971.)[1]

• The intrinsic connection between the use of program and the purpose of social work became increasingly recognized and appreciated, at least "officially," by social work's national organizations and by group workers themselves, if not by social work practitioners generally (although many continued to regard the use of activity with disdain). In a 1959 curriculum statement on the characteristics of the group work method, the Council on Social Work Education wrote:

---

[1] Full citation information can be found in Appendix C for those references not listed in the Readings section of this unit.

> The group worker is concerned simultaneously with program content, and with the ways in which persons relate to each other. Achievement, however, cannot be measured in content and process themselves, but in relation to the social work goal, enhancement of members' social functioning, as far as this can be observed in changes in thinking and behavior. (Murphy, 1959, p. 39)

Thus, group work's uniqueness was seen as related to the knowledge its practitioners had about the skillful and purposeful use of program and activity to meet human needs.

• Group work's unique use of activity began to vanish in the 1960s when the Council on Social Work Education, in an effort to more sharply define social work's identity as an autonomous profession, moved toward curriculum standards that required social work programs to emphasize generic social work practice. In most such social work practice courses, little time was devoted to the specific beliefs, knowledge, and skills that were the hallmark of group work. The use of program and activity was generally ignored altogether, and the professional education of an entire generation of social workers failed to include any training in this area of practice.

• An opposite trend also began in the 1960s. The emergence of expressive therapies—art, music, and dance therapy—gave activity new cachet for many in social work who seemed to accept the therapeutic focus of these newer disciplines. At the same time, social workers began increasingly to use play therapy in their one-on-one work with children. However, the differences between the populations, purposes, and methods of group work and those of the expressive therapies were generally unrecognized and unappreciated.

• Amazingly, given the neglect of this area in social work education, the use of program and activity in group work practice has refused to disappear. Perhaps because of the tremendous value that program and activity can have, social workers who work with groups today continue to discover their importance, sometimes on their own. Evidence of this can be found in the substantial number of articles on their use in the journal *Social Work with Groups*, since its inception in 1978, and the many presentations on activity that have been made at the yearly symposia of the Association for the Advancement of Social Work with Groups, which began in 1979.

Value of Programs and Activities

We next discuss with the class the value that program and activity can have for group members. Our intent is to help students gain respect for the many ways in which program can benefit both individual group members and the total group. We describe four values to the class and present examples to illustrate each.

First, we emphasize that all persons have a need to be creative, to have the power and ability to create something with imagination, expressiveness, and originality. Participation in activity can help to fulfill that need, as the following record, which we read to the class, shows.

A social work student whose internship was at an inpatient psychiatric facility expressed interest in forming a singing group. "Why a singing group?" her group work instructor asked. The student explained that she had a personal interest in singing and had sung professionally before coming to social work school. "But why a singing group with the patients?" the instructor persisted. "For one thing, I never see the patients having any fun. A singing group would be fun." The instructor concurred. "Any other reasons for a singing group?" "Well, the patients here are never given any choices. In a singing group, if nothing else, at least they could have some choices about what they wanted to sing." Both the instructor and the members of the class smiled in agreement.

The student went on to form a singing group, despite much questioning on the part of her supervisor and hospital administrators, who challenged the need for a social worker to lead such a group. This attitude was illustrated by her supervisor, who told the student, "Don't bother to write process recording on the singing group. Just give me process on your therapy group." The singing group was a voluntary group that turned out to be a huge success. Patients on the unit had to be reminded about other groups, but they needed no reminders or coaxing to attend the singing group. In fact, often they would approach the student and hopefully ask, "Today's the singing group, right?" Many of the patients had had long histories of multiple hospitalizations and few successes in their lives. Yet it turned out that every member of the singing group, when they were younger, had been a member of a high school singing group of some sort. For them, the singing group represented and called upon strengths that they possessed.

Second, we stress that activity provides rich and powerful opportunities for direct observation of group dynamics by the worker. Individual behavior and interaction among group members are immediately available to the worker, who sees these components in action. The advantage of seeing first-hand what members actually *do*, as opposed to what they report, is invaluable. It is of use to the group worker, who can apply observations either immediately in the group or at a later point with individual group members, the total group, or both.

A social worker in a community center decided to form a men's cooking group when she realized that there were a number of single or widowed men at the center who were spending a large proportion of their fixed incomes on restaurant meals, because they did not know how to cook or how to do even simple tasks in the kitchen. The group developed both a cooking and a social focus. Over the course of a late-afternoon/early-evening meeting, the men would shop, prepare a meal, eat together, clean up, and plan the meal for the following week.

Mr. Broglio was a member of the group whom the worker also saw individually because he was an isolated person who had no friends in the community. Mr. Broglio reported to the worker that he wanted and tried to make friends, but that others were not nice to him. He tried to reach out to others, he said, but was always rebuffed and did not understand why this was so.

The worker could understand Mr. Broglio's situation only after she had the chance to observe the way he interacted with the other members of the cooking group. In his interactions, he would become almost tyrannical, putting other people down as he "dictated" to them what to do and how to do it. "Don't stir it that way, you're doing it all wrong," he would say loudly to another group member, as he literally tore the mixing bowl out of his hands. At other times, he would talk over and seem oblivious to the other members as he tried to get his way in planning the exact menu he wanted. His

behavior in the group surprised the worker. Such actions were not apparent to her when he would discuss
his situation with her one-on-one. Observing Mr.
Broglio's behavior in the group allowed her to raise
issues with him that she thought were problematic in
his efforts to make friends and to illustrate the issues
she raised with specific examples.

Third, we underscore that for many people who find it difficult to articulate their thoughts and feelings in words, the use of
activity is especially helpful. Such persons can express their ideas
directly in the activity, or they can use an activity as a concrete
aid to help them subsequently express in words ideas that may be
abstract. Activity can also be used to help group members express
themselves about issues that are emotional for them. With many
group members, insistence that they express themselves verbally
can exacerbate feelings of inadequacy and inarticulateness, as
we show the class.

In an elementary school, a social worker was working with a group of fifth-grade girls who were having
behavioral and academic difficulties. She found that the
girls had trouble sustaining discussions in the group.
Often, they responded to her questions with shrugs
and one-word answers. To help them express their ideas
and feelings, she thought it would be a good idea to
engage them in an activity that would aid them in doing so. She divided the group into two subgroups and,
using magazines that she brought, she asked each subgroup to do a collage, one on what's good about being
in the fifth grade and the other on what's bad about
being in the fifth grade. The group members set to work
and seemed to enjoy the task. Much discussion took
place among members about what pictures to include. The
group spent the entire meeting working on the collages.

At the next meeting, the worker asked each subgroup
to explain to the others what pictures they had included
in their collage and their reasons for doing so. The
group members were quite able to talk about this. The
pictures aided them in expressing their ideas verbally
and served as a jumping-off point that enabled them to
do so. Had the worker simply asked the girls to discuss
what is good and bad about being in the fifth grade,
they would have had great difficulty doing so. It was

interesting that many of the same pictures ended up appearing in both the 'good' and 'bad' collages. The group members thus expressed their ambivalent feelings around the increasing independence that was starting to occur for them. The collages helped them to express that ambivalence.

Finally, we elaborate on the value of activities and projects that require members to work together over an extended period of time toward the accomplishment of a substantial and multifaceted task. Such long-term projects demand cooperation, hard work, and mutual aid on the part of group members. If the quality of the product that results from group members' efforts is high, the members can emerge from their work with a sense of accomplishment and mastery, improved self-esteem, and the satisfaction of having participated usefully in something larger than themselves. Along with a feeling of individual accomplishment, members can also experience a sense of mutuality and cohesiveness that is both powerful and pervasive.

After having met for six months, a photography group composed of members of a senior center decided they would like to create an exhibit at the center that captured the work they had done over the year. The social worker who worked with the group agreed, thinking that the creation of such an exhibit could provide an excellent ending for the group that could involve group members in a range of individual and collective efforts. Creation of the exhibit involved a variety of tasks and activities. As a group, the members reviewed all the pictures they had taken since the group's beginning. Such a review provided wonderful opportunities for group members to reminisce about all that had taken place in the group over time. Members decided which pictures to include in the exhibit and how to group them according to themes. Next, the group took two trips to see different exhibits of photographs on display in the city. Specifically, they looked at how the photographs in these exhibits were arranged and captioned. Returning to the center, they worked in pairs to develop captions for the photographs chosen for their own exhibit. Pairing the members to work on captions allowed some members who did not write particularly well to contribute ideas for the content of the captions. Other members went to a local lumber store to purchase material for the flats which they then built for the display. The entire group got involved in creating the arrangement of the titles, pictures, and captions. Finally, the group selected one of its members to emcee the opening of the exhibit at the center. All in the group made suggestions about things they wanted to be sure she included in her remarks about the group and the exhibit.

The quality of the exhibit resulted in group members receiving a great deal of recognition from others for their work. Perhaps even more important, the members themselves took pride in their creation and derived from it a sense of mastery and accomplishment for their complex efforts.

We end this part of the unit by distributing a handout (see pp. 118–120), taken directly from Sondra Brandler and Camille Roman's book, *Group Work: Skills and Strategies for Effective Interventions* (1991). In a comprehensive manner, it effectively summarizes the varied purposes of program/activity.

To encourage students to think about the purposeful use of program and activity with groups, we divide the class into four subgroups. Our aim is to help class members see how program can be used purposefully to address a range of group needs. We tell each subgroup that they are social workers with a group where the use of activity would make sense, and we assign one of the following groups:

• A group of high school seniors, all of whom are persons of color, who will be going next year to out-of-town colleges where they are likely to be one of only a few persons of color on campus. The group has spent a great deal of time, using both discussion and activity, examining the concerns that group members have about this and the dilemmas that they foresee. This group has met for seven sessions and has three sessions remaining.

• A group of parents of developmentally disabled adult children who live at home. The parents are particularly concerned about what will happen to their children as they age and as they are less able to actively care for them. This is the second meeting of the group. The first meeting was spent with the parents introducing themselves, describing the developmentally disabled child who lives with them, and identifying some of the concerns that they have.

The Varied Purposes of Activities

1. To reach out to clients who are uncomfortable or unable to express themselves verbally. Multi-family group members learn a great deal about themselves through a programmatic technique called family sculpting. In this method, group members who are unable to verbalize feelings about each other place their family members in poses which illustrate their relationships.

2. To teach specific coping skills. A cooking-and-shopping-for-one group might be an important part of a program for widowers. While providing an opportunity to share feelings in a period of bereavement, this group also teaches specific skills needed for survival in a changed environment.

3. To help clients to feel competent, worthwhile, and, through mastery, spiritually, emotionally, and intellectually rejuvenated. A newspaper writing group in a nursing home allows patients to express themselves, be creative, and feel capable of making a contribution to the larger nursing home community.

4. To sufficiently distance threatening subject matter in order to address it and problem solve around it. A popular group for psychiatric in-patients uses soap opera programs as engagement material. The patients are able to talk about the television characters with an openness impossible if they were asked to speak about themselves. The discussion, which begins with the fantasy, progresses to real-life situations and the patients' issues. The group provides its members with a socialization experience, develops problem-solving skills, and can hopefully lead to insights for patients concerning their own functioning.

5. To learn to share and work cooperatively toward common goals. Many groups that have specific concrete goals fail to reach them because group members find it difficult to share tasks and work together in a constructive manner. These difficulties may be seen in employee groups within organizations, in social action groups, and in volunteer groups. Training exercises, group puzzle assignments, and other activities may be useful in mobilizing a tenants' rights group, for example, to accomplish a unified effort to a common end.

6. To engage clients selectively around an area in which particularly problematic or painful material creates resistance. Adolescents struggling with sexual identity issues may find such matters hard to discuss. A co-ed basketball game may be a way

to bring boys and girls together in a game which involves some physical closeness within clear rules for conduct. For adolescents less able to tolerate the physical intimacy of a game like co-ed basketball, another sport such as baseball may be appropriate. The recreational element can lessen the discomfort and provide an arena for discussion later.

7. To help clients express socially unacceptable or conflictual feelings in a socially accepted manner. A puppetry group allows abused children to act out frightened, violent, and angry feelings. Unexpressed, some of these feelings are likely to manifest themselves in problematic anti-social behavior or in severe depression.

8. To help develop higher levels of frustration tolerance. With emotionally disturbed youngsters, waiting for one's turn, concentrating on a task, and being competitive yet in control, are essential skills. A simple game of Pick-up Sticks can help children to master these skills. In the game, each child takes a turn at dropping a stack of colored sticks on a table and then attempting to pick up each stick one at a time from the pile without disturbing the other sticks. The player to collect the most sticks in his turn without moving the remaining sticks is the winner. For more sophisticated groups, sticks with certain colors may be given point values. For young children or those with great difficulty in tolerating frustration, the game can be modified to allow two or three mistakes before passing the sticks on to the next player.

9. To provide individuals with an opportunity to experience new roles and unexplored parts of themselves. Psychodrama activities have been used successfully in many groups to stimulate discussion and help individuals to new levels of understanding about themselves. Role playing enhances multi-family and parenting groups in which walking in someone else's shoes provides a valuable new perspective that hopefully improves communication.

10. To act as a prelude to permitting successful movement toward verbal communication. Organized physical exercise programs can be useful in reducing tensions, releasing energy, and relaxing group members who may be agitated and unable to focus. Dancing or listening to music may also be therapeutic and assist in calming clients (including psychiatric patients and hyperactive children) in a manner which paves the way for more introspective work. Similarly, activities may be used as a

reinforcement or reward after a productive discussion. A game and snack period might follow a gradually lengthened discussion period. The game may also be used as a way to practice the skills expressed verbally. For example, the group may talk about conflict and then work it out in a competitive game.

11. To aid in diagnosis, interpretation and treatment. By seeing clients engaged in group activities, the worker can assess patterns of functioning, some of which may reveal behavior in other social settings.

Note: From Sondra Brandler & Camille P. Roman (1991), *Group Work: Skills and Strategies for Effective Interventions* (pp. 128–131). Binghamton, NY: Haworth.

• A group of social workers based at a state hospital for the mentally ill, who meet for group supervision and who are also all members of interdisciplinary teams. During group meetings, a number of the social workers have expressed annoyance and frustration because they feel that the other team members—psychiatrists, nurses, and psychologists, primarily—do not hear them or take them or their ideas seriously. This is an ongoing group in its middle stage.

• A group of formerly homeless men, mentally ill and chemically addicted, who now live in a single-room occupancy hotel. The group members are all participating in a work program at a cooperating agency and are striving for self-sufficiency. All group members are currently clean and sober, but drug use at the hotel is widespread. They fear they will not be able to stay clean as a result of the stress of continuous exposure to drugs. The group is in its middle stage.

Although we assign these four group situations, the instructor need not feel bound by these suggestions. Other situations that reflect the life and work experience of the class members can be developed.

We ask each subgroup to plan a program that would be relevant to their assigned group, given its substantive concerns and its stage of development. We ask them to envision a specific need that the members of their group might have and to design an activity whose purpose would be to help meet that need. Thus, the activity that they plan does not have to be all-encompassing (e.g., to help group members avoid drug use), but would involve encouraging members to develop personal or group characteristics that would be a step toward their achievement of that larger purpose (e.g., enhance self-esteem or increase interaction among group members). We advise students that the Varied Purposes of Activities handout will help them carry out this exercise.

To accomplish this task, each subgroup will need 30–60 minutes. Discussion in each group may start slowly, but it is likely to build as students become more involved and begin to appreciate the complexities of developing a program that is both purposeful and timely, and as they recognize the potential benefits activity can have. Once they have completed their program plan, each subgroup presents its suggestions to the entire class. Their suggested activities will likely range greatly, from games and exercises to reading, art, drawing, and writing to role plays and improvisational drama.

As the class is asked to critique each subgroup's proposed activity, we keep the focus on two questions: What is the purpose of the proposed activity? Does the activity make sense, given the group's stage of development? The handout on the purposes of activity is helpful in looking at the first question, and Robert D. Vinter's (1985, pp. 226–250) "Program Activities: An Analysis of their Effects on Participant Behavior" is especially helpful for the second question. Vinter identifies six dimensions of activities that relate to group needs and abilities based on its stage of development.

- *Prescriptiveness:* the degree and range of rules or other guides for conduct;
- *Institutionalized controls:* who enforces the rules or controls the behavior of participants—for example, an umpire, the group leader, the team captain, or the person who plays 'It';
- *Provision for physical movement:* the extent to which participants are required or permitted to move about in an activity setting;
- *Competence required for performance:* the minimum level of skill required to participate in the activity, but not the competence required to excel or win—skills may be physical, cognitive, emotional, and/or social;
- *Provision for participant interaction:* the degree and type of interaction among participants that is required or provoked— verbal/nonverbal, cooperative/competitive, degree of intimacy or personal disclosure/emotional distance;

- *Reward structure:* the types of rewards available—intrinsic, offered by leader, offered by other members—and the abundance or scarcity of rewards or punishments and how they are distributed.

As each group presents its suggested activity, we encourage the class to look at these dimensions and their relationship to both the activity's purpose and the group's developmental stage. Involving the class in this task encourages students to appreciate the value of program and activity and to respect the thoughtfulness that needs to go into their planning and implementation.

In the final section of this unit, we ask the students to participate in an activity that involves the entire class. We want them to experience—to see and to feel—the impact that participation in an activity can have.

We turn to the work of Marc Kaminsky, a social worker with expertise in the group work method and an accomplished writer and poet. Kaminsky uses the program component extensively in his work with older adults. We select an excerpt from his book, *What's Inside You It Shines Out of You* (1974), which presents the conceptual foundation and uses the creation of a collaborative poem as a type of program.

In affecting fashion, the excerpt provides an example of this creative process and lends itself to a dramatic reading. We distribute a passage (see pp. 123–128) to a number of students, asking them to read designated roles. We have the students arrange their chairs in a row in the front of the class.

In discussion after reading the excerpt, students have reported that they felt intensely involved because the content and structure of the reading touched their emotional core. As they analyze the process, they come to understand that the experience provided them with an opportunity to take part in an affective activity and see the potential for using this kind of program with other groups.

Building on this reading and the students' reactions to it, we next involve the class in creating a group poem. We ask them to reflect on the class over the semester and to express their thoughts aloud. We select a student whom we know to be agile with words and writing to be the person who "catches" the comments and writes them down. The lines contributed by the students usually combine class content and process. Some repeat key words and phrases that have become themes in the class; others describe more seriously things they have learned; still others reflect on their per-

Class Exercise – Collaborative Poem
(Adapted from Marc Kaminsky, 1974, *What's Inside You
It Shines Out of You*, pp. 16–20.)

Instructor

Six women joined me in the classroom. Hilda was one of them. I remember that her friend, the teacher, was among them. There was also an extremely old and elegant woman named Mary; a tall Austrian woman, a great lady with a long black dress and a string of pearls; an anxious American-born woman, who kept asking me to explain things to her; and a woman whose name and face I forget.

Together with them in a room that neither dwarfed nor pumped up human proportions, I relaxed. I felt back in the world, among people who were familiar to me, engaged in an activity which is so much a part of what I am. I felt a burst of energy, and enjoyed the thought of what was about to take place: the creation of a poem by a group of old people.

I said, "Today we're going to make up a poem together."

They were startled—and interested. They also didn't believe it.

How, they wanted to know, were we going to accomplish this miracle?

Student 1

If my older colleague had recipes for vegetable soup, I had recipes for poems. Many recipes: they had come, initially, from Kenneth Koch's great cookbook on the subject, *Wishes, Lies and Dreams: Teaching Children to Write Poetry*. After I had worked a while with Koch's recipes for collaborative poems, I had begun to make up poem-recipes of my own; and then I had sought ways to help people learn to make poems without the use of anything so fixed as a recipe.

Koch's recipes for poems are brilliant and simple devices for releasing the poetry in people. They provide the security of a prefabricated structure. They remove people's anxiety about poetry by turning the making of poems into a fun game: each player need only provide a single line, and that one line can completely rely upon the lines which Koch has already laid down. Moreover, the line need not even be written. It may be dictated to the person conducting the workshop. Responsibility for creative autonomy is kept to a minimum.

This is not necessarily a bad thing. Responsibility in any area of our lives can only be assumed gradually. Koch's basic workshop methods tends to create confidence, to free people for more difficult and hazardous work. The formulas which he devised can be depended upon to produce good and interesting results. That is their virtue. But they must be used tactfully. There is a fine line between supporting a novice and infantilizing him, and one must be sensitive and cautious not to cross it. If slavishly imitated, the advantages of Koch's poem-formulas become serious limitations. They end up stifling the person who attempts to administer them, and they hinder the growth of persons who, after a steady diet of collaborative poems produced by formula, are ready for a declaration of creative independence.

Instructor

Once one has learned to work with formula-poems skillfully, they become fine tools in the poet's bag of tricks. When the old women asked me how we would make up a poem together, I said, "By talking to each other. A poem is really a way of talking to another person, it's like having a good talk, you can only have a good talk if you feel that the other person can really understand you, then you feel free to say what's on your mind, and you suddenly find you have a lot to talk about."

Student 2

"Well," asked the teacher, "what should we talk about?"

Instructor

"How about dreams?" I said. "They're usually pretty interesting."

Student 3

The great lady with the string of pearls wasn't crazy about the idea. She thought dreams were pure nonsense, and she had no desire to discuss pure nonsense.

Student 4

The anxious woman asked if dreams really did have a meaning. Yes. Well, then, what did they mean?

Instructor

I asked her if she could remember any dream of her own that had been meaningful to her. No, she couldn't remember.

Student 5

Then Mary said: "I dreamed that my husband all dressed up in his gentle voice came back to me and told me, 'Take care of yourself.'"

Instructor

I and the group were stunned. My pen, which had been waiting in ambush for a good line, seized it verbatim. I copied Mary's words onto the yellow scratch pad that had been lying in front of me, and I read them back to the group.

Student 6

Hilda said that it was a good dream, and Mary must have had a good husband.

Student 5

Mary said that he was, and that the dream had eased her. She spoke of her insomnia: most nights she lay awake till three or four in the morning.

Student 2

"What do you do when you can't sleep?" the teacher asked.

Student 5

"I read the New York Times. From cover to cover."

Instructor

The other women accorded Mary a marked degree of respect and sympathy. They all addressed themselves to her, drew her out, and listened to her with greater interest than they listened to anyone else in the room. She was the oldest among them, eighty-five, a woman of obvious strength and dignity. I was impressed by her, and deeply moved. I later found out that she was the president of the club.

I said that what I found beautiful in Mary's line was that her husband was "all dressed up in his gentle voice." It seemed to me such a distinguished and lovely way to be dressed.

I then asked if anyone else had a dream that she remembered.

Student 4

The one who had asked me to explain the meanings of dreams said that she still couldn't remember anything in particular, but something did in fact, come back. "I dream all the time of water, always in my dream there's water—muddy water, pools—but there's always water."

She then asked me what water meant.

Instructor

I said it might mean many things, that there wasn't a simple "key" to interpreting dreams.

Student 4

Still, she wanted to know the meaning of water in dreams.

Instructor

I said that water was often a symbol of life, and spoke briefly of several things that came to mind—flowing and standing water in Blake and Coleridge, rites of purification, baptism, transition from one place of the soul to another, "death by water." She seemed satisfied. Water meant life, and I seemed to know a thing or two about this and that, so my word could be trusted.

Student 6

Hilda, who had followed all the turns of the conversation intently, now spoke up. She said that dreams were like prophecy: they could tell you what would happen in the future or what was happening now in some far-off place. Mary's dream had clearly touched off her remembering a dream of profound significance for her: "I dreamed that when I was alone in this country my parents appeared before me, and my father blessed me; and I knew it was their last time, I knew they were perished, it was just before Shavuos, 1942."

Instructor

I took down her words. The moment someone started speaking of a dream, I started writing; and I left off taking dictation when the talk turned aside from the subject of the poem.

After Hilda said something more about her parents, who perished in a Nazi concentration camp, I read the three lines I had gathered thus far.

Student 3
The great lady was willing to concede there was something to all this fiddle-faddle; and she was certainly not going to be left out. But she made it clear that she wanted to offer a corrective to the questionable niceness of the other lines. She reared herself up and delivered her "beautiful lines" in a rebuking tone: "I dream about the beautiful things – the colors of nature, and music, and I see Haifa and Israel and the mountains of Switzerland."

Instructor
These, of course, are the only words in the collaborative poem that approach being pure nonsense. What was clear was that she feared her actual dreams and wished to dream beautiful ones. She had admitted earlier that she thought too much delving into these things could make you crazy. So naturally, I had not pushed her, and I received her lines as they were intended to be taken—as a gift of beauty. It was a lot, considering her initial resistance, for her to have contributed a line at all. And I welcomed her contribution—even if it was a fake one.

Whether by accident or not, the pattern of a distinct and strongly felt dream following an obtuse one continued. The one whose name and face I no longer remember said,

Student 7
"I dreamed when I was sleeping at a window near the fire-escape a hand came and choked me, and in the morning I saw the watch was there and I knew no one had come."

Student 6
Hilda asked the woman how she had felt after this nightmare, and she answered,

Student 7
"Glad to be alive."

Instructor

The dead had appeared in Hilda's and Mary's dreams, to give news of death and a gift for survival. Then the hand of death itself had come into the poem, and choked the speaker. The woman's death had approached, forced her into waking up to her mortality, and left her intact. This dream, she told us, had occurred when she was fifteen, and she had remembered it vividly all her life. She spoke of her relief when in the daylight she saw that "the watch," time itself, was still there for her; and death, the thief who steals all our watches, had not come for her after all.

Student 2

The teacher, who had thus far not spoken of a dream, ended the discussion and the poem on a lighter note: "Whenever I dream of my folks, I know I have to call the rest of the family." The group laughed—and we broke up because it was noon and time for the group worker's vegetable soup.

The collaborative poem follows and is read in its entirety.

Dreams

I dreamed that my husband, all dressed up in his gentle voice, came back to me and told me "Take care of yourself."

I dreamed all the time of water, always in my dream there is water—muddy water, pools—but there is always water.

I dreamed that when I was alone in this country my parents appeared before me, and my father blessed me; and I knew it was their last time; I knew they were perished, it was just before Shavuos, 1942.

I dream about the beautiful things—the colors of nature, and music—and I see Haifa and Israel and the mountains of Switzerland.

I dreamed when I was sleeping at a window near the fire escape a hand came and choked me, and in the morning I saw the watch and I knew no one had come.

Whenever I dream of my folks, I know I have to call the rest of my family.

sonal reactions to the class. The collaborative poem that results is a blend of humor, thoughtfulness, and heartfelt reactions.

After this class session, the group poem can be typed and distributed to all class members. Students thus emerge from the program experience with a tangible memento of their effort and of the class.

This unit employs a range of teaching methods, from lecture to small-group problem solving to participation in a class activity. The combination helps students to understand and appreciate the importance of program and activity, to "see" their use and value, and to view their own use of activity with groups now and in the future with positive anticipation.

Readings

Brandler, Sondra, & Roman, Camille P. (1991). *Group Work: Skills and Strategies for Effective Interventions* (pp. 125-150). Binghamton, NY: Haworth.

Coyle, Grace. (1946). Social Group Work in Recreation. In *Proceedings of the National Conference of Social Work 1946* (pp. 195-208). New York: Columbia University Press.

Kaminsky, Marc. (1974). *What's Inside You It Shines Out of You*. New York: Horizon.

Lynn, Maxine, & Nisivoccia, Danielle. (1995). Activity-Oriented Group Work with the Mentally Ill: Enhancing Socialization. *Social Work with Groups, 18*(2/3), 95-106.

Malekoff, Andrew. (1997). *Group Work with Adolescents: Principles and Practice* (pp. 146-165). New York: Guilford.

Middleman, Ruth. (1980). The Use of Program: Review and Update. *Social Work with Groups, 3*(3), 5-23.

Middleman, Ruth. (1982). *The Non-verbal Method in Working with Groups*. Hebron, CT: Practitioners Press. Originally published in 1968, New York: Association Press.

Murphy, Marjorie. (1959). *The Social Group Work Method in Social Work Education. A Project Report of the Curriculum Study*. XI, Werner Boehm, Director and Coordinator. New York: Council on Social Work Education.

Northen, Helen. (1988). *Social Work with Groups* (2nd ed., pp. 78-97). New York: Columbia University Press.

Pollio, David E. (1995). Hoops Group: Group Work with Young 'Street' Men. *Social Work with Groups, 17*(2/3), 107-122.

Potocky, Miriam. (1993). An Art Therapy Group for Clients with Chronic Schizophrenia. *Social Work with Groups*, *16*(3), 73-82.

Ross, A. L., & Bernstein, N. D. (1976). A Framework for the Therapeutic Use of Group Activities. *Child Welfare*, *55*(9), 627-640.

Schnekenburger, Erica. (1995). Waking the Heart Up: A Writing Group's Story. *Social Work with Groups*, *18*(4), 19-40.

Shulman, Lawrence. (1971). "Program" in Group Work: Another Look. In William Schwartz & Serapio Zalba (Eds.), *The Practice of Group Work* (pp. 221-240). New York: Columbia University Press.

Shulman, Lawrence. (1992). *The Skills of Helping Individuals, Families, and Groups* (pp. 561-568). Itasca, IL: Peacock.

Vinter, Robert. (1985). Program Activities: An Analysis of Their Effects on Participant Behavior. In Martin Sundel, Paul Glasser, Rosemary Sarri, & Robert Vinter (Eds.), *Individual Change through Small Groups* (2nd. ed., pp. 226-236). New York: Free Press.

Waite, Lesley Meirovitz. (1993). Drama Therapy in Small Groups with the Developmentally Disabled. *Social Work with Groups*, *16*(4), 95-108.

Whittaker, James K. (1985). Program Activities: Their Selection and Use in a Therapeutic Milieu. In Martin Sundel, Paul Glasser, Rosemary Sarri, & Robert Vinter (Eds.), *Individual Change through Small Groups* (2nd ed., pp. 237-250). New York: Free Press.

Wilson, Gladys, & Ryland, Gertrude. (1949). *Social Group Work Practice*. Boston: Houghton-Mifflin.

Unit 10
Endings

Students often find the ending stage of group development particularly difficult to effect successfully when they work with groups. Because of their student status, they are often forced to bring their groups to premature closure because of the vagaries of their schedules. But even when the timing of a group's ending is appropriate, its final stage is often filled with emotion, both for the members and for the student. The ending of groups often comes at a time when group members and the worker are feeling a sense of comfort and ease with one another, when both are able to be truly themselves. In addition, with increased knowledge about group members and their needs, the student may become intent on accomplishing too much before the group ends.

This unit seeks to teach students about the ending stage of group development and the worker's role and functions. The objectives of this teaching unit for students are three:

1. To become familiar with the characteristics, member needs, and worker roles in the ending stage.
2. To develop practice skills for use with groups in the ending stage.
3. To be able to skillfully and purposefully intervene with groups in the ending stage.

We begin by asking the class to think about members of groups they are working with, or have worked with, and to identify members' feelings about ending a group. As students identify these feelings, we list them on the board. Often, students concentrate on the negative reactions that group members have toward ending. We remind them that group members have positive reactions toward ending as well. The list is extensive.

We next ask the students which of these reactions apply to them, as well. The response often is swift: students quickly and easily acknowledge that many of the feelings of group members also hold true for them.

We emphasize that group endings raise many feelings common to both members and worker, and often this makes the ending stage of group development emotionally complex. For the group members, behavior during the ending stage will be shaped by the many reactions they have about the group's termination. Given the likely behavior of the members and the tasks that need to be accomplished at this time in the group, the worker's role will change to meet these new conditions. While the worker was active in the beginning and became less central in the group's middle stage, the worker now needs to become more active again to help the group members bring successful closure to this group experience and to provide a positive frame of reference for members who are approaching new groups and other situations.

We distribute the "Stages of Group Development—Ending" handout (see Appendix J) and again point out that the handout on endings uses the same format as the ones they received for beginnings (see Appendix G) and middles (see Appendix I). They are reminded that if they wish to view the progression of any one dimension over time (i.e., where the members are, what needs to happen, or the role of the worker), they can read down a column from beginning to middle to ending. In reviewing the new handout with the class, we emphasize:

• Endings with groups are particularly complicated because they occur on three levels: the relationship between group members and the worker is coming to an end; the relationships among group members are ending; and the group as an entity is concluding and will cease to exist. The worker needs to be cognizant simultaneously of the multiple meanings of endings on all three levels.

• Often, workers find that expression of feelings from group members about the group's ending seems to be unnatural and to lack depth, even when the members seem to use the "right" words and express the "right" feelings. Frequently such lip service to feelings occurs because the worker has forced the issue of endings and members are unable to respond with genuine feeling. The worker, for instance, might say to the group, "We have five meetings left. How do you feel about that?" The members' responses are likely to come in the form of one-word answers ("bad," "okay," "good") or empty phrases ("it's too bad that we're almost done," "it doesn't bother me").

• The worker needs to call early attention to the imminence of endings as an important and intrinsic part of group life, so that the process will unfold in an unforced and natural manner. Group members' positive and negative feelings are best expressed spontaneously and over time, thus providing the worker and the group opportunities to explore and consider them.

• The members' (and the worker's) articulations of feelings about endings are important. The most effective way of inviting such expression is to encourage the group to reminisce—to relive and talk about the group's common experiences, meaningful content and events, observations about one another, progress and changes over time, etc. Genuine feelings become expressed during such discussion, and reminiscence thus helps the group members bring closure to the experience.

• Evaluation of the group experience is a corollary to reminiscence. In addition to bringing continuity and closure, evaluation allows members to transfer their learning from this group to other situations. Discussion of each member's participation in the group also allows each person to identify areas of progress and areas for future growth. The evaluative process—both group and individual—provides a frame of reference that members can use as they move on to new situations.

• A dangerous tendency in the ending stage is for the worker and/or the clients to try to cram extensive new material in at the last moment. Perhaps the familiarity with the group that both the members and the worker now have contributes to this tendency. Or perhaps the difficulty in saying goodbye and a longing to continue what has been important to the members, the worker, or both leads to such behavior. Either way, it is best to use the last meetings of the group to consolidate the learning and what has taken place, and to eschew the desire to impart some final "pearls of wisdom."

Next, we lead a discussion of the kinds of behavior that students might see, or have seen, as the group moves into the ending stages. We emphasize three kinds of behavior.

• *Denial.* Students, knowing the importance of endings, may have been planful in introducing the idea of termination, even in the group's very beginning and then periodically throughout the group's life. In beginning the group, they may have let members know what the duration of the group would be. Then, periodically, they may have reminded the group about the amount of time that remained. Nevertheless, when the group's ending is imminent and the worker again reminds the group of that, it is not unusual to be met with statements from members such as, "This group's going to be ending? You never told us that." Or, "You didn't tell us you were leaving." The members' reactions to losing the group and the worker may thus be raised via their denial of the group's ending and of the fact that the worker ever mentioned it.

• *Regression.* Facing the loss of the group and the worker, group members may return to previous patterns of behavior that were seen in earlier stages of the group. Members may seem unable to cope with tasks already mastered or with relationships that have been established. They may even act as they did in the group's beginnings. This reaction can be understood as one way that members make a plea for the group to continue and for the worker to remain. In essence, the members are saying, "We still need this group and we still need you."

• *Flight.* As the group nears its end, the attendance of some members may become sporadic, while other members may stop attending altogether. Perhaps this is because it is difficult for them to deal with the feelings and reactions they are experiencing in the face of loss. Since ending is imminent, they see no point in continuing. It is as if such members are saying, "I might as well leave this group and you, the worker, before you and the group leave me." In the face of such premature flight, it is important that a worker actively reach out to such members and urge them to return to the group so that a helpful and appropriate ending can take place. It is important that the worker not allow group members to trickle off and let the group end by default. (The flight of group members may also be expressed constructively. As a group is ending, members may use their experience to begin to establish connections with other groups and different relationships.)

The worker may find many of the above behaviors exasperating. They may cause her or him to question whether anything was accomplished in the group, since members seem not to have remembered what was said, not to have changed their behavior patterns, or not to care. Students need to recognize that such behavior is expectable and is very much connected to the group's ending.

Students also should be alert to the possibility that unusual or exasperating behavior at this stage of the group's development may well be connected to endings. In fact, they need to remember that at this time in the life of the group *any* behavior that elicits strong feelings on their parts may have to do with endings. It is easy for students to forget that possibility.

We illustrate such a failure to recognize the salience of endings by recounting an incident that occurred in one of the author's group work classes.

> There were only three more classes left in a year-long course on group work. In the class, we had discussed endings with groups a number of weeks prior to this class session. On this day, we were looking at class members' actual practice interventions. During the discussion, Luis, one of the members of the class, commented, 'You know, in this class we never really talked about co-leadership.' I agreed. Joan added, 'And we never talked about supervisory groups.' Again, I agreed. The floodgates opened. The areas that we had not covered were shouted from all parts of the room by different class members. I felt increasingly horrible, as areas that had gone uncovered were accurately identified. "What had we been doing all year?" I asked myself as I sank deeper into my chair and the onslaught continued. At that point, Margie stopped the action. "Hey, wait a minute," she said. "I think what's going on here has to do with termination." Bells rang in my head. Here I was, the 'expert' on endings and, as this was happening to *me*, not once had I made the connection to our class's ending. Margie's realization of that connection was important to me and to the class members.

Although a worker should not ascribe *all* unusual or exasperating behavior to endings, she or he needs not to forget that the group's coming to an end may be an important factor in the behavior, thoughts, and feelings expressed.

To help the students examine the role of the worker in the ending stage, we use two process records that illustrate endings in two very different groups. We distribute the first record (see pp. 136–138), which is of a group of girls, ages 10 and 11, in a community-based after-school program. As students follow along, we read this record aloud.

Goodbye and Good Riddance

During the week preceding this meeting, I had not been at the community center because it was my spring vacation. However, the program continued and all the other counselors were at the center, since they were required to be in attendance.

Because it was spring vacation for the public schools, as well, the center had planned several trips, all of which my group was able to participate in because they were not "club" activities, but "center" activities. All children from the junior program who had signed up for the trips went together as a large group. Counselors were arbitrarily assigned to accompany the children on these activities. Thus, each child did not necessarily have a chosen counselor to accompany her or him on the trip. However, all counselors were at the center for most of the week, and some had planned extra activities for their own group.

When I spoke to the girls on the phone the evening before our meeting, I strongly sensed their anger. I therefore had some idea of their feelings going in to our next meeting.

As I was waiting at the door to greet the girls, Patty and Sylvia brushed right past me and walked into the clubroom. Patty said, "The only reason I came was to tell you that I'm not going to come to this crummy old place anymore!"

"Yeah," said Sylvia. "We're not going to stay with you anymore. We're going to another group."

Patty yelled, "And it's going to be far away from here!"

"Wow, you two girls sure are angry," I said. "We talked a little over the phone and so I think I kind of know what it's about. But maybe you could help me and make it a little clearer for me."

"Help you?" cried Patty. "Why should we help you? You don't care anything about us! All you ever do is go on your vacations."

"Yes, I was on my spring vacation last week, as I told you I would be," I said.

At that point Lori walked in and looked at me with great disdain and said, "Oh, you're here."

Sylvia said to Lori, "We were telling her that we're not coming anymore because she's never here."

"Yeah," said Lori to me. "Brenda was here last week and Frances was here and Ella was here—everyone was here but you. We were the only group that didn't have a counselor last week. We were the only group that couldn't do anything."

I reminded them that I had come to the center on Monday, but that it must feel to them like I hadn't been in at all because the other counselors were here for all of the week.

"They're always here more than you are," said Patty. "All the other groups meet twice a week, but we only get to meet on Fridays. The center won't let us do anything that everyone else gets to do."

"Yeah," said Lori. "This dumb old place won't let us do anything. I bet if you wanted to you could meet with us another day, but you just don't want to."

"You said it," Patty said. "You know why that is? Because she's too busy taking her vacations."

Sylvia said, "Maybe we could go and ask Brenda if we could be in her group. She won't say no. She *likes* kids."

"Yeah," said Lori. "She's not like our counselor."

"You know, you girls are right about something," I said. "The other groups meet twice a week and we only meet once. And I think that you think that means that I only like you half as much, and that I don't care about you as much as the other counselors care about their groups."

"Well, you don't," Patty said. "If I were in a burning building you would just leave me there. And I would die, and you wouldn't even care."

"Do you girls feel the same way that Patty does?" I asked.

"Why should we tell you how we feel? Before we could tell you, you'll say the meeting's over," said Lori.

"Do any of you think I've done that before?" I asked.

"Why can't we meet twice a week like all the other girls?" Sylvia asked.

"Yeah, why can't we meet twice a week like them? I bet it's just because you don't want to," said Patty.

"You know, we've talked about this before," I said, "and I guess I didn't realize how strongly you felt about it. It seems now that you girls think we're doing this to punish you, or because we don't care as much about you as the other children."

"Well, why else can't we meet as much as everyone else?" asked Sylvia.

"You know, I remember that I told you that Alan and I decided that we would go by the decision that the first group had made and meet only on Fridays. But I think that you're telling me something very important now. You're saying that you really do need to meet more than one time a week, and that maybe it would be a very good idea for you to meet twice a week in the fall. Do you think we can work together to see if we can make that happen?"

"That isn't the real reason that we couldn't meet on Tuesdays. You just think we're stupid! Well, we think you're stupid!"

"I'm telling you the truth, Patty, and I think that you know deep down that I don't think the group is stupid, but I think that it's very hard for you girls to remember that now, because when we get angry at people, it's pretty tough to think about other things besides that we're angry at them."

"We're not mad at you," Lori said. "We just think you stink. How come we had to get a student?" [Lori makes a twisted face.] "All the other groups get regular people. They can come all the time, but you have to always be in school."

I told them that I cared about the group very much, but it was true that I spent less time here than the other counselors. I said that the time that we do spend together, though, was very important to me, and very special. And I had the feeling that they felt that way too.

"That's not true. You're lying!" Patty said. "If we were so special you would stay for the summer."

"It sounds to me that maybe you're feeling some of the sadness that I am feeling about our group ending soon. It's very hard to have things that are about end. Sometimes we try very hard not to let them end, because it hurts a lot."

"It doesn't hurt me," said Lori. "You can just leave right now for all I care."

"Well, it makes me sad that our group is ending," I said. "And I certainly don't want to leave now. I know how angry you girls are, but I hope that you won't leave now either. But after three more times, the group will have to end."

"Well, so we don't care," Sylvia said.

"Yeah, we don't care," Betty said. "Let's go to Brenda's room."

At that, they all ran out of the clubroom and into Brenda's room.

We then discuss the record with the class, focusing on the worker's interventions.

> I began the discussion, "This meeting ended very destructively for both the worker and the girls. What brought this about?" "I'm glad that wasn't me, that's for sure," Marcus said. "Those kids were really giving that worker a hard time." "I can imagine how that worker felt when the kids ran out of the room," Sylvana said. "I'd be devastated. I'd feel like an absolute failure." "I'd be angry," Jennifer added.
>
> "OK, that's how you'd feel," I said. "But let me ask again, why do you think this meeting came to such a destructive end?" "I think the worker was having trouble," Marisol said. "But she was really trying. Maybe she sounded too programmed. But I don't know what else she could have done." I asked, "What were these kids really asking this worker? What did they want from her?" "They didn't want her to leave," Lonny said. Fran added, "They wanted to know if she liked them. They keep asking her that in different ways." "And does she answer them?" I asked. "Well, yes," Julie said. "She says she cares." "Where in the record does she do that?" I asked. "Toward the end," Julie said. "She says, 'I told them that I cared....'" [She continues to read that paragraph.] "Yeah, but look at all the words she uses," Walter commented. "The feeling of caring doesn't come through very strongly and doesn't sound very genuine." I said, "I think these kids are *screaming* for the worker to tell them that she really likes them, to express that feeling unreservedly and with emotion. And she never really does that."

In class discussion, we make a number of teaching points about this record that are applicable to the ending stage generally.

• In the face of the group's ending and the worker's imminent departure, the behavior of the girls exhibits both regression and flight. The hostility they express is their way of saying to the worker, "We don't care. We'll leave you before you leave us."

• The girls' behavior escalates and becomes increasingly out of control. The worker needs to limit them and stop their destructive behavior.

• One way the worker could interrupt the girls' destructive behavior is by pointing out to the group, clearly and with feeling, that this group has been a wonderful one.

• Equally important is that the worker clearly express her own feelings. She needs to let the girls know, simply and clearly, with feeling and emotion, how much she likes them. In fact, genuine expression of feelings by the worker often helps the members of a group to then express their feelings.

• Once the girls' destructive behavior is interrupted, the group members and the worker can discuss the group and its ending through reminiscence and evaluation.

The second record that we distribute is of a group of blind elderly participants in a day program (see pp. 141–143). This record describes the first meeting of the group following a lengthy transit strike during which group members were unable to travel to the program. We ask students to read aloud the parts of the members and the worker.

Review of this record enables us to reemphasize many of the points that were brought out in the discussion of the Goodbye and Good Riddance record.

> I began the discussion, "I've asked you to look at these two records in tandem. Aside from the fact that they both concern endings, what would you say is the commonality between them?" "The members of this group don't want the worker to leave either," Julie said. "That was also true for the kids." "And this worker also forces the issue and doesn't sound genuine," Jose added. "I think these members are really asking the worker whether she liked them, just like the kids were asking in the first record," Walter said. "And this worker doesn't really express her feelings either." "Exactly," I said. "Here are the blind elderly asking the worker the same question that the 10- and 11-year-olds were asking. Each group asks that question differently but quite loudly. And in each group, the worker's response is not adequate, because it is distant, evasive, clouded by too many words, and not expressed with genuine feeling. In this record, how might the worker have responded?"

Both case records provide the instructor opportunity to emphasize that clear expression of feelings on the part of the worker

Do You Think Old, Blind People Are Different?

Setting: Day program for the elderly blind

Worker: Alison (student intern)

The problem came to my attention on April 11. The Passover/ Easter holidays were over and the transit strike was finally settled. The group was meeting for the first time in three weeks and was very happy to be back together again. During the strike, I had maintained contact with the members by phone. Since time was going by and I knew we had only five weeks left together, I felt pressured to discuss termination with the group.

Louise: It's good to be back. I really missed coming here.

Sonia: Me too. I get very lonesome not coming here. This program is the most important thing in my life.

Greg: I missed this group the most and I especially missed you, Alison.

Louise: I did too and I really appreciated your calling. It made my day. You know when you can't get out by yourself and you don't have too many people calling you, you're really glad when someone cares.

Worker: *I'm glad you're all back. I missed you too and I know it's hard when a major activity is cut out of your lives.*

Greg: I'm such a creature of habit. Any change throws me off.

Worker: *Change is hard for everybody, Greg. And speaking of change, I want to discuss something with the group which is hard for me. In five weeks I will be leaving, and even though this may seem to be a bad time to bring it up because we are just coming back, I think it's real important for us to talk about my leaving.*

Louise: What do you mean you're leaving? Why?

Tom: Because she's a student. It happens every year.

Sonia: I didn't know you were a student. Why didn't you tell us?

Worker: *I did tell you, Sonia, but sometimes people forget things they don't want to hear.*

Ellen: Of course you knew, Sonia. The students were all introduced to us the first day at the community meeting.

Tom: Don't listen to Sonia, Alison. It's alright. We all knew you were leaving. We just didn't realize it was so soon.

Louise: I never knew.

Worker: *I know it comes as a surprise because we have all been apart for a while and now at our first meeting back, you are zapped with my leaving first thing. Louise, you are relatively new to the program so you may not have known the policies about students. In that case, I'm sorry for not mentioning it to you when you first joined the group.*

Tom: Every year it's the same thing. By the time we finally get to know the students, they leave. But that's life. There's nothing we can do about it, so what's the point of talking about it.

Worker: *That's true, we can't change the policy, but we can certainly talk about how we feel about it. For example, even though students leave every year, I would like to know how you feel about my leaving this year.*

Ellen: We have all discussed you, and everybody agrees that this year's students were the best we ever had.

Greg: Especially you and Abigail. We love you.

Tom: I'd like to ask you a question. How did you like working with us this year?

Ellen: Do you think old, blind people are different from old, sighted people?

Worker: *That's an interesting question. I guess you want to know how I feel about you.*

Tom: No, not about us. Just in general—people at the agency.

Worker: *You know, we have talked a lot in this group about the differences and similarities between older, blind people and older, sighted people. I think maybe it might be good for the group to kind of summarize our past meetings and to answer that question yourselves.*

Ellen: Why won't you answer the question?

Louise: Maybe you don't like us because we're blind.

Tom: I'll answer the question. I think blind old people are a lot ruder than sighted old people. The people here at

> the agency constantly interrupt because they can't see who's speaking and don't pick up non-verbal cues.
>
> Greg: That's ridiculous, Tom. People who interrupt are just impolite. It has nothing to do with blindness or age.
>
> Tom: [raising his voice] Stupid! Of course it does.
>
> Worker: *Hold on a minute, Tom. What's going on here? Louise doesn't think I like you anymore because you're blind. Tom, you are screaming and getting excited at Greg for just expressing a difference in opinion. I have a feeling that this is all linked up to my leaving. You know, Tom, I think you may be angry at me and are just taking it out on Greg right now.*
>
> Tom: Don't be silly. Don't start psychoanalyzing me again.
>
> Ellen: Alison, what *is* your opinion of us? Do you think we're different?
>
> Ken: What did you think when you first met us?
>
> Worker: *First of all, let me say that I will really miss all of you very much. As far as what I thought of you at the beginning, I was a little nervous because I had never known or been around blind people before, but I very quickly got over that feeling. I now think of you as individuals as opposed to being blind. But I'm just wondering if these questions have to do with my leaving, whether you feel safer now to ask me, or maybe you're even wondering whether I would leave if you weren't blind.*
>
> Tom: Oh, oh, there she goes again.

encourages group members to express their own feelings about the group, the other group members, the worker, and the ending stage. Such expressions then enable the group to engage in reminiscence and evaluation.

In the material on beginnings (Unit 4) and middles (Unit 6), we identified and discussed skills that were of particular use in those stages of group development. These skills were selected from Middleman and Wood's (1990) *Skills for Direct Practice in Social Work*. The skills that are useful in one stage of development often continue to be important as the group evolves. We remind the class of the skills already described that seem particularly important in the ending stage as well.

Beginnings	*Middles*
Referring to purpose	Reaching for consensus
Building on strengths	Reaching for difference
Reaching for a feeling link	Confronting situations
Inviting full participation	Reaching for feelings
	Amplifying subtle messages
	Reporting own feelings

To these skills, we now add some others that have particular relevance in the ending stage.

- *Summarizing:* stating the essence of a particular discussion or series of discussions, action or series of actions;
- *Getting with feelings:* indicating to the other person that the essence of her or his inner experience has been communicated and understood;
- *Talking in the idiom of the other:* "responding to another person's disguised or veiled messages, using the same context or symbols, treating these as if they were real rather than unreal, and as if they were overt rather than covert expressions" (Middleman & Wood, 1990, p.66);
- *Partializing feelings:* dividing emotional experience into smaller, more manageable components;
- *Voicing group achievements:* verbally summarizing with appreciation any indications of progress or growth which the worker has noticed;
- *Preserving group history and continuity:* reminding members of previous experiences in the group by deliberately linking the current session to previous ones.

Students have been using the material and practice skills from Middleman and Wood in their practice. Therefore, it is not necessary for the instructor to spend significant time at this point in an exercise that uses these skills. The instructor may briefly describe the skills that have not been discussed previously. If any seem difficult for students to grasp, the instructor may refer to the exemplars that are used in the *Skills for Direct Practice in Social Work* text as the basis for discussion.

The skill of talking in the idiom of the other may prove difficult for students to understand, and thus they might benefit from the following example from Middleman and Wood (1990, p. 67, author's italics):

> In the example below, the social worker not only talks in the idiom of the other, she reaches for feelings in the other person's idiom. Then, still in the other person's

idiom, she checks to see if the idiom remains necessary.

> After a staff meeting in which the psychologist's plan for a new service was turned down, she asked me if I ever thought about how long it takes a spider to spin a web and how fast it can be wiped out of the corner with a dust rag. *I said that it sounded very demoralizing.* She looked at me with a sad expression on her face and nodded. *I said that spider webs were very vulnerable*, and she said that spiders were very vulnerable, too. I nodded. Then *I said that sometimes people were vulnerable, giving her a chance to be more direct if she were ready to be.* And apparently she was ready, because she said she should never have allowed herself to get so invested in that project.

We also present to students three points of caution. First, the worker should not make false promises about continuing the relationship with the group or with individual members. To say "I will visit" or "I will write" or "I'm sure I will see you again" is a strong temptation and a way that workers often avoid the difficulty and discomfort of saying goodbye.

Second, we caution the students about what we call "the big bash syndrome" in endings, by which we mean using the final meeting of the group for a big party, group trip, or some sort of major event. Such an event does not allow the group to end meaningfully. A "big bash" is a way for group members and for the worker to avoid saying goodbye. It is not that we are against marking the group's ending with some sort of celebration. Our suggestion is that the group's last meeting should give it an opportunity to finish its task—to value the experience, what has been learned, what was difficult, and what can be useful as the members move on.

William Schwartz discussed the tendency for the worker and members to avoid endings through what he called the "farewell party syndrome":

> The farewell party syndrome is a condition that has to be examined carefully; it is generally a collaboration between worker and members, for the feeling is shared and the evasions of the opportunity to *finish with work*— to use the last moments as part of the contract, rather than something different—anticlimactic. For the worker, the inability to *resolve* his function—"the client is dead, long live the client" – makes it difficult for him to end with feeling, even as he looks forward to the next beginning, with new people. (pp. 184-185, in Berman-Rossi, 1994)

Finally, we raise the issue of endings with groups which the worker has not liked or with groups whose purposes have not been fully achieved and in which there is not a great sense of accomplishment. We caution the student not to make false statements about their feelings or about the group's achievements. Such false statements will be easily recognized as such by the group members. With such groups, it is important that the worker think in advance about what she or he can and wants to say to the group. The parts of the experience that were useful and positive can be recognized and acknowledged, and the content of the worker's statements can be directed toward what members have learned from this group experience and ways members can use such learning in future experiences.

Readings

Berman-Rossi, Toby. (1994). *Social Work: The Collected Writings of William Schwartz* (pp. 181-186). Itasca, IL: Peacock.

Brandler, Sondra, & Roman, Camille P. (1991). *Group Work: Skills and Strategies for Effective Interventions* (pp. 75-103). Binghamton, NY: Haworth.

Brown, Leonard N. (1991). *Groups for Growth and Change* (pp. 218-233). New York: Longman.

Garland, James, Jones, Hubert, & Kolodny, Ralph. (1973). A Model for Stages of Development in Social Work Groups. In Saul Bernstein (Ed.), *Explorations in Group Work* (pp. 17-71). Boston: Milford House.

Garvin, Charles D. (1997). *Contemporary Group Work* (pp. 208-221). Boston: Allyn and Bacon.

Henry, Sue. (1992). *Group Skills in Social Work: A Four-Dimensional Approach* (2nd ed., pp. 192-220). Pacific Grove, CA: Brooks/Cole.

Malekoff, Andrew. (1997). *Group Work wth Adolescents: Principles and Practice* (pp. 166-188). New York: Guilford.

Middleman, Ruth R., & Wood, Gale Goldberg. (1990). *Skills for Direct Practice in Social Work* (pp. 91-154). New York: Columbia University Press.

Northen, Helen. (1988). *Social Work with Groups* (2nd ed., pp. 298-332). New York: Columbia University Press.

Shulman, Lawrence. (1992). *The Skills of Helping Individuals, Families and Groups* (3rd ed., pp. 173-206, 573-594). Itasca, IL: Peacock.

Toseland, Ronald W., & Rivas, Robert F. (1998). *An Introduction to Group Work Practice* (3rd ed., pp. 363-439). Boston: Allyn and Bacon.

Unit 11
Group Work versus Casework in a Group [*]

All practice with groups is not social work with groups. True group work practice is characterized by the depth of mutual aid that emerges among group members. This aid is the benchmark of group work, because the issues and concerns that one member brings to the group provide opportunities for all members to examine their own situations and concerns. A level of mutual aid that goes beyond superficial advice can then result when members reflect on themselves and the other person's situation. Such a process thus benefits both the receiver and the giver, and, as we teach students in this unit, the worker plays a key role by making a demand that members apply another person's issues or problems to themselves and their own experiences.

Casework in a group, on the other hand, is typified by members offering a kind of instant and shallow advice to peers, advice that is not rooted in examination of their own experiences. The worker who practices casework in a group does not ask members to apply the issues raised by one member to themselves, but instead has what amounts to an individual meeting with a group member in the presence of others in the group.

This unit is intended to help students practice group work rather than casework in a group. The objectives of this teaching unit for students are three:

1. To understand the distinction between group work and casework in a group.

2. To appreciate the uniqueness of group work (versus casework in a group) in relation to the group's inherent strengths, participatory democracy, and, especially, the essential power of mutual aid.

---

[*] This unit draws upon material in the authors' article "Group Work vs. Casework in a Group: Principles and Implications for Teaching and Practice" (Kurland & Salmon, 1992).

147

3. To be able to intervene in a group in such a way that members practice real group work, rather than casework in a group.

We first want students to recognize that often what practitioners identify as group work is really not that at all. To do this, we make the following teaching points:

• The notion that putting people together in a group equals group work has been dispelled by a number of group work theorists.

• Getting people together and responding to each one individually in the presence of the others—what Hartford (1978, p. 9) calls "aggregational therapy of individuals"—is *not* working with a group and *not* maximizing the group's potential.

• Putting a group member on a "hot seat" by having the leader engage in extended back-and-forth discussion with that person while others watch or engage in extended criticism of that person is, similarly, *not* group work (see Middleman, 1978).

• Group process that is dominated by the worker and used to enhance conformity—where dissenters are humiliated, "revealing" is required, and punishment is given if refusal takes place—violates the basic tenets of social group work (Konopka, 1990).

Next, we want students to recognize major differences between group work and casework in a group, some of which are obvious and others more subtle. To help them understand these differences, we make a second set of teaching points:

• The worker who views each group member only as an individual and who applies individual personality theories and dynamics without appreciating or understanding the impact of such concepts as group size, roles, norms, communication patterns, member interaction and influence, and group stages, to name but a few, is practicing casework in a group.

• The worker who allots time to each individual group member, in turn and in round-robin fasion, to talk about progress on issues of concern and who does not maximize group interaction and mutual aid practices casework in a group rather than group work.

• Group work requires the worker to engage in "thinking group," a consideration of the group as a whole, first, and individual participants, second, when initiating or responding to others (Middleman & Wood, 1990).

• Active participation by group members in the form of giving advice to solve a group member's problem can remain casework in a group, even though it might seem the group is attending to member issues. In such an instance, all the group members become "caseworkers" in an attempt to solve the problem of one group member.

• Group work takes place when there is an emphasis on the commonalities of problems and situations among members and on the concomitant commonality of feelings to which they give rise.

• An effective group worker draws out for members the applicability of problems, elicits their commonalities, and asks members to examine reflectively the issues of others. Thus, such a worker helps group members view and use the issues raised by one member as an opportunity for all.

Once the class understands the theoretical distinction between group work and casework in a group, we focus on how to put their understanding into practice. We ask students to describe how they would go about assuring that real group work takes place when a member of a group with which they are working brings an individual issue to the forefront. We ask them to identify the steps involved in such group work practice by drawing on the problem-solving process of John Dewey, which was discussed in Unit 5.

Using Dewey's model, students are able to identify with ease the first three steps in the progression:

1. An individual group member raises a problem/issue/situation of concern.
2. The problem is clearly identified by the individual and the group.
3. The problem is explored.

We then ask the students to raise any concerns they have about carrying out these first three steps.

> Glenn said, "What do we really mean when we say the problem is explored? That's easier said than done. I get very anxious with exploration. When an individual in the group is talking about something, I never know how long to stay with that person. I worry that if I stay with one member, I'll lose the rest of the group." Louise immediately responded, "I worry about the opposite— that I'll stay with an individual too long so that person feels as if she's on a hot seat and being grilled." Dena said, "What's even worse is when the group members

ask a million questions of one person. Then that person really feels like they're being roasted." Tanya thoughtfully responded, "It seems to me that if we're really going to do group work rather than casework in a group, then we also have to think about when to ask others in the group to look at their own experiences in relation to whatever the individual has raised and that the group's ability to do that would be related to how well they understand the individual's issue."

The issues raised by these students are pertinent and common. We respond to their concerns by emphasizing that the timing of the third step in this progression—exploration of the individual's problem—is crucial and should not be rushed. The group must spend enough time exploring the individual's problem to allow other group members to understand and develop empathy for the individual member and the situation. Only if members understand the problem will they be able to recount relevant experiences and dilemmas of their own. Too much time spent in exploration with the individual, on the other hand, can contribute to a sense of being on a hot seat and of being grilled by other members.

We continue by asking students to identify the rest of the steps in the progression, with which they are familiar based on their knowledge of Dewey's progression.

4. The worker asks group members to recount situations they have experienced and dilemmas they have faced that are relevant to the problem raised.

5. Possible "solutions" to the individual's problem are identified, drawing upon the experiences recounted by other group members.

6. The worker and group members help the individual decide on a course of action or solution and how to implement it.

7. The worker asks all members what they have taken out of the discussion that has transpired.

8. At future group meetings, the group as a whole follows up with the individual about the problem and how things are going.

We emphasize the importance of the fourth step in the progression—asking group members to recount relevant situations and dilemmas they have experienced. When the group is in a rush to offer advice, this crucial step is often omitted altogether, thus depriving the group members of the opportunity to draw upon and learn from their own experiences.

To further help the class distinguish between group work and casework in a group, and to see the worker's role in assuring that real group work takes place, we distribute a two-part record.

Jim—Part 1

Jim is a member of a group on coping skills in a day program for the mentally ill. Jim is a lonely and reclusive 29-year-old man who has trouble making friends. He has been diagnosed as paranoid schizophrenic. Jim lives in his own apartment. He frequently annoys the group by talking of masturbation and walking around with his pants unzipped, by making inane comments that interrupt the group, and by pretending to fall asleep and lying across three chairs during the meeting.

At the group's 10th meeting, Jim asks a question of the worker. "I want to know what you think, Debbie. Hypothetically speaking, suppose you had a friend and you don't have any other friends, but this friend every time he comes over he smokes pot or does a couple of lines of coke in your living room. I mean he is a good listener and is your only friend and you don't do drugs or anything, what would you do?"

Before the worker could even respond, group members quickly jumped in to offer advice. Jerry immediately said he'd just tell the guy to get out of his house with the drugs. Allen said drugs are dangerous and this guy's no good. Pam said she wouldn't want anyone doing drugs in her house. Ron said that the guy must not be a very good friend. Will said a friend wouldn't take advantage of you or get you in trouble. Finally, Jim said defensively, "You know, I don't really care if he does drugs in my house." He seemed dissatisfied with the discussion that had taken place. Others in the group seemed frustrated as well. As the meeting ended, Pam asked Jim, "Why did you waste our time if there is no problem?"

In discussion of this record, we point out to students that key steps in the problem-solving progression were ignored. The students are able to see that the problem was neither identified nor explored, that "solutions" were offered to Jim in a seemingly belligerent fashion, without empathy or understanding, and that members' relevant experiences went untapped. As a result, Jim, the group, and the worker emerged feeling highly dissatisfied. Such dissatisfaction led the worker to raise this issue again with the group at the first opportunity.

Jim—Part 2

The worker asked the group if they remembered the meeting where Jim spoke of his friend who did drugs at his house. Everyone did remember it. She acknowledged that the discussion had been frustrating for everyone. The group agreed. She asked the group's permission to discuss the issue again in the hope that the group could be helpful to Jim and engage in a discussion that would be more satisfying for everyone. The group agreed.

Jim recounted the situation. This time, though, the worker's questions and comments helped Jim be more specific. When she observed that this issue seemed important to him, Jim responded by telling the group, "I don't have any other friends and having this one friend is very important to me. This guy I've known all my life. We went to high school together. This guy is a college graduate with a good job. He has his own apartment. This guy is somebody."

The group began to understand and empathize. The tone of their questions and comments changed from belligerent to supportive. Jim's responses, in turn, became less defensive and more honest. He could now hear the group's comments better. Even his physical posture changed as he sat upright and faced the group. Allen asked Jim if he was worried about the police. "Yes, I am," Jim responded. "But I don't want to end the friendship. I don't want to get caught either with my friend doing drugs." Pam asked Jim if he ever talked to his friend about being caught when he does drugs at his house. "I told him it bothered me," Jim said. "He stopped for a while, but then he started doing it again."

The worker then asked the group if they could remember situations they'd experienced that were related to that with which Jim was struggling now. Ron recounted a time a year ago when he told a friend who wanted him to use cocaine that he would not do it. Others spoke of similar situations—times they'd tried to convince friends or relatives to do something, times others tried to convince them to do something, friends they'd valued and lost, people who'd gotten them into trouble. Everyone listened attentively to one another until the session finished.

At the next meeting, the group returned to Jim's particular situation and helped him develop a plan to talk with his friend about his concerns. Drawing on their own experiences, some gave Jim suggestions of what he might say and words he might use. The group even engaged in some role play, with Jim playing his friend and various members playing Jim.

As we help the class understand the reasons that the second meeting was more successful, they are able to identify the essential factors that led to this result. The worker's role was decisive. She asked Jim to expand on the issue. Her doing so served as a model for the group members, and they had questions to ask of Jim as well.

As Jim elaborated, the group began to empathize. When the worker asked the group to recall similar situations with which they had struggled, they were able to respond with highly relevant and even painful experiences from their own lives. The commonalities became clear. Their remarks and suggestions then had more power and were more helpful both for Jim and for themselves.

The class is thus able to appreciate that part one of this record is an example of casework in a group and that in the second part effective group work took place. It was the worker's clear demand for attention to the third and fourth steps in the progression that make this a helpful process for everyone in the group.

In the last segment of this unit, we want students to look at their practice interventions as they work to engage the members of a group in real group work. To do this, we present a situation which, clearly, is casework in a group. Through the use of a role play, we ask students to demonstrate how the same situation would be handled if group work were to take place. We read aloud the following example of casework in a group to the class:

> In a pre-vocational skills group in a day treatment program, Sara explains that she is nervous about going back to work. She tells the group that she's gained weight and that her clothes do not fit; she's worried that she won't be able to get a job because of the bad economy; and she doesn't know what to say about the

gap in her employment history. "What am I going to say I did for two years—that I was hospitalized and under psychiatric care and doing nothing?" she exclaims. On the other hand, she also says she'd like to have some money and that she feels useless staying home, especially when her sister pressures her to go to work.

Group members jump in to offer advice. Doris says maybe Sara is not ready to go back to work yet. Robert advises her to go on a diet. John tells her not to listen to her sister. Chris and Lisa suggest she "go for it" and have an interview. Frank tells her to lie on her application and say she was working in her sister's office. Sara rejects all these suggestions. "I couldn't lie on my application. I just couldn't do that," she says. "And if I went on an interview and didn't get the job, I couldn't handle it. I'd be sick for weeks." Finally, she says in frustration, "I don't want to talk about this any more. Let's talk about something else." The group then moves on to discuss difficulties Frank is having with his girlfriend.

We underscore to the class that all the issues that Sara raises—readiness to work, feelings of inadequacy, fear of failure, how to explain having been hospitalized—are applicable to other members of this group. Yet the focus is maintained solely on Sara. The group is active. In fact, six members explicitly offered advice. But the problems mentioned, highly relevant to all and ones with which many members have had experience, do not seem to touch the others as they try to help Sara.

We challenge the class to take this situation and, using role play, to make it *group work*. We ask for volunteers to play the part of the worker, of Sara, and of group members. As usual, the students and instructor can feel free to stop the role play to make comments or ask questions. We prepare the class to expect particularly active intervention from the instructor in this exercise.

Even though students by this time have a good conceptual grasp of the difference between group work and casework in a group, they often have a hard time putting their understanding into practice in the role play. The student who plays the role of the worker tends to make one of two different kinds of mistakes.

Often, because of worry about focusing on one member (Sara) for too long, the student who plays the worker will ask the other group members too quickly to relate their own relevant experiences. The student worker will do this before the other group members really understand or develop empathy for Sara's concerns and feelings. When that happens, the instructor needs to halt the action and direct the worker to stay longer with Sara's issue and not widen it prematurely to the group.

The second kind of mistake that the student worker will often make is exactly the opposite. He or she will hold a one-on-one interview, questioning Sara at length while the members of the group observe silently. The tendency to do this comes from the student's desire to be sure that Sara's concerns and feelings are fully expressed so that they are understood and are accessible to the group. When that happens, the instructor again needs to halt the action and direct the student to help the other members become involved in interacting with Sara to elicit her concerns and feelings.

This role play is an essential learning opportunity for students, and the instructor's active participation is crucial. The role play gives students an opportunity for the rehearsal that they need to bring their conceptual understanding and practice skills together. The instructor's clear directions help this evolution to occur.

As the student playing the role of Sara is allowed and encouraged to describe her concerns, there is an important point at which the empathy of the other group members for Sara's situation becomes tangible. Students in the class are usually able to see and appreciate this. When this happens in the role play, the instructor can then encourage the student to widen the issue to the group and ask members to recount situations involving feelings similar to Sara's. The quality of the group members' responses changes as they are able to reflect on their own experiences and ultimately offer suggestions and comments that come from their own life experiences. The students who are playing the roles of group members see and feel the organic connection between their personal experiences and their ability to offer help to Sara.

This role play provides an important teaching moment in which students truly begin to understand, both intellectually and practically, the difference between group work and casework in a group. Casework in a group does not engage group members in a mutual aid process. Group work, on the other hand, demands depth of member participation and a multiplicity of helping relationships. The process of mutual aid is unique to group work. This unit is central in helping students appreciate and be able to activate real mutual aid among group members.

We bring the course to an end with this unit. An understanding of the difference between group work and casework in a group will allow students to achieve a level of quality in their practice that comes only when the foundation for good and effective group work practice has been established. The practice that this unit describes epitomizes the uniqueness of social group work method and its firm belief in the strengths of individual group members.

Readings

Hartford, Margaret E. (1978). Groups in Human Services: Some Facts and Fancies. *Social Work with Groups*, 1(1), 7-13.

Konopka, Gisela. (1990). Past/Present Issues in Group Work with the Emotionally Disabled: Part II, Thirty-Five Years of Group Work in Psychiatric Settings. *Social Work with Groups*, 13 (1), 13 -15.

Kropotkin, Peter. (1989). *Mutual Aid: A Factor of Evolution*. Montreal, Canada: Black Rose. Originally published 1903.

Kurland, Roselle, & Salmon, Robert. (1992). Group Work vs. Casework in a Group: Principles and Implications for Teaching and Practice. *Social Work with Groups*, 15(4), 3-14. Also published in *Groupwork*, 6(1), 1993, 5-16.

Middleman, Ruth R. (1978). Returning Group Process to Group Work. *Social Work with Groups*, 1(1), 15-26.

Middleman, Ruth R., & Wood, Gale Goldberg. (1990). *Skills for Direct Practice in Social Work* (pp. 91-154). New York: Columbia University Press.

Shulman, Lawrence. (1992). *The Skills of Helping Individuals, Families, and Groups*. (3rd ed., pp. 279-282). Itasca, IL: Peacock.

Steinberg, Dominique Moyse. (1996). She's Doing All the Talking, So What's in It for Me? (The Use of Time in Groups). *Social Work with Groups*, 19(2), 5-16.

APPENDIX A
MODELS OF GROUP WORK PRACTICE

The limited classroom time available in a one-semester basic methods course in social group work precludes extensive discussion of the models of group work practice, and therefore a teaching unit on this subject matter has not been offered in this volume. However, theory about groups and group behavior certainly informs and provides the foundation for an instructor's presentation to students. This appendix provides background information and some sources on group work models to which instructors might wish to refer as they prepare their courses. All of the group work models draw from classic or enduring works from research and theory in the various fields upon which social work draws.

Comparisons and discussions of models of social group work practice have appeared with regularity in the literature.[1] This is understandable because an enduring theme in group work's short but creative history has been the consistent concern with purposes and goals. Group work theorists and practitioners seeking to clarify what people in the profession do and should do have worked to provide a conceptual base for the method. Significant in these efforts was the article by Catherine Papell and Beulah Rothman, "Social Group Work Models: Possession and Heritage" (1962). Middleman and Wood (1990, p. 5) underscore its impor-

---

[1] See, for example: Catherine Papell & Beulah Rothman (1962), "Social Group Work Models: Possession and Heritage"; Emanuel Tropp (1977), "The Developmental Approach"; William Schwartz, (1977), "The Interactionist Approach"; Paul Glasser & Charles Garvin (1977), "The Organizational and Environmental Approach"; Charles Garvin & Paul Glasser (1971), "The Preventive and Rehabilitative Approach"; Robert Roberts & Helen Northen (1976), *Theories of Social Work with Groups*; Catherine Papell & Beulah Rothman (1980), "Relating the Mainstream Model of Social Work with Groups to Group Psychotherapy and the Structured Group Approach"; Charles Garvin (1997), *Contemporary Group Work* (3rd ed.); Andrew Malekoff (1997), *Group Work with Adolescents: Principles and Practice*; Ronald W. Toseland & Robert F. Rivas (1998), *An Introduction to Group Work Practice* (3rd ed.); and Marian F. Fatout (1992), *Models for Change in Social Work*.

tance by focusing on how Papell and Rothman draw upon extant group work theory:

> The *social goals* model which [Papell and Rothman] elaborate draws upon the work of several early theorists, including Coyle (1948), Wilson and Ryland (1949), Phillips (1957), and Kaiser (1958). This model aimed to influence groups toward democratic values, social conscience, and social action toward the 'common good,' to encourage socialization, and to enhance individual growth, development and learning. The *remedial model*, formulated primarily by Vinter (1959), was grounded in social role theory, psychoanalytic concepts, and ego psychology, and used the group to alter and reinforce individual behavior change. The *reciprocal model*, conceptualized by Schwartz (1961), was based on social systems theory and field theory, and directed the worker to mediate the engagement between the individual and society as each reached toward the others for his/her mutual self-fulfillment. This model introduced the terms *contract* and *mutual aid* into the vocabulary of social group workers.

Another important contribution to group work theory was the volume edited by Robert W. Roberts and Helen Northen, *Theories of Social Work with Groups* (1976). Eleven chapters were devoted to the presentation of various contributors' theoretical models of group work, and the editors' 12th chapter addressed the status of group work theory generally and analyzed the work of the contributors. Some of the models discussed in this collection that continue to influence group work's practice approach include those of Paul H. Glasser and Charles D. Garvin ("An Organizational Model"), Helen Northen ("Psychosocial Practice in Small Groups"), William Schwartz ("Between Client and System: The Mediating Function"),[2] and Emanuel Tropp ("A Developmental Theory").

---

[2] Prominent educators have carried forth the legacy of William Schwartz. Alex Gitterman and Lawrence Shulman edited a special issue of the journal *Social Work with Groups* (1986), *8*(4), titled "The Legacy of William Schwartz: Group Practice as Shared Interaction." Also, Toby Berman-Rossi (1994) has edited a comprehensive volume of his collected works, *Social Work: The Collected Writings of William Schwartz*.

Developmental and Behavioral Models

Two more theoretical models first described in the 1960s and 1970s and not included in the Roberts and Northen book are the Boston Model and the Behavioral Approach. They continue to have a strong impact on current group work practice. The Boston Model developed out of research at Boston University's School of Social Work, whose group work specialization was chaired by Saul Bernstein, and is perhaps best known for the article "A Model for Stages of Development in Social Work Groups" by James Garland, Hubert Jones, and Ralph Kolodny.[3] Earlier writers in social work and the social sciences did research and published on group phases,[4] but the creative work of Garland, Jones, and Kolodny caught the imagination of group workers. Their work on stages of development is a key reference in many group work articles and presentations. The model consists of five stages of group development: Preaffiliation, Power and Control, Intimacy, Differentiation, and Separation. The central theme characterizing this developmental model is the differential degree of emotional closeness that exists and is possible at each stage of a group.

The emphasis on stage theory in group work is unique among social work practice methods, and researchers and practitioners alike often turn to it to understand member and group behavior. Today, most group work writers and educators use group stages to organize their writing, thinking, and teaching about group work practice. Different writers and teachers might delineate different numbers of group stages, breaking them down more or less finely. But however many stages might be identified, most of the group work literature agrees that progression in stages occurs in groups and is important to consider in practice. As the units and handouts show, we delineate three stages, Beginnings, Middles and Endings, and examine each in three dimensions: *Where the Members Are*, *What Needs to Happen*, and the *Role of the Worker*.

---

[3] That article, first published in 1965, was later reissued in *Explorations in Group Work* (Bernstein, 1973, pp. 17–71).

[4] See Margaret E. Hartford (1971), *Groups in Social Work: Application of Small Group Theory and Research to Social Work Practice*. In Chapter 3, "Phases of Group Development" (pp. 63–93), she provides extensive references to others' work on stages of development and presents her own five-phase scheme.

Linda Yael Schiller (1995) recently provided a thought-pro-voking theoretical article on stages of group development by de-parting from the Boston Model to propose alternative developmental stages for women's groups. Drawing on recent feminist research into women's psychological development, she introduces a *Relational Model* that deemphasizes the importance of power and control.

Behavioral group work has moved to the foreground in recent years with the emergence of cognitive-behavioral approaches to practice. Rooted in theories of behavior modification, cognitive-behavioral approaches view thought processes as stimuli of be-havior and target group members' thinking as objectives for change. An important contributor to behavioral group work is Sheldon Rose, whose work, along with that of some of his col-leagues, differs from many other psychological behaviorists in that it draws upon small group theory and principles of mutual aid (Garvin, 1997).

The cognitive-behavioral approach seems to fit into the cur-rent social environment with its interest in short-term, time-lim-ited efforts and its need for results that can be clearly measured. The approach often is used in assertiveness training groups, in situations of addiction, and with groups addressing social skills deficits. The staff of New York City's probation department, for example, is currently being trained by social group work faculty in the use of a cognitive-behavioral group work program for pro-bationers.

The Process of Model Development

Finally, there is current growing interest in feminist group work, with writers from a number of countries working in this area.[5] Feminist ideas and the ways in which they can be utilized

---

[5] See, for example, Sandra Butler and Claire Wintran (1991), *Feminist Group Work*; Charles D. Garvin and Beth G. Reed (1995), "Sources and Visions for Feminist Group Work: Reflective Processes, Social Justice, Diversity, and Correction"; Judith A. B. Lee (1994), "Fifocal Vision: Developing Ethclass, Feminist, and Critical Perspectives"; Elizabeth Lewis (1992), "Regaining Promise: Feminist Perspectives for Social Group Work Practice"; Anna Travers (1995), "Adversity, Diversity, and Empower-ment: Feminist Group Work with Women in Poverty"; and Charles Zastrow (1997), "Feminist Intervention in Groups."

in group work practice is an important development, particularly in relation to sexism and racism, oppression, and gender issues in the life of the group. There is every expectation that model development in feminist group work will expand and flourish in the future.

Model development is ongoing. Group work approaches continue to develop, mature, and change, in response to the time in which we live and the existing environment of our practice. Middleman and Wood commented on this process in the 17th edition of the *Encyclopedia of Social Work* (1977, p. 717).

> Much of the social goals model was incorporated with an existential/humanistic/phenomenological twist into the developmental model advanced by Tropp (1977). The remedial model evolved into the organizational/environmental approach (Glasser & Garvin, 1977), which included concepts other than those strictly concerned with individual change. The reciprocal model became the mediating model and finally the interactional model (Schwartz, 1977). This name change reflected a shift in emphasis from the philosophical base to the worker's role and from the worker's role to the nature of the group process.

Other changes, innovations, and adaptations will take place as theorists continue to turn their attention to the development of more effective ways to serve groups, individual group members, and society.

References

Berman-Rossi, Toby. (Ed). (1994). *Social Work: The Collected Writings of William Schwartz*. Itasca, IL: Peacock.

Butler, Sandra, & Wintran, Claire. (1991). *Feminist Group Work*. London: Sage.

Coyle, Grace. (1948). *Group Work with American Youth*. New York: Harper.

Fatout, Marian F. (1992). *Models for Change in Social Work*. New York: Aldine de Gruyter.

Garland, James, Jones, Hubert, & Kolodny, Ralph. (1973). A Model for Stages of Development in Social Work Groups. In Saul Bernstein (Ed.), *Explorations in Group Work* (pp. 17-71). Boston: Milford House.

Garvin, Charles. (1997). *Contemporary Group Work* (3rd ed., pp. 1-22). Boston: Allyn and Bacon.

Garvin, Charles, & Glasser, Paul. (1971). The Preventive and Rehabilitative Approach. In Robert Morris (Ed.), *Encyclopedia of Social
Work* (16th ed., pp. 263-1273). Washington, DC: National Association
of Social Workers.

Garvin, Charles D., & Reed, Beth G. (1995). Sources and Visions for
Feminist Group Work: Reflective Processes, Social Justice, Diversity, and Correction. In Nan Ven Den Bergh (Ed.), *Feminist Visions
for Social Work*. Washington, DC: NASW Press.

Gitterman, Alex, & Shulman, Lawrence. (Eds). (1986). The Legacy of
William Schwartz: Group Practice as Shared Interaction [Special
issue]. *Social Work with Groups, 8*(4).

Glasser, Paul, & Garvin, Charles. (1977). The Organizational and
Environmental Approach. In John B. Turner (Ed.), *Encyclopedia of
Social Work* (17th ed., pp. 1338-1350). Washington, DC: National
Association of Social Workers.

Hartford, Margaret E. (1971). Phases of Group Development. In
*Groups in Social Work: Application of Small Group Theory and Research
to Social Work Practice* (pp. 63-93). New York: Columbia University
Press.

Kaiser, Clara. (1958). The Social Group Work Process. *Social Work,
3*(2), 67-75.

Lee, Judith A. B. (1994). Fifocal Vision: Developing Ethclass, Femi-
nist, and Critical Perspectives. In *The Empowerment Approach to
Social Work Practice* (pp. 99-118). New York: Columbia University
Press.

Lewis, Elizabeth. (1992). Regaining Promise: Feminist Perspectives
for Social Group Work Practice. *Social Work with Groups, 15*(2/3),
271-284.

Malekoff, Andrew. (1997). *Group Work with Adolescents: Principles
and Practice* (pp. 40-50). New York: Guilford.

Middleman, Ruth, & Wood, Gale Goldberg. (1990). Reviewing the
Past and Present of Group Work and the Challenge of the Future.
Social Work with Groups, 13(3), 3-19.

Papell, Catherine, & Rothman, Beulah. (1962). Social Group Work
Models: Possession and Heritage. *Journal of Education for Social
Work, 2*(2), 66-77.

Papell, Catherine, & Rothman, Beulah. (1980). Relating the Mainstream
Model of Social Work with Groups to Group Psychotherapy and the
Structured Group Approach. *Social Work with Groups, 3*(2), 5-23.

Phillips, Helen U. (1957). *Essentials of Social Group Work Skill*. New
York: Association Press.

Roberts, Robert, & Northen, Helen. (Eds). (1976). *Theories of Social Work with Groups*. New York: Columbia University Press.

Schiller, Linda Yael. (1995). Stages of Development in Women's Groups: A Relational Model. In Roselle Kurland & Robert Salmon (Eds), *Group Work Practice in a Troubled Society: Problems and Opportunities* (pp. 117-138). New York: Haworth.

Schwartz, William. (1961). The Social Worker in the Group. *The Social Welfare Forum*. New York: Columbia University Press.

Schwartz, William. (1977). The Interactionist Approach. In *Encyclopedia of Social Work* (17th ed., pp. 1328-1338). Washington, DC: National Association of Social Workers.

Toseland, Ronald W., & Rivas, Robert F. (1998). *An Introduction to Group Work Practice* (3rd ed., pp. 47-65). Boston: Allyn and Bacon.

Travers, Anna. (1995). Adversity, Diversity, and Empowerment: Feminist Group Work with Women in Poverty. In Roselle Kurland & Robert Salmon (Eds.), *Group Work in a Troubled Society: Problems and Opportunities* (pp. 139-158). New York: Haworth.

Tropp, Emanuel. (1971). The Developmental Approach. In *Encyclopedia of Social Work* (17th ed., pp. 1321-1328). Washington, DC: National Association of Social Workers.

Vinter, Robert. (1959). Group Work: Perspectives and Prospects. *Social Work with Groups* (pp. 128-148). New York: National Association of Social Workers.

Wilson, Gertrude, & Ryland, Gladys. (1949). *Social Group Work Practice*. Cambridge, MA: Houghton Mifflin.

Zastrow, Charles. (1997). Feminist Intervention in Groups. In *Social Work with Groups* (4th ed., pp. 391-400). Chicago: Nelson-Hall.

APPENDIX B
ISSUES CONFRONTING GROUP WORK

Many of the issues that confront group work today have their roots in the history and evolution of the method (see Unit 2). Issues exist in three interrelated arenas: in the social work profession at large, in education, and in practice.

As was true of group work in its earlier days, many in our profession today do not understand or appreciate group work. Many social workers have a lack of respect for the method, believing that group work is simply casework multiplied and that if a social worker knows how to work with individuals, then he or she knows how to work with a group. The unique values, knowledge, and skills that are the basis of group work often go unrecognized professionally. As one recent graduate, whose first job was in a hospital social work department, stated:

> I was surprised to find that very few people really know about group work....[They] think that social group work is casework in a group. You just throw the group together and talk to each person and you control everything and that's fine....I also found surprising how much group work is looked down upon by other social workers and even by administrators. Its special training, theories, and skills are not acknowledged.

Others in the profession believe that group work is superficial, that only in individual work does true depth occur, and that the use of program and activity (see Unit 9) is a way to avoid exploration of difficult content and that real insight occurs only if problems are discussed.

The lack of understanding and appreciation of group work is reflected in our profession's national forums, at its national conferences, and in its most widely circulated journals, where the voice of group work is frequently but a whisper. In a keynote address on constructivism at Symposium XVII of the Association for the Advancement of Social Work With Groups, Gale Goldberg Wood and Ruth Middleman (1997) stated that professional leaders, such as journal editors and conference chairpersons, have power to determine what is acceptable and desirable in a profession. The decisions of those on program committees and editorial boards have demonstrated the profession's devaluation of group work, for too often they have underrepresented group work in professional conferences and journals. In fact, such omissions led group workers 20 years ago to establish their own journal and national organization where group work practice and theory could be addressed. In the 1940s, social group workers felt similarly isolated and compelled to establish a separate professional organization (see Unit 2).

In education, generic practice continues to be the rule in schools of social work, with the result that group work has been neglected in the training of more than a generation of social work professionals. Because group workers were always a small minority of social work faculty, generic practice courses are taught largely by persons with expertise in work with individuals and with little or no social group work experience. The emphasis in such courses too often is on either work with individuals or on a kind of group work practice that focuses on individual group members, to the neglect of the total group, and on psychological aspects of the individual, to the neglect of social factors. Such neglect of group work is also present for most students in field work where, if they work with groups at all, their practice is supervised by professionals who, similarly, do not have real expertise in social group work practice.

The three-decade neglect of group work in education becomes magnified in the implications that it has for the method's future. The paucity of group work content in schools of social work means that the development of those who will become the future teachers and supervisors of group work is not taking place.

The neglect has an additional consequence. Those students who enter schools of social work with value orientations and a worldview that predispose them toward the group work method often question whether they belong in the social work field. Often, they feel left out and do not find in their practice courses support for an approach to work with people with which they are comfortable. Such an approach, characteristic of group work practice, includes an emphasis on clients' strengths, mutual aid, shared responsibility, active use of self, and comfort with authority and conflict. The educational accent on the generic and on the commonalities of practice too often leaves out specific beliefs, qualities, and principles—in short, the differences that distinguish each practice method and the world views that attract students to specific practice methods. It is ironic that today, at a time when our profession is placing great emphasis on cultural, racial, and sexual diversity and difference, we are simultaneously ignoring the diversity of world views that exist among ourselves and our students.

The neglect of group work in schools of social work can be seen plainly in the diminished quality of group work practice. Many groups are being led today by workers untrained in social group work practice, and that gap in their education makes a difference in the essence of their work with groups. In a study that looked at the group work practice of those with substantial graduate social work education in group work and those with minimal or no such training, Steinberg (1993) identified some key differences. Those with minimal education in group work tended to see the group as a place for individual change. They tended to play a central role throughout the group's life, to direct many of their interventions to individual group members, and to assume a great deal of control. Those with substantial group work education, on the other hand, expected group members to integrally affect and effect the shape and movement of the group. They saw group purpose as central. They tended to direct many of their interventions and expectations to the group as a whole and to be aware of the impact that stages of group development had over time on their role and their use of themselves. Steinberg also found important differences regarding conflict (see Unit 8). While those with substantial group work education expected conflict to occur as a natural result of group life and viewed conflict as an opportunity for important work in the group, those with minimal education in group work tended to regard conflict as an intrusion into the group's affairs, an unwelcome interruption, a threat to the group, and a hurdle that needed to be quickly resolved so that the group could move on. Finally, Steinberg identified differences in the workers' emphases on mutual aid. Those with minimal group work education tended to practice casework in a group (see Unit 11), while those with substantial group work education maximized mutual aid among group members in their practice.

The move toward managed care in the 1990s—arrangements whereby an individual's health plan determines agency reimbursements for group services—is another practice issue for group work. Managed care is likely to affect group work practice in the future in areas of group work with chronically mentally ill populations in after-care and day treatment settings. Although managed care encourages work with groups because it can be economical, it places a premium on short-term work and the setting of specific treatment goals. Such an emphasis can sometimes be incongruent with more traditional approaches of group work and their emphases on group process and the facilitative—rather than directorial—role of the worker.

Some of the issues discussed here may have been touched on previously in the teaching units of this volume. However, as is true of the material in Appendix A on group work practice models, there will unlikely be time in a basic group work methods course to discuss in depth the current issues that confront the method. Thus, the material in this appendix aims to augment instructors' perspectives as they develop courses and work with students.

References and Selected Readings

Birnbaum, Martin. (1990, October). *Group Work, the Spotted Owl: An Endangered Species in Social Work Education.* Presentation at Symposium XII, Association for the Advancement of Social Work with Groups, Miami, FL.

Birnbaum, Martin, & Auerbach, Charles. (1994). Group Work in Graduate Social Work Education: The Price of Neglect. *Journal of Social Work Education*, 30, 325-335.

Birnbaum, Martin, Middleman, Ruth, & Huber, Ruth. (1989, October). *Where Social Workers Obtain Their Knowledge Base in Group Work.* Presentation at Annual Meeting, National Association of Social Workers.

Garvin, Charles D. (1997). *Contemporary Group Work* (3rd ed.). Boston: Allyn and Bacon.

Kurland, Roselle, & Salmon, Robert. (1996, October). *Education for the Group Worker's Reality: The Special Qualities and World View of Those Drawn to Work with Groups.* Presentation at Symposium XVIII, Association for the Advancement of Social Work With Groups, Ann Arbor, MI.

Kurland, Roselle, & Salmon, Robert. (1992). Group Work vs. Casework in a Group: Principles and Implications for Teaching and Practice. *Social Work with Groups.* 15(4), 3-14.

Kurland, Roselle, & Salmon, Robert. (1996). Making Joyful Noise: Presenting, Promoting and Portraying Group Work to and for the Profession. In Benjamin L. Stempler & Marilyn Glass (Eds.), *Social Group Work Today and Tomorrow* (pp. 19-32). Binghamton, NY: Haworth.

Middleman, Ruth R. (1992). Group Work and the Heimlich Maneuver: Unchoking Social Work Education. In David F. Fike & Barbara Rittner (Eds.), *Working from Strengths: The Essence of Group Work* (pp. 16-40). Miami, FL: Center for Group Work Studies.

Steinberg, Dominique Moyse. (1993). Some Findings from a Study on the Impact of Group Work Education on Social Work with Groups. *Social Work with Groups, 16*(3), 41-54.

Wood, Gale Goldberg, & Middleman, Ruth R. (1997). Constructivism, Power, and Social Work with Groups. In Joan K. Parry (Ed.), *From Prevention to Wellness through Group Work* (pp. 1-14). Binghamton, NY: Haworth.

Appendix C
Selected Bibliography

Selections are grouped by topic, with some occurring more than once. Reference to chapters or pages relevant to the topic are made in some cases.

I. Basic Texts

Middleman, Ruth R., & Wood, Gale Goldberg. (1990). *Skills for Direct Practice in Social Work*. New York: Columbia University Press.

Northen, Helen. (1988). *Social Work with Groups* (2nd ed.). New York: Columbia University Press.

Shulman, Lawrence. (1992). *The Skills of Helping Individuals, Families and Groups* (3rd ed.). Itasca, IL: Peacock.

II. Other Group Work Text Books

Anderson, Joseph. (1997). *Social Work with Groups: A Process Model*. New York: Longman.

Brandler, Sondra, & Rothman, Camille P. (1991). *Group Work: Skills and Strategies for Effective Interventions*. Binghamton, NY: Haworth.

Brown, Leonard N. (1991). *Groups for Growth and Change*. New York: Longman.

Ephross, Paul H., & Vassil, Thomas. (1988). *Groups That Work: Structure and Process*. New York: Columbia University Press.

Garvin, Charles D. (1997). *Contemporary Group Work*. Boston: Allyn and Bacon.

Gitterman, Alex, & Shulman, Lawrence. (Eds). (1994). *Mutual Aid Groups, Vulnerable Populations, and the Life Cycle* (2nd ed.). New York: Columbia University Press.

Glassman, Urania, & Kates, Len. (1990). *Group Work: A Humanistic Approach*. Newbury Park, CA: Sage.

Greif, Geoffrey L., & Ephross, Paul H. (Eds.). (1997). *Group Work with Populations at Risk*. New York: Oxford University Press.

Hartford, Margaret E. (1971). *Groups in Social Work: Application of Small Group Theory and Research to Social Work Practice*. New York: Columbia University Press.

Henry, Sue. (1992). *Group Skills in Social Work: A Four-Dimensional Approach* (2nd ed.). Pacific Grove, CA: Brooks/Cole.

Malekoff, Andrew. (1997). *Group Work with Adolescents: Principles and Practice*. New York: Guilford.

Phillips, Helen. (1957). *Essentials of Social Group Work Skill*. New York: Association Press.

Rose, Sheldon D. (1989). *Working with Adults in Groups: Integrating Cognitive Behavioral and Small Group Strategies*. San Francisco: Jossey-Bass.

Rose, Sheldon D., & Edelson, Jeffrey L. (1987). *Working with Children and Adolescents in Groups*. San Francisco: Jossey-Bass.

Schwartz, William, & Zalba, Serapio R. (Eds.). (1971). *The Practice of Group Work*. New York: Columbia University Press.

Steinberg, Dominique M. (1997). *The Mutual-Aid Approach to Working with Groups: Helping People Help Each Other*. Northvale, NJ: Aronson.

Sundel, Martin, Glasser, Paul, Sarri, Rosemary, & Vinter, Robert. (Eds.). (1985). *Individual Change through Small Groups* (2nd ed.). New York: Free Press.

Toseland, Ronald W., & Rivas, Robert F. (1998). *An Introduction to Group Work Practice* (3rd ed.). Boston: Allyn and Bacon.

Wilson, Gertrude, & Ryland, Gladys. (1949). *Social Group Work Practice*. Boston: Houghton-Mifflin.

Zastrow, Charles. (1997). *Social Work with Groups* (4th ed.). Chicago: Nelson-Hall.

III. Orienting Knowledge

Addams, Jane. (1910). *Twenty Years at Hull House*. New York: MacMillan.

Anderson, Joseph. (1985). Working with Groups: Little Known Facts That Challenge Well-Known Myths. *Small Group Behavior*, *16*(3), 267-283.

Bales, Robert F. (1950). *Interaction Process Analysis: A Method for the Study of Small Groups*. Reading, MA: Addison-Wesley.

Bennis, Warren G., & Shepard, H. A. (1961). Theory of Group Development. In Warren G. Bennis (Ed.), *The Planning of Change* (pp. 321-339). New York: Holt, Rinehart & Winston.

Berman-Rossi, Toby. (1993). The Tasks and Skills of the Social Worker across Stages of Group Development. *Social Work with Groups*, *16*(1/2), 69-81.

Breton, Margot. (1994). On the Meaning of Empowerment and Empowerment-Oriented Social Work Practice. *Social Work with Groups,* *17*(3), 23-37.

Breton, Margot. (1995). The Potential for Social Action in Groups. *Social Work with Groups, 18* (2/3), 5-14.

Caplan, Gerald, & Killilea, Marie. (1976). *Support and Mutual Help* (pp. 19-93). New York: Grune and Stratton.

Coser, Lewis A. (1955). *The Functions of Social Conflict.* Glencoe, IL: Free Press.

Dewey, John. (1910). *How We Think.* Boston: Heath.

Falck, Hans. (1988). *Social Work: The Membership Perspective.* New York: Sprough.

Falck, Hans. (1989). The Management of Membership: Social Group Work Contributions. *Social Work with Groups, 12*(3), 19-32.

Falck, Hans S. (1995). Central Characteristics of Social Work with Groups—A Sociocultural Analysis. In Roselle Kurland & Robert Salmon (Eds.), *Group Work Practice in a Troubled Society: Problems and Opportunities* (pp. 63-72). Binghamton, NY: Haworth.

Garvin, Charles. (1997). *Contemporary Group Work* (3rd ed., chapter 1). Boston: Allyn and Bacon.

Gitterman, Alex. (1989). Building Mutual Support in Groups, *Social Work with Groups, 12*(2), 5-21.

Hare, A. Paul. (1985). *Social Interaction as Drama.* Beverly Hills, CA: Sage.

Hartford, Margaret E. (1971). *Groups in Social Work.* New York: Columbia University Press.

Homans, George C. (1950). *The Human Group.* New York: Harcourt.

Kamerman, Sheila B., et al. (1973). Knowledge for Practice: Social Sciences in Social Work. In Alfred J. Kahn (Ed.), *Shaping the New Social Work* (pp. 97-146). New York: Columbia University Press.

Kropotkin, Peter. (1989). *Mutual Aid: A Factor of Evolution.* Montreal: Black Rose. Originally published 1903.

Kurland, Roselle, & Salmon, Robert. (1993). Not Just One of the Gang: Group Workers and Their Role as an Authority. In Stanley Wenocur et al. (Eds.), *Social Work with Groups: Expanding Horizons* (pp. 153-169)..Binghamton, NY: Haworth. Also in *Social Work with Groups, 16*(1/2), 153-169.

Lee, Judith A. B. (1994). *The Empowerment Approach to Social Work Practice* (chapters 1–4). New York: Columbia University Press.

Middleman, Ruth R., & Wood, Gale Goldberg. (1995). Contextual Groupwork: Apprehending the Elusive Obvious. In Roselle Kurland & Robert Salmon (Eds.), *Group Work Practice in a Troubled Society: Problems and Opportunities* (pp. 5-18). Binghamton, NY: Haworth.

Mills, Theodore. (1967). *The Sociology of Small Groups* (chapters 1–2). Englewood Cliffs, NJ: Prentice-Hall.

Morris, Van Cleve, & Pai, Young. (1976). *Philosophy and the American School* (pp. 149-152). Boston: Houghton Mifflin.

Northen, Helen. (1987). Selection of Groups as the Preferred Modality of Practice. In Joseph Lassner, Kathleen Powell, & Elaine Finnegan (Eds.), *Social Group Work: Competence and Values in Practice* (pp. 19-34). Binghamton, NY: Haworth.

Pinderhughes, Elaine. (1989). *Understanding Race, Ethnicity and Power: The Key to Efficacy in Clinical Practice.* New York: Free Press

Ridgeway, Ceilia L. (1983). *The Dynamics of Small Groups.* New York: St. Martin's.

Rogers, Carl R. (1961). *On Becoming a Person.* Boston: Houghton Mifflin.

Shaw, Marvin E. (1981). *Group Dynamics: The Psychology of Small Group Behavior* (3rd ed.). New York: McGraw Hill.

Solomon, Barbara Bryant. (1976). Characteristics of the Nonracist Practitioner. In *Black Empowerment: Social Work in Oppressed Communities* (pp. 299-313). New York: Columbia University Press.

Toseland, Ronald W., & Rivas, Robert F. (1998). *An Introduction to Group Work Practice* (3rd ed., pp. 46-90). New York: Allyn and Bacon.

Wood, Gale Goldberg, & Middleman, Ruth R. (1989). *The Structural Approach to Direct Practice in Social Work* (pp. 1-16, 182-211). New York: Columbia University Press.

Wood, Gale Goldberg, & Middleman, Ruth R. (1997). Constructivism, Power, and Social Work with Groups. In Joan K. Parry (Ed.), *From Prevention to Wellness through Group Work* (pp. 1-14). Binghamton, NY: Haworth.

IV. Historical Origins and Evolution of Group Work

Berman-Rossi, Toby, & Miller, Irving. (1994). African-Americans and the Settlements during the Late Nineteenth and Early Twentieth Centuries. *Social Work with Groups, 16*(3), 77-95.

Birnbaum, Martin. (1990, October). *Group Work, the Spotted Owl: An Endangered Species in Social Work Education.* Presentation at Symposium XII, Association for the Advancement of Social Work with Groups, Miami, FL.

Birnbaum, Martin, & Auerbach, Charles. (1994). Group Work in Graduate Social Work Education: The Price of Neglect. *Journal of Social Work Education, 30,* 325-335.

Birnbaum, Martin, Middleman, Ruth, & Huber, Ruth. (1989, October). *Where Social Workers Obtain Their Knowledge Base in Group Work.* Presentation at Annual Meeting, National Association of Social Workers.

Breton, Margot. (1990). Learning From Social Group Work Traditions. *Social Work with Groups, 13*(1), 21-45.

Briar, Scott. (1971). Social Case Work and Social Group Work: Historical Foundations. In Robert Morris (Ed.), *Encyclopedia of Social Work,* (16th ed., pp. 1237-1245). New York: National Association of Social Workers.

Coyle, Grace. (1947). On Becoming a Professional. In *Group Experience and Democratic Values* (pp. 81-97). New York: The Woman's Press.

Coyle, Grace. (1947). Group Work as a Method in Recreation. In *Group Experience and Democratic Values* (pp. 69-80). New York: The Woman's Press.

Coyle, Grace. (1948). *Group Work with American Youth.* New York: Harper and Brothers.

Galinksy, Maeda J., & Schopler, Janice H. (Eds.). (1995). Support Groups [Special issue]. *Social Work with Groups, 18*(1).

Garvin, Charles, D. (1997). *Contemporary Group Work* (3rd ed., pp. 23-32). Boston: Allyn and Bacon.

Hartford, Margaret E. (1964). Social Group Work 1930-1960: The Search for a Definition. In Margaret E. Hartford (Ed.), *Working Papers Toward a Frame of Reference for Social Group Work* (pp. 62-76). New York: National Association of Social Workers.

Hartford, Margaret E. (1978). Groups in Human Services: Some Facts and Fancies. *Social Work with Groups, 1*(1), 7-13.

Konopka, Gisela. (1960). Social Group Work: A Social Work Method. *Social Work, 5,* 53-61.

Konopka, Gisela. (1983). *Social Group Work: A Helping Process* (3rd ed.). Englewood Cliffs, NJ: Prentice Hall.

Konopka, Gisela. (1990). Past/Present Issues in Group Work with the Emotionally Disabled: Part II, Thirty-Five Years of Group Work in Psychiatric Settings. *Social Work with Groups, 13*(1), 13-15.

Kurland, Roselle, & Salmon, Robert. (1996, October). *Education for the Group Worker's Reality: The Special Qualities and World View of Those Drawn to Work With Groups.* Presentation at Symposium XVIII, Association for the Advancement of Social Work with Groups, Ann Arbor, MI.

Kurland, Roselle, & Salmon, Robert. (1996). Making Joyful Noise: Presenting, Promoting and Portraying Group Work to and for the Profession. In Benj. L. Stempler & Marilyn Glass (Eds.), *Social Group Work Today and Tomorrow: Moving from Theory to Advanced Training and Practice* (pp. 19-32). Binghamton, NY: Haworth.

Lee, Judith. (1987). Social Work with Oppressed Populations: Jane Addams Won't You Please Come Home? In Joseph Lassner et al. (Eds.), *Social Group Work: Competence and Values in Practice* (pp. 1-16). Binghamton, NY: Haworth.

Lindeman, Eduard. (1980). Group Work and Democracy—A Philosophical Note. In Albert S. Alissi (Ed.), *Perspectives on Social Group Work Practice* (pp. 77-83). New York: Free Press.

Middleman, Ruth R. (1978). Returning Group Process to Group Work. *Social Work with Groups, 1*(1), 15-26.

Middleman, Ruth R. (1990). Group Work and the Heimlich maneuver: Unchoking Social Work Education. In David F. Fike & Barbara Rittner (Eds.), *Working From Strengths: The Essence of Group Work* (pp. 16-40). Miami Shores, FL: Center for Group Work Studies.

Middleman, Ruth R., & Goldberg, Gale. (1987). Social Work Practice with Groups. In Anne Minahan (Ed.), *Encyclopedia of Social Work* (18th ed., pp. 714-729). Silver Spring, MD: National Association of Social Workers.

Middleman, Ruth R., & Wood, Gale Goldberg. (1990). From Social Group Work to Social Work with Groups. *Social Work with Groups, 13*(3), 3-20.

Newstetter, Wilbur. (1935). What Is Social Group Work? *Proceedings of the National Conference of Social Work* (pp. 291-299).

Northen, Helen. (1988). *Social Work with Groups* (pp. 16-45). New York: Columbia University Press.

Perlman, Helen Harris. (1965). Social Work Method: A Review of the Past Decade. *Social Work, 10*(4), 166-178.

Phillips, Helen U. (1957). *Essentials of Social Group Work Skill* (pp. 15-115). New York: Association Press.

Reynolds, Bertha. (1951). *Social Work and Social Living.* New York: Citadel Press.

Schwartz, William. (1959). Group Work and the Social Scene. In Alfred J. Kahn (Ed.), *Issues in American Social Work* (pp. 11-37). New York: Columbia University Press.

Schwartz, William. (1969). Private Troubles and Public Issues: One Job or Two? In *The Social Welfare Forum, 1969* (pp. 22-43). New York: Columbia University Press.

Shulman, Lawrence. (1994). Group Work Method. In Alex Gitterman & Lawrence Shulman (Eds.), *Mutual Aid Groups, Vulnerable Populations, and the Life Cycle* (2nd ed., pp. 29-58). New York: Columbia University Press.

Shulman, Lawrence. (1996). Social Work with Groups: Paradigms Shifts for the 1990's. In Benj. L. Stempler & Mariilyn Glass (Eds.), *Social Group Work: Today and Tomorrow* (pp. 1-18). Binghamton, NY: Haworth.

Shulman, Lawrence, & Gitterman, Alex. (1994). The Life Model, Mutual Aid, Oppression, and the Mediating Function. In Alex Gitterman & Lawrence Shulman (Eds.), *Mutual Aid Groups, Vulnerable Populations, and the Life Cycle* (2nd ed., pp. 3-28). New York: Columbia University Press.

Somers, Mary Louise. (1976). Problem-Solving in Small Groups. In Robert W. Roberts & Helen Northen (Eds.), *Theories of Social Work with Groups* (pp. 331-367). New York: Columbia University Press.

Smalley, Ruth. (1967). *Theory for Social Work Practice*. New York: Columbia University Press.

Steinberg, Dominique Moyse. (1993). Some Findings from a Study on the Impact of Group Work Education on Social Work Practitioners' Work with Groups. *Social Work with Groups, 16*(3), 23-39.

Trecker, Harleigh. (1944). Group Work: Frontiers and Foundations—In Wartime. *The Compass, 25*(3), 4.

Trecker, Harleigh. (1955). *Group Work: Foundations and Frontiers*. New York: Whiteside and William Morrow.

Vinikand, Abe, & Levin, Morris. (Eds.). (1991). Social Action in Group Work [Special issue]. *Social Work with Groups, 14* (3/4).

Vinter, Robert D. (1959). Group Work: Perspectives and Prospects. In *Social Work with Groups, Selected Papers from the National Conference on Social Welfare* (pp. 128-149). New York: National Association of Social Workers.

Weinberg, Nancy, Schmale, John D., Uken, Janet, & Wessel, Keith. (1995). Computer-Mediated Support Groups. *Social Work with Groups, 17*(4), 43-54.

Weiner, Hyman J. (1964). Social Change and Group Work Practice. *Social Work, 9,* 106-112.

Wenocur, Stanley, & Reisch, Michael. (1989). *From Charity to Enterprise: The Development of American Social Work in A Market Economy* 9PP. 225-269). Urbana, IL: University of Illinois Press.

Wilensky, Harold L., & Lebeaux, Charles N.(1958). *Industrial Society and Social Welfare* (pp. 283-332). New York: Russell Sage Foundation.

Wilson, Gertrude. (1976). From Practice to Theory: A Personalized History. In Robert W. Roberts & Helen Northen (Eds.), *Theories of Social Work with Groups* (pp. 1-44). New York: Columbia University Press.

Wilson, Gertrude, & Ryland, Gladys. (1949). *Social Group Work Practice* (pp. 3-35, 60-100). Boston: Houghton Mifflin.

V. Ethics and Values

Bernstein, Saul. (1962). Self-Determination: King or Citizen in the Realm of Values, *Social Work, 5*(1), 3-8.

Bernstein, Saul. (1973). Values and Group Work. In Saul Bernstein (Ed.), *Further Explorations in Group Work* (pp. 145-179). Boston: Milford House.

Bernstein, Saul B. (1993). What Happened to Self-Determination? *Social Work with Groups, 16*(1/2), 3-15.

Compton, Beulah R., & Galaway, Burt. (1994). *Social Work Processes* (5th ed., pp. 219-262). Pacific Grove, CA: Brooks/Cole.

Dolgoff, Ralph, & Skolnik, Louise. (1992). Ethical Decision Making, the NASW Code of Ethics and Group Work Practice: Beginning Explorations. *Social Work with Groups, 15*(4), 99-112.

Dolgoff, Ralph, & Skolnik, Louise. (1996). Ethical Decision Making in Social Work with Groups: An Empirical Study. *Social Work with Groups, 19*(2), 49-65.

Freedberg, Sharon. (1989). Self-Determination: Historical Perspectives and Effect on Current Practice. *Social Work, 34*(1), 33-38.

Getzel, George A. (1978). A Value Base for Interactionist Practice: A Proposal. *The Social Worker, 46*(4), 116-120.

Glassman, Urania, & Kates, Len. (1990). *Group Work: A Humanistic Approach* (pp. 21-72). Newbury Park, CA: Sage.

Konopka, Gisela. (1978). The Significance of Social Group Work Based on Ethical Values. *Social Work with Groups, 1*(2), 123-131.

Kurland, Roselle, & Salmon, Robert. (1992). Self-Determination: Its Use and Misuse in Group Work Practice and Social Work Education. In David F. Fike & Barbara Rittner (Eds.), *Working from Strengths: The Essence of Group Work* (pp. 105-121). Miami, FL: Center for Group Work Studies.

Kurland, Roselle, & Salmon, Robert (1997). When Worker and Member Expectations Collide: The Dilemma of Establishing Group Norms in Conflictual Situations. In Albert S. Alissi & Catherine G. Corto Mergins (Eds.), *Voices from the Field: Group Work Responds* (pp. 43-53). Binghamton, NY: Haworth.

Lee, Judith A. B. (1994). The Concept of Mutual Aid. In Alex Gitterman & Lawrence Shulman (Eds.), *Mutual Aid Groups, Vulnerable Populations, and the Life Cycle* (2nd ed., pp. 413-429). New York: Columbia University Press.

Loewenberg, Frank M., & Dolgoff, Ralph. (1996). *Ethical Decisions for Social Work Practice* (pp. 120-130, 176-211). Itasca, IL: Peacock.

Malekoff, Andrew. (1997). *Group Work with Adolescents: Principles and Practices* (pp. 244-265). New York: Guilford.

Middleman, Ruth R., & Rhodes, Gary B. (1985). *Competent Supervision: Making Imaginative Judgments* (pp. 152-159, 245-260). Englewood Cliffs, NJ: Prentice Hall.

Northen, Helen. (1988). *Social Work with Groups* (2nd ed., pp. 1-15). New York: Columbia University Press.

Northen, Helen. (1995). *Clinical Social Work Knowledge and Skills* (2nd ed., pp. 65-87). New York: Columbia University Press.

Shulman, Lawrence. (1992). *The Skills of Helping Individuals, Families, and Groups* (pp. 27-49). Itasca, IL: Peacock.

Skolnik, Louise, & Attinson, Lisa. (1978). Confidentiality in Group Work Practice. *Social Work with Groups, 1*(1), 65-74.

Vigilante, Joseph. (1983). *Professional Values.* In Aaron Rosenblatt & Diana Waldfogel (Eds.), *Handbook of Clinical Social Work* (pp. 58-69). San Francisco: Jossey-Bass.

Zastrow, Charles. (1997). *Social Work with Groups* (4th ed., pp. 501-524). Chicago: Nelson-Hall.

VI. Pre-Group Planning and Group Formation

Bertcher, Harvey J., & Maple, Frank. (1985). Elements and Issues in Group Composition. In Paul Glasser et al. (Eds.), *Individual Change through Small Groups* (pp. 180-202). New York: Free Press.

Boer, Annette K., & Lantz, James E. (1974). Adolescent Group Therapy Membership Selection. *Clinical Social Work Journal, 2*(3), 172-181.

Brager, George. (1960). Goal Formation: An Organizational Perspective. *Social Work with Groups 1960* (pp. 2-36). New York: National Association of Social Workers.

Brandler, Sondra, & Roman, Camille P. (1991). *Group Work: Skills and Strategies for Effective Interventions* (pp. 104-124). Binghamton, NY: Haworth.

Brown, Leonard N. (1991). *Groups for Growth and Change* (pp. 144-160). New York: Longman.

Croxton, Tom A. (1985). The Therapeutic Contract. In Martin Sundel, Paul Glasser, Rosemary Sarri, & Robert Vinter (Eds.), *Individual Change through Small Groups* (2nd ed., pp. 159-179). New York: Free Press.

Davis, Frederick B., & Lohr, Naomi E. (1971). Special Problems with the Use of Co-therapists. *International Journal of Group Psychotherapy*, 21(2), 143-158.

Davis, Larry E. (1979). Racial Composition of Groups. *Social Work*, 24(3), 208-213.

Davis, Larry E. (1980). Racial Balance: A Psychological Issue. *Social Work with Groups*, 3(2), 75-85.

Ephross, Paul H., & Vassil, Thomas V. (1988). *Groups that Work: Structure and Process* (pp. 56-74). New York: Columbia University Press.

Fike, David. (1980). Evaluating Group Intervention. *Social Work with Groups*, 3(2), 41-51.

Galinsky, Maeda J., & Schopler, Janice H. (1971). The Practice of Group Goal Formulation in Social Work Practice. In *Social Work Practice* (pp. 24-32). New York: Columbia University Press.

Garvin, Charles. (1969). Complementarity of Role Expectations in Groups: The Member–Worker Contract. In *Social Work Practice* (pp. 127-145). New York: Columbia University Press.

Garvin, Charles D. (1997). *Contemporary Group Work* (3rd ed., pp. 50-75). Boston: Allyn and Bacon.

Gitterman, Alex. (1994). Developing a New Vulnerable Populations, Group Work Service. In Alex Gitterman & Lawrence Shulman (Eds.), *Mutual Aid Groups, and the Life Cycle* (pp. 58-77). New York Columbia University Press.

Hartford, Margaret E. (1971). *Groups in Social Work* (chapters 3-6). New York: Columbia University Press.

Hellwig, Karen, & Memmott, Rae Jeanne. (1974). Co-Therapy: The Balancing Act. *Small Group Behavior*, 5(2), 175-181.

Henry, Sue. (1992). *Group Skills in Social Work: A Four-Dimensional Approach* (2nd ed., pp. 43-69). Pacific Grove, CA: Brooks/Cole.

Kurland, Roselle. (1978). Planning: The Neglected Component of Group Development. *Social Work with Groups, 1*(2), 173- 178.

Kurland, Roselle. (1982). *Group Formation: A Guide to the Development of Successful Groups*. New York: United Neighborhood Centers of America.

Lang, Norma C. (1978). The Selection of the Small Group for Service Delivery: An Exploration of the Literature on Group Use in Social Work. *Social Work with Groups, 1*(3), 247-264.

Lowy, Louis. (1973). Goal Formulation in Social Work with Groups. In Saul Bernstein (Ed.), *Further Explorations in Group Work* (pp. 116-144). Boston: Milford House.

Malekoff, Andrew. (1997). *Group Work with Adolescents: Principles and Practice* (pp. 53-80). New York: Guilford.

Maluccio, Anthony N., & Marlow, Wilma D. (1974). The Case for the Contract, *Social Work, 19*(1), 28-36.

McGee, Thomas, & Schuman, Benjamin N. (1970). The Nature of the Co-Therapy Relationship. *International Journal of Group Psychotherapy, 20*(1), 25-36.

Meadow, Diane Ammund. (1981). The Preparatory Interview. *Social Work with Groups, 4* (3/4), 135-144.

Mistry, Tara, & Brown, Allan. (1991). Black/White Co-Working in Groups. *Groupwork, 4*(2), 101-118.

Northen, Helen. (1987). Selection of Groups as the Preferred Modality of Practice. In Joseph Lassner et al. (Eds.), *Social Group Work: Competence and Values in Practice* (pp. 19-33). Binghamton, NY: Haworth.

Northen, Helen. (1988). *Social Work with Groups* (2nd ed., pp. 98-184). New York: Columbia University Press.

Paradise, Robert, & Daniels, Robert. (1973). Group Composition as a Treatment Tool with Children. In Saul Bernstein (Ed.), *Further Explorations in Group Work* (pp. 34-54). Boston: Milford House.

Paulson, Irene, et al. (1976). Co-Therapy: What is the Crux of the Relationship? *International Journal of Group Psychotherapy, 26*(2), 213-224.

Rose, Steven R. (1985). Time-Limited Treatment Groups for Children. *Social Work with Groups, 8*(2), 17-27.

Schmidt, Julianna T. (1969). The Use of Purpose in Casework Practice. *Social Work, 14*(1), 77-84.

Schopler, Janice H., & Galinsky, Maeda J. (1981). When Groups Go Wrong. *Social Work, 26*(5), 424-429.

Schopler, Janice H., & Galinsky, Maeda J. (1985). Goals in Social Group Work Practice: Formulation, Implementation and Evaluation. In Martin Sundel, Paul Glasser, Rosemary Sarri, & Robert Vinter (Eds.), *Individual Change through Small Groups* (2nd ed., pp. 140-158). New York: Free Press.

Shalinsky, William. (1969). Group Composition as an Element of Social Group Work Practice. *Social Service Review*, 43(1), 42-49.

Shulman, Lawrence. (1992). *The Skills of Helping Individuals, Families and Groups* (pp. 53-78, 291-314). Itasca, IL: Peacock.

Toseland, Ronald W., & Rivas, Robert F. (1998). *An Introduction to Group Work Practice* (3rd ed., pp. 143-171). New York: MacMillan.

Waldman, Ellen, (1980). Co-Leadership as a Method of Training: A Student's Point of View. *Social Work with Groups*, 3(1), 51-58.

VII. Beginnings

Berman-Rossi, Toby. (1993). The Tasks and Skills of the Social Worker across Stages of Group Development. *Social Work with Groups*, 16(1/2), 69-82.

Brandler, Sondra, & Roman, Camille P. (1991). *Group Work: Skills and Strategies for Effective Interventions* (pp. 14-36). Binghamton, NY: Haworth.

Brown, Leonard N. (1991). *Groups for Growth and Change* (pp. 161-188). New York: Longman.

Garland, James, Jones, Hubert, & Kolodny, Ralph. (1973). A Model for Stages of Development in Social Work Groups. In Saul Bernstein (Ed.), *Explorations in Group Work* (pp. 17-71). Boston: Milford House.

Garvin, Charles D. (1997). *Contemporary Group Work* (3rd ed., pp. 76-98). Boston: Allyn and Bacon.

Glassman, Urania, & Kates, Len. (1990). *Group Work: A Humanistic Approach* (pp. 73-104). Newbury Park, CA: Sage.

Hartford, Margaret E. (1971). *Groups in Social Work* (pp. 63-94). New York: Columbia University Press.

Henry, Sue. (1992). *Group Skills in Social Work: A Four-Dimensional Approach* (2nd ed., pp. 70-126). Pacific Grove, CA: Brooks/Cole.

Malekoff, Andrew. (1997). *Group Work with Adolescents: Principles and Practice* (pp. 81-101). New York: Guilford.

Middleman, Ruth R., & Wood, Gale Goldberg. (1990). *Skills for Direct Practice in Social Work* (pp. 91-154). New York: Columbia University Press.

Northen, Helen. (1988). *Social Work with Groups* (2nd ed., pp. 185-221). New York: Columbia University Press.

Shulman, Lawrence. (1992). *The Skills of Helping Individuals, Families and Groups* (3rd ed, pp. 79-102, 315-400). Itasca, IL: Peacock.

Stempler, Benj. L. (1992). There Are So Many of Them and Only One of Me: Developing And Utilizing Natural Strengths in Learning to Lead Mutual Aid Groups. In David F. Fike & Barbara Rittner (Eds.), *Working from Strengths: The Essence of Group Work* (pp. 162-181). Miami Shores, FL: Center for Group Work Studies.

Toseland, Ronald W., & Rivas, Robert F. (1998). *An Introduction to Group Work Practice* (3rd ed., pp. 173-232). Boston: Allyn and Bacon.

VIII. Middles

Bernstein, Saul. (1973). Conflict and Group Work. In Saul Bernstein (Ed.), *Explorations in Group Work* (pp. 72-106). Boston: Milford House.

Brandler, Sondra, & Roman, Camille P. (1991). *Group Work: Skills and Strategies for Effective Interventions* (pp. 37-74). Binghamton, NY: Haworth.

Brandler, Sondra, & Roman, Camille P. (1995). Uncovering Latent Content in Groups. In Roselle Kurland & Robert Salmon (Eds.), *Group Work Practice in a Troubled Society: Problems and Opportunities* (pp. 19-32). Binghamton, NY: Haworth.

Brown, Leonard N. (1991). *Groups for Growth and Change* (pp. 189-233). New York: Longman.

Colman, Arthur D. (1995). *Up from Scapegoating: Awakening Consciousness in Groups.* Wilmette, IL: Chiron.

Compton, Beulah R., & Galaway, Burt. (1994). *Social Work Processes* (5th ed., pp. 43-84). Pacific Grove, CA: Brooks/Cole.

Cowger, Charles D. (1979). Conflict and Conflict Management in Working With Groups. *Social Work with Groups, 2*(4), 309-320.

Douglas, Tom. (1995). *Scapegoats: Transferring Blame.* London: Routledge.

Galinsky, Maeda, & Schopler, Janice H. (1985). Patterns of Entry and Exit in Opened Group. *Social Work with Groups, 8*(2), 67-80.

Galinsky, Maeda, & Schopler, Janice.(1989). Developmental Patterns in Open-Ended Groups. *Social Work with Groups, 12*(2), 99-114.

Garland, James, Jones, Hubert, & Kolodny, Ralph. (1973). A Model for Stages of Development in Social Work Groups. In Saul Bernstein (Ed.), *Explorations in Group Work* (pp. 17-71). Boston: Milford House.

Garland, James, & Kolodny, Ralph. (1973). Characteristics and Resolutions of Scapegoating. In Saul Bernstein (Ed.), *Further Explorations in Group Work* (pp. 55-74). Boston: Milford House.

Garvin, Charles D. (1997). *Contemporary Group Work* (3rd ed., pp. 99-137). Boston: Allyn and Bacon.

Gitterman, Alex. (1989) Building Mutual Support in Groups. *Social Work with Groups, 12*(2), 5-21.

Glassman, Urania, & Kates, Len. (1990). *Group Work: A Humanistic Approach* (pp. 169-192). Newbury Park, CA: Sage.

Goodman, Harriet. (1997). Social Group Work in Community Corrections. *Social Work with Groups, 20*(1), 51-64.

Hartford, Margaret E. (1971). *Groups in Social Work* (pp. 193-276). New York: Columbia University Press.

Henry, Sue. (1992). *Group Skills in Social Work: A Four-Dimensional Approach* (2nd ed., pp. 127-191). Pacific Grove, CA: Brooks/Cole.

Hirayama, Hisashi, & Hirayama, Kasumi. (1997). Bullying and Scapegoating in Groups: Process and Interventions. In Joan K. Parry (Ed.), *From Prevention to Wellness through Group Work* (pp. 89-100). Binghamton, NY: Haworth.

Kurland, Roselle, & Salmon, Robert. (1992). Group Work vs. Casework in a Group: Principles and Implications for Teaching and Practice. *Social Work with Groups, 15*(4), 3-14. Also published in *Groupwork* (1993), *6*(1), 5-16.

Kurland, Roselle, & Salmon, Robert (1992). Self-Determination: Its Use and Misuse in Group Work Practice and Social Work Education. In David F. Fike & Barbara Rittner (Eds.), *Working From Strengths: The Essence of Group Work* (pp. 105-121). Miami Shores, FL: Center for Group Work Studies.

Kurland, Roselle, & Salmon, Robert. (1993). Not Just One of the Gang: Group Workers and Their Role as an Authority. *Social Work with Groups, 16*(1/2), 153-167.

Malekoff, Andrew. (1997). *Group Work with Adolescents* (chapter 7). New York: Guilford.

Middleman, Ruth R., & Wood, Gale Goldberg. (1990). *Skills for Direct Practice in Social Work* (pp. 91-154, 164-171). New York: Columbia University Press.

Mondros, Jacqueline, Woodrow, Richard, & Weinstein, Lois. (1992). The Use of Groups to Manage Conflict. *Social Work with Groups, 15*(4), 43-58.

Northen, Helen. (1988). *Social Work with Groups* (pp. 47-49, 240-254, 279-282). New York: Columbia University Press.

Nosko, Anna, & Wallace, Robert. (1997). Female/Male Co-Leadership in Groups. *Social Work with Groups*, 20(2), 3-16.

Reid, Kenneth E. (1997). Conflict Management in Group Treatment: Get Out of My Face, You S.O.B.! In Joan K. Parry (Ed.), *From Prevention to Wellness through Group Work* (pp. 61-78). Binghamton, NY: Haworth.

Schiller, Linda Yael. (1995). Stages of Development in Women's Groups: A Relational Model. In Roselle Kurland & Robert Salmon (Eds.), *Group Work Practice in a Troubled Society: Problems and Opportunities* (pp. 117-138). Binghamton, NY: Haworth.

Schopler, Janice H., & Galinsky, Maeda J. (1984). Meeting Practice Needs: Conceptualizing the Open-Ended Group. *Social Work with Groups*, 7(2), 3-22.

Shulman, Lawrence. (1967). Scapegoats, Group Workers, and Pre-Emptive Intervention. *Social Work*, 12(2), 37-43.

Shulman, Lawrence. (1992). *The Skills of Helping Individuals, Families and Groups* (pp. 103-172, 401-572). Itasca, IL: Peacock.

Steinberg, Dominique Moyse. (1996). She's Doing All the Talking, So What's in It for Me? (The Use of Time in Groups). *Social Work with Groups*, 19(2), 5-16.

Toseland, Ronald W., & Rivas, Robert F. (1998). *An Introduction to Group Work Practice* (3rd ed., pp. 233-362). Boston: Allyn and Bacon.

IX. Endings

Berman-Rossi, Toby. (1993). The Tasks and Skills of the Social Worker across Stages of Group Development, *Social Work with Groups*, 16(1/2), 69-82.

Brandler, Sondra, & Roman, Camille P. (1991). *Group Work: Skills and Strategies for Effective Interventions* (pp. 75-103). Binghamton, NY: Haworth.

Brown, Leonard N. (1991). *Groups for Growth and Change* (pp. 218-233). New York: Longman.

Garland, James, Jones, Hubert, & Kolodny, Ralph. (1973). A Model for Stages of Development in Social Work Groups. In Saul Bernstein (Ed.), *Explorations in Group Work* (pp. 17-71).. Boston: Milford House.

Garvin, Charles D. (1997). *Contemporary Group Work* (pp. 208-221). Boston: Allyn and Bacon.

Greenfield, Wilma L., & Rothman, Beulah (1987). Termination or Transformation? Evolving Beyond Termination in Groups. In Joseph Lassner, Kathleen Powell, & Elaine Finnegan (Eds.), *Social Group Work: Competence and Values in Practice* (pp. 51-65). Binghamton, NY: Haworth.

Henry, Sue. (1992). *Group Skills in Social Work: A Four-Dimensional Approach* (2nd ed., pp. 192-220). Pacific Grove, CA: Brooks/Cole.

Malekoff, Andrew. (1997). *Group Work with Adolescents: Principles and Practice* (pp. 166-185). New York: Guilford.

Middleman, Ruth R., & Wood, Gale Goldberg. (1990). *Skills for Direct Practice in Social Work* (pp. 91-154). New York: Columbia University Press.

Northen, Helen. (1988). *Social Work with Groups* (2nd ed., pp. 298-332). New York: Columbia University Press.

Schiller, Linda Yael. (1995). Stages of Development in Women's Groups: A Relational Model. In Roselle Kurland & Robert Salmon (Eds.), *Group Work Practice in a Troubled Society: Problems and Opportunities* (pp. 117-138). Binghamton, NY: Haworth.

Shulman, Lawrence. (1992). *The Skills of Helping Individuals, Families and Groups* (3rd ed., pp. 173-206, 573-594). Itasca, IL: Peacock.

Toseland, Ronald W., & Rivas, Robert F. (1998). *An Introduction to Group Work Practice* (3rd ed., pp. 363-439). Boston: Allyn and Bacon.

X. Diversity in Group Work Practice

Ball, Steven, & Lipton, Benjamin. (1997). Group Work with Gay Men. In Geoffrey L. Greif & Paul H. Ephross (Eds.), *Group Work with Populations at Risk* (pp. 2589-277). New York: Oxford University Press.

Bentelspacher, Carl E., DeSilva, Evelyn, Goh, Terrence Leng Chuang, & LaRowe, Karl D. (1996). A Process Evaluation of the Cultural Compatibility of Psychoeducational Family Group Treatment With Ethnic Asian Clients. *Social Work with Groups, 19*(3/4), 41-55.

Bilides, David. (1990). Race, Color, Ethnicity and Class: Issues of Biculturalism In School-Based Adolescent Counseling Groups. *Social Work with Groups, 13*(4), 43-58.

Brower, Aaron M., Garvin, Charles D., Hobson, Josephine, Reed, Beth Glover, & Reed, Harvey. (1987). Exploring the Effects of Leader Gender and Race on Group Behavior. In Jospeh Lassner, Kathleen Powell, & Elaine Finnegan (Eds.), *Social Group Work: Competence and Values in Practice* (pp. 129-148). Binghamton, NY: Haworth.

Brown, Allan, & Mistry, Tara. (1994). Group Work with Mixed Membership Groups: Issues of Race and Gender. *Social Work with Groups*, *17*(3), 5-21.

Chau, Kenneth L. (1990). Ethnicity and Biculturalism: Emerging Perspectives of Social Group Work [Special issue]. *Social Work with Groups*, *13*(4).

Chau, Kenneth L. (1992). Needs Assessment for Group Work with People of Color: A Conceptual Formulation. *Social Work with Groups*, *15*(2/3), 53-66.

Davis, Larry E. (1984). Essential Components of Group Work with Black Americans. *Social Work with Groups*, *7*(3), 97-109.

Davis, Larry E. (Ed.). (1984). Ethnicity in Social Group Work Practice [Special issue]. *Social Work with Groups*, *7*(3).

Davis, Larry E. (1995). The Crisis of Diversity. In Marvin D. Feit, John H. Ramey, John S. Wodarski, & Aaron R. Mann (Eds.), *Capturing the Power of Diversity* (pp. 47-58). Binghamton, NY: Haworth.

Delgado, Melvin, & Humm-Delgado, Denise. (1984). Hispanics and Group Work: A Review of the Literature. *Social Work with Groups*, *7*(3), 85-96.

Englehardt, Bonnie. (1997). Group Work with Lesbians. In Geoffrey L. Greif & Paul H. Ephross (Eds.), *Group Work with Populations at Risk* (pp. 278-294). New York: Oxford University Press.

Fagan, Jay, & Stevenson, Howard. (1995). Men as Teachers: A Self-Help Program on Parenting for African-American Men. *Social Work with Groups*, *17*(4), 29-42.

Flavio, Francisco Marsiglia. (1997). Horizontes: Using Social Work with Groups in the Classroom to Serve the Needs of Latino College Students. In Albert S. Alissi & Catherine G. Corto Mergins (Eds.), *Voices from the Field: Group Work Responds* (pp. 113-138). Binghamton, NY: Haworth.

Garvin, Charles D., & Reed, Beth G. (1995). Sources and Visions for Feminist Group Work: Reflective Processes, Social Justice, Diversity, and Correction. In Nan Van Den Bergh (Ed.), *Feminist Visions for Social Work*, Silver Springs, MD: National Association of Social Worker.

Getzel, George. (1997). Group with Gay Men and Lesbian Women. In Gary Mallon (Ed.), *Foundations of Social Work Practice with Gay Men and Lesbian Women*. Binghamton, NY: Haworth.

Gitterman, Alex, & Schaeffer, Alice. (1972). The White Professional and the Black Client. *Social Casework*, *53*(5), 280-291.

Glasgow, Godfrey F., & Gouse-Sheese, Janice. (1995). Themes of Rejection and Abandonment in Group Work with Caribbean Adolescents. *Social Work with Groups, 17*(4), 3-27.

Gottlieb, Naomi, Burden, Dianne, McCormick, Ruth, & Nicarthy, Ginny. (1983). The Distinctive Attributes of Feminist Groups. *Social Work with Groups, 6*(3/4), 81-93.

Groves, Patricia, & Schondel, Connie. (1996). Lesbian Couples Who Are Survivors of Incest: Group Work Utilizing A Feminist Approach. *Social Work with Groups, 19*(3/4), 93-103.

Gutierrez, Lorraine. (1990). Working with Women of Color: An Empowerment Perspective. *Social Work, 35*(2), 149-153.

Gutierrez, Lorraine, & Ortega, Robert. (1991). Developing Methods to Empower Latinos: The Importance of Groups. *Social Work with Groups, 4*(2), 23-44.

Hardy-Fanta, Carol, & Montana, Prinscila. (1983). The Hispanic Female Adolescent: A Group Therapy Model. In Norman Goroff (Ed.), *Reaping from the Field* (pp. 542-600). Hebron, CT: Practitioners Press.

Lewis, Elizabeth. (1992). Regaining Promise: Feminist Perspectives for Social Group Work Practice. *Social Work with Groups, 15*(2/3), 271-284.

Liu, Fanny W. C. L. (1995). Towards Mutual Aid in a Chinese Society. In Roselle Kurland & Robert Salmon (Eds.), *Group Work Practice in a Troubled Society: Problems and Opportunities* (pp. 89-100). Binghamton, NY: Haworth.

Malekoff, Andrew. (1997). Prejudice Reduction, Intergroup Relations, and Group Identity. In *Group Work with Adolescents: Principles and Practice* (pp. 189-214). New York: Guilford.

Muston, Ros, & Weint, Jeremy. (1991). Race and Groupwork: Some Experiences in Practice and Training, *Groupwork, 4*(2), 30-40.

Norman, Alex. (1991). The Use of the Group and Group Work Techniques in Resolving Interethnic Conflict. *Social Work with Groups, 14*(3/4), 75-186.

Reed, Beth G., & Garvin, Charles, D. (Eds.). (1983). Group Work with Women/Group Work With Men: An Overview of Gender Issues [Special issue]. *Social Work with Groups, 6*(3).

Schopler, Janice H., Galinsky, Maeda, J., Davis, Larry E., & Despard, Mathieu. (1996). The RAP Model: Assessing a Framework for Leading Multiracial Groups. *Social Work with Groups, 19*(3/4), 21-29.

Solomon, Barbara Bryant. (1976). *Black Empowerment: Social Work in Oppressed Communities*. New York: Columbia University Press.

Travers, Anna. (1995). Adversity, Diversity and Empowerment: Feminist Group Work with Women in Poverty. In Roselle Kurland & Robert Salmon (Eds.), *Group Work in a Troubled Society: Problems and Opportunities* (pp. 139-158). Binghamton, NY: Haworth.

Travers, Anna. (1996). Redefining Adult Identity: A Coming out Group for Lesbians. In Benj. L. Stempler & Marilyn Glass (Eds.), *Social Group Work: Today and Tomorrow* (pp. 103-118). Binghamton, NY: Haworth.

Van Den Bergh, Nan. (1990). Managing Biculturalism At the Workplace: A Group Approach, *Social Work with Groups, 13*(4), pp. 71-84.

Wilson, Hugh. (1991). The Black Experience in Suburbia: Prospects and Possibilities for Group Work Intervention. *Social Work with Groups, 14*(1), 17-28.

Waites, Cheryl. (1992). The Tradition of Group Work and Natural Helping Networks in the African American Community. In David F. Fike & Barbara Rittner, (Eds.), *Working from Strengths: The Essence of Group Work* (pp. 220-235). Miami Shores, FL: Center for Group Work Studies.

Zastrow, Charles. (1997). Feminist Intervention In Groups. In *Social Work with Groups* (4th ed., pp. 391-400). Chicago: Nelson-Hall.

XI. Populations at Risk

Albert, Jeffrey. (1994). Rethinking Difference: A Cognitive Therapy Group for Chronic Mental Patients, *Social Work with Groups, 17*(1/2), 105-121.

Albert, Jeffrey. (1994). Talking Like Real People: The Straight Ahead Prison Group. In Alex Gitterman & Lawrence Shulman (Eds.), *Mutual Aid Groups, Vulnerable Populations, and the Life Cycle* (2nd ed., pp. 199-214). New York: Columbia University Press.

Altman, Marjorie, & Crocker, Ruth. (Eds.). (1982). Social Group Work and Alcoholism [Special issue]. *Social Work with Groups. 5*(1).

Amelio, Robert C. (1993). An AIDS Bereavement Support Group: One Model of Intervention in a Time of Crisis. *Social Work with Groups, 16*(1/2), 43-54.

Auerbach, Sandra, & Moses, Charles. (1987). Groups for Wives of Gay and Bisexual Men. *Social Work, 32*(4), 321-325.

Avery, Nancy, & Wayne, Julianne. (1978). Group Development and Grief Therapy for Non-nurturing Mothers. *Social Work with Groups, 1*(3), 287-298.

Berman-Rossi, Toby. (1994). The Fight against Hopelessness and Despair: Institutionalized Aged. In Alex Gitterman & Lawrence Shulman,

(Eds.). *Mutual Aid Groups, Vulnerable Populations, and the Life Cycle* (2nd ed., pp. 385-409). New York: Columbia University Press.

Berman-Rossi, Toby, & Cohen, Marcia B. (1988). Group Development and Shared Decision-Making with Homeless Mentally Ill Women. *Social Work with Groups, 11*(4), 63-78.

Bilides, David G. (1992). Reaching Inner-City Children: A Group Work Program Model for a Public Middle School. *Social Work with Groups, 15*(2/3), 129-144.

Biskind, Sylvia E. (1966). The Group Method with Clients, Foster Families and Adoptive Families: The Group Method in Services to Adoptive Parents. *Child Welfare, 45*(10), 561-564.

Bonkowski, Sara E., & Wanner-Westly, Brenda. (1979). The Divorce Group: A New Treatment Modality. *Social Casework, 60*(9), 552-557.

Brady, Donna E. (1989). Substance Abuse: The Use of Groups in Relapse Prevention. In Estelle Hopmeyer, Alice Home, & Lise Darveau-Fournier (Eds.), *Social Work with Groups and the Challenge of Societal Change* (pp. 620-631). Montreal, Canada: Symposium XI Social Work with Groups.

Breton, Margot. (1979). Nurturing Abused and Abusive Mothers: The Hair-Dressing Group. *Social Work with Groups, 2*(2), 161-174.

Breton, Margot. (1988). The Need for Mutual-Aid Groups In a Drop-In Center for Homeless Women: The Sistering Case. *Social Work with Groups, 11*(4), 47-61.

Brooks, Anne. (1978). Group Work on the 'Bowery.' *Social Work with Groups, 1*(1), 53-63.

Brown, Jennifer. (1984). Group Work With Low-Income Black Youths. *Social Work with Groups, 7*(3), 111-124.

Brown, Jennifer A. (1994). Agents of Change: A Group For Women in a Shelter. In Alex Gitterman & Lawrence Shulman (Eds.), *Mutual Aid Groups, Vulnerable Populations, and the Life Cycle* (2nd ed., pp. 272-296). New York: Columbia University Press.

Caplan, Tom, & Thomas, Harle. (1995). Safety and Comfort, Content and Process: Facilitating Open Group Work With Men Who Batter. *Social Work with Groups, 18*(2/3), 33-52.

Cardarelle, James A. (1975). A Group For Children with Deceased Parents, *Social Work, 20*(4), 328-329.

Cassano, D. Rosemary. (1989). Multi-Family Group Therapy In Social Work Practice. *Social Work with Groups, 12*(1), 3-14.

Child, Rachel, & Getzel, George S. (1989). Group Work With Inner City People With AIDS. *Social Work with Groups, 12*(4), 65-80.

Cohen, Marcia B. (1994). Who Wants to Chair the Meeting? Group Development and Leadership Patterns in a Community Action Group of Homeless People. *Social Work with Groups, 17*(1/2), 71-87.

Cox, Enid Opal. (1988). Empowerment of the Low-Income Elderly Through Group Work, *Social Work with Groups, 11*(4), 111-126.

Crosby, Constance. (1978). A Group Experience for Elderly Socially Isolated Widows. *Social Work with Groups, 1*(4), 345-354.

Davis, Kenneth R., & Shapiro, Linda J. (1979). Exploring Group Process as a Means of Reaching the Mentally Retarded. *Social Casework, 60*(6), 330-337.

Drews, Jeanette R., & Bradley, Tamara T. (1989). Group Treatment for Adults Molested as Children: An Educational and Therapeutic Approach. *Social Work with Groups, 12*(3), 57-75.

Finn, Jerry, & Lavitt, Melissa. (1994).. Computer-Based Self-Help Groups for Sexual Abuse, Survivors, *Social Work with Groups, 17*(1/2), 21-46.

Freeman, Edith M., & McRoy, Ruth. (1986). Group Counseling Program for Unemployed Black Teenagers. *Social Work with Groups, 9*(1), 73-89.

Gambe, Richard, & Getzel, George S. (1989). Group Work With Gay Men With AIDS. *Social Casework, 70*(3), 172-179.

Getzel, George. (1991). Survival Modes of People With AIDS in Groups. *Social Work, 36,* 7-11.

Getzel, George. (1994). No One Is Alone: Groups During the AIDS Pandemic. In Alex Gitterman & Lawrence Shulman (Eds.), *Mutual Aid Groups, Vulnerable Populations, and the Life Cycle* (2nd ed., pp. 185-197). New York: Columbia University Press.

Getzel, George. (1996). AIDS and Group Work: Looking at the Second Decade of the Pandemic. In Benj. L. Stempler & Marilyn Glass (Eds.), *Social Group Work: Today and Tomorrow* (pp. 33-44). Binghamton, NY: Haworth.

Getzel, George. (1997). Group Work Practice with People with AIDS. In Geoffrey L. Greif & Paul H. Ephross (Eds.), *Group Work with Population At Risk* (pp. 42-55). New York: Oxford University Press.

Gitterman, Alex, & Shulman, Lawrence. (Eds). (1994). *Mutual Aid Groups, Vulnerable Populations, and the Life Cycle* (2nd ed.). New York: Columbia University Press.

Gladstone, James, & Reynolds, Tom. (1997). Single Session Group Work Intervention in Resonse to Employee Stress during Workforce Transformation. *Social Work with Groups, 20*(1), 33-49.

Goldberg, Elisa Valladares, & Simpson, Thomas. (1995). Challenging Stereotypes in Treatment of the Homeless Alcoholic and Addict: Creating Freedom through Structure in Large Groups. *Social Work with Groups, 18*(2/3), 79-94.

Goodman, Harriet. (1997). Social Group Work in Community Corrections. *Social Work with Groups, 20*(1), 51-64

Goodman, Harriet, Getzel, George S., & Ford, William. (1996). Group Work with High Risk Urban Youth on Probation. *Social Work, 14*, 375-381.

Greene, Darrell C., McVinney, L. Donald, & Adams, Sallie. (1993). Strengths in Transition: Professionally Facilitated HIV Support Groups and the Development of Client Symptomatology. *Social Work with Groups, 16*(3), 41-54.

Greif, Geoffrey L., & Ephross, Paul H. (Eds.). (1997). *Group Work with Populations at Risk.* New York: Oxford University Press.

Haran, Judy. (1988). Use of Group Work to Help Children Cope with the Violent Death of a Classmate. *Social Work with Groups, 11*(3), 79-94.

Hardman, Karen L. J. (1997). A Social Work Group for Prostituted Women with Children. *Social Work with Groups, 20*(1), 19-49.

Hepler, Juanita B. (1995). Utilizing a Group Approach to Improve the Social Skills of Children with Learning Disabilities. In Marvin Feit, John H. Ramey, John S. Wodarski, & Aaron R. Mann (Eds.), *Capturing the Power of Diversity* (pp. 115-126). Binghamton, NY: Haworth.

Irrizary, Carol, & Appel, Yetta H. (1994). In Double Jeopardy: Preadolescents in the Inner City. In Alex Gitterman & Lawrence Shulman (Eds.), *Mutual Aid Groups, Vulnerable Populations, and the Life Cycle* (2nd ed., pp. 119-149). New York: Columbia University Press.

Israel-Ikeman, Beverly, & Rotholz, Tryna. (1987). The Single Session Waiting Room Group. In Joseph Lassner, Kathleen Powell, & Elaine Finnegan (Eds.), *Social Group Work: Competence and Values in Practice* (pp. 113-125). Binghamton, NY: Haworth.

Joyce, Patricia A. (1995). Group Work With Mothers of Sexually Abused Children. In Roselle Kurland & Robert Salmon (Eds.), *Group Work Practice in a Troubled Society: Problems and Opportunities* (pp. 165-176). Binghamton, NY: Haworth.

Jones, Margaret J. (1994). Speaking the Unspoken: Parents of Sexually Victimized Children. In Alex Gitterman & Lawrence Shulman (Eds.), *Mutual Aid Groups, Vulnerable Populations, and the Life Cycle* (2nd ed., pp. 239-255). New York: Columbia University Press.

Kixmiller, I., & Onserud, H. F. (1995). A Community Center Model for Current Urban Needs. In Roselle Kurland & Robert Salmon (Eds.), *Group Work Practice in a Troubled Society: Problems and Opportunities* (pp. 203-216). Binghamton, NY: Haworth.

Knight, Carolyn. (1993). The Use of a Therapy Group for Adult Men and Women Sexually Abused in Childhood. *Social Work with Groups*, 16(4), 81-94.

Kolodny, Ralph, & Garland, James. (Eds.). (1984). Group Work with Children and Adolescents [Special issue]. *Social Work with Groups*, 7(4).

Kosberg, Jordan I., & Kaye, Lenard W. (1997). Support Groups for Older Men: Building on Strengths and Facilitating Relationships. In Jordan I. Kosberg & Lenard W. Kaye (Eds.), *Elderly Men: Special Problems and Professional Challenges* (pp. 262-278). New York: Springer Publishing Company.

Laterza, Esther, et al. (1979). An Eclectic Approach to Group Work with the Mentally Retarded. *Social Work with Groups*, 2(3), 235-245.

Lee, Judith A. B. (Ed.). (1988). Group Work with the Poor and Oppressed [Special issue]. *Social Work with Groups*, 11(4).

Lee, Judith A. B. (1994). No Place to Go: Homeless Women. In Alex Gitterman & Lawrence Shulman (Eds.), *Mutual Aid Groups, Vulnerable Populations, and the Life Cycle* (2nd ed., pp. 297-313). New York: Columbia University Press.

LePantois, Joan. (1986). Group Therapy for Children of Substance Abusers. *Social Work with Groups*, 9(1), 39-51.

Levine, Baruch. (Ed.). (1990). Group Work with the Emotionally Disabled [Special issue]. *Social Work with Groups*, 13(1).

Levinsky, Lois, & McAleer. (1994). Listen to Us. Young Adolescents in Urban Schools. In Alex Gitterman & Lawrence Shulman (Eds.), *Mutual Aid Groups, Vulnerable Populations, and the Life Cycle* (2nd ed., pp. 151-162). New York: Columbia University Press.

Lewis, Elizabeth A. (1996). What Works in the Treatment of MICA Clients: A Journey Through the Evolution of an Outpatient MICA Program. In Roselle Kurland & Robert Salmon (Eds.), *Group Work Practice in a Troubled Society: Problems and Opportunities* (pp. 217-242). Binghamton, NY: Haworth.

Lopez, Jose. (1991). Group Work as a Protective Factor for Immigrant Youth. *Social Work with Groups* 14(1), 29-42.

Lovell, Madeline L., Reid, Kathy, & Richey, Cheryl A. (1992). Social Support Training for Abusive Mothers. *Social Work with Groups*, 15(2/3), 95-107.

Lowy, Louis. (1992). Social Group Work with Elders: Linkages and Intergenerational Relationships. *Social Work with Groups, 15*(2/3), 109-127.

Lurie, Abraham, Rosenberg, Gary, & Pinsky, Sidney. (1982). *Social Work with Groups in Health Settings.* New York: Prodist.

Malekoff, Andrew. (Ed.). (1991). Group Work With Suburban Children: Differences, Acceptance and Belonging [Special issue]. *Social Work with Groups, 14*(1).

Malekoff, Andrew. (1994). A Guideline for Group Work With Adolescents. *Social Work with Groups, 17*(1/2), 5-19.

Mancoske, Ronald, & Lindhorst, Taryn. (1991). Mutual Assistance Groups in a Shelter for Persons with AIDS. *Social Work with Groups, 14*(2), 75-86.

Martin, Marsha, & Nayowith, Susan A. (1988). Creating Community: Groupwork to Develop Social Support Networks with Homeless Mentally Ill. *Social Work with Groups, 11*(4), 79-93.

McNeil, John S., & McBride, Mary L. (1979). Group Therapy With Abusive Parents. *Social Casework, 60*(1), 36-42.

Miller, David B. (1997). Parenting Against the Odds: African-American Parents in the Child Welfare System—A Group Approach. *Social Work with Groups, 20*(1), 5-18.

Miller, Irving, & Solomon, Renee. (1980). The Development of Group Services for the Elderly. *Journal of Gerontological Social Work, 2*(3), 241-257.

Morris, Sylvia. (Ed.). (1982). The Use of Group Services in Permanency Planning for Children [Special issue]. *Social Work with Groups. 5*(4).

Nightengale, Jane. (1990). Discharge Planning: Promoting Patient Involvement through Group Process. *Social Work with Groups, 13*(2), 83-94.

Nosko, Anna, & Wallace, Bob. (1988). Group Work with Abusive Men: A Multidimensional Model. *Social Work with Groups, 11*(3), 33-52.

Parsons, Ruth J. (1988). Empowerment for Role Alternatives for Low-Income Minority Girls: A Group Work Approach. *Social Work with Groups, 11*(4), 27-46.

Peters, Andrew J. (1997). Themes in Group Work with Lesbian and Gay Adolescents. *Social Work with Groups, 20*(2), 51-69.

Pollio, David E., McDonald, Sharon M., & North, Carol S. (1996). Combining a Strengths-Based Approach and Feminist Theory in Group Work with Persons 'On the Streets.' *Social Work with Groups, 19*(3/4), 5-20.

Pollio, David E. (1994). Wintering at the Earle: Group Structures in the Street Community. *Social Work with Groups, 17*(1/2), 47-70.

Pollio, David E. (1995). Hoops Group: Group Work with Young 'Street' Men. *Social Work with Groups, 18*(2/3), 107-122.

Portner, Doreen. (1981). Clinical Aspects of Social Group Work With the Deaf. *Social Work with Groups, 4*(3/4), 123-133.

Poynter-Berg, Dorothy. (1994). Getting Connected: Institutionalized Schizophrenic Women. In Alex Gitterman & Lawrence Shulman (Eds.), *Mutual Aid Groups, Vulnerable Populations, and the Life Cycle* (2nd ed., pp. 315-333). New York: Columbia University Press.

Rittner, Barbara, & Hammons, Kim. (1992). Telephone Group Work with People with End Stage AIDS. *Social Work with Groups, 15*(4), 59-72.

Rothenberg, Eleanor Dubin. (1994). Bereavement Intervention with Vulnerable Populations: A Case Report on Group Work with the Developmentally Disabled. *Social Work with Groups, 17*(3), 61-75.

Rounds, Kathleen A., Galinsky, Maeda J., & Stevens, L. (1991). Linking People with AIDS in Rural Communities: The Telephone Group. *Social Work, 36*(1), 13-18.

Ryan, Deborah, & Doubleday, Elizabeth. (1995). Group Work: A Lifeline for Isolated Elderly. *Social Work with Groups, 18*(2/3), 65-78.

Sachs, Jerome. (1991). Action and Reflection in Work With A Group of Homeless People. *Social Work with Groups, 14*(3/4), 187-202.

Saul, Shura. (Ed.). (1982). Social Group Work with the Frail Elderly [Special issue]. *Social Work with Groups. 5*(2).

Schiller, Linda Yale, & Zimmer, Bonnie. (1994). Sharing Secrets: Women's Groups for Sexual Abuse Survivors. In Alex Gitterman & Lawrence Shulman (Eds.), *Mutual Aid Groups, Vulnerable Populations, and the Life Cycle* (2nd ed., pp. 215-238). New York: Columbia University Press.

Schopler, Janice H., & Galinsky, Maeda J. (Eds.). (1990). Groups in Health Care Settings [Special issue]. *Social Work with Groups, 13*(3).

Seskin, Jane. (1988). Sounds of Practice II: Group Work with Battered Women. *Social Work with Groups, 11*(3), 101-108.

Shapiro, Joan. (1986). *Transcending the Fear of the Stranger*. New York: United Neighborhood Houses.

Shields, Sally Ann. (1985/1986). Busted and Branded: Group Work with Substance Abusing Adolescents in Schools. *Social Work with Groups, 8*(3/4), 61-81.

Stein, Lynne, Rothman, Beulah, & Nakanishi, Manuel. (1993). The Telephone Group: Accessing Group Service to the Homebound. *Social Work with Groups, 16*(1/2), 203-215.

Steinberg, Dominique Moyse. (1990). A Model of Pregnancy Prevention through te Use of Small Groups. *Social Work with Groups*, *13*(2), 57-68.

Subramanian, Karen, Hernandez, Sylvia, & Martinez, Angie. (1995). Psychoeducational Group Work for Low-Income Latina Mothers with HIV Infection. *Social Work with Groups*, *18*(2/3), 53-64.

Trimble, Dale. (1994). Confronting Responsibility: Men Who Batter Their Wives. In Alex Gitterman & Lawrence Shulman (Eds.), *Mutual Aid Groups, Vulnerable Populations, and the Life Cycle* (2nd ed., pp. 257-271). New York Columbia University Press.

Vastola, Joyce, & Associates. (1994). The Lost and Found Group: Group Work and Bereaved Children. In Alex Gitterman & Lawrence Shulman (Eds.), *Mutual Aid Groups, Vulnerable Populations, and the Life Cycle* (2nd ed., pp. 81-96). New York: Columbia University Press.

Wagner, Robin A. (1992). Group Work with Mainstreamed Adolescents Who Are Differently Abled Physically Abled. In David F. Fike & Barbara Rittner (Eds.), *Working from Strengths: The Essence of Group Work* (pp. 267-287). Miami Shores, FL: Center for Group Work Studies.

Wayne, Julianne, & Fine, Susan B. (1986). Group Work With Retarded Mothers. *Social Casework*, *67*(4), 195-202.

Weisberg, Alma. (1987). Single Session Group Practice In A Hospital. In Joseph Lassner, Kathleen Powell, & Elaine Finnegan (Eds.), *Social Group Work: Competence and Values In Practice* (PP. 99-112). Binghamton, NY: Haworth.

Weisman, Celia, & Schwartz, Paula. (1990). Worker Expectation in Group Work with the Frail Elderly: Modifying the Models for a Better Fit. *Social Work with Groups*, *13*(3), 47-56.

Wood, Gale Goldberg, & Middleman, Ruth R. (1992). Re-Casting the Die: A Small Group Approach to Giving Batterers a Chance to Change. *Social Work with Groups*, *15*(1), 5-18.

Xenarios, Susan. (1988). Sounds of Practice I: Group Work with Rape Survivors. *Social Work with Groups*, *11*(3), 95-100.

XII. Use of Program and Activity

Brandler, Sondra, & Roman, Camille P. (1991). *Group Work: Skills and Strategies for Effective Interventions* (pp. 125-163). Binghamton, NY: Haworth.

Canfield, Jack, & Wells, Harold Clive. (1994). *100 Ways to Enhance Self-Concept in the Classroom*. Boston, MA: Allyn and Bacon.

Coyle, Grace L. (1949). *Group Work with American Youth* (pp. 169-216). New York: Harpers.

Fluegelman, Andrew. (Ed.). (1976). *The New Games Book.* New York: Doubleday.

Fluegelman, Andrew. (Ed.). (1981). *More New Games.* New York: Doubleday.

Kaminsky, Marc. (1974). *What's Inside You It Shines Out of You.* New York: Horizon.

Kaminsky, Marc. (Ed.). (1984). The Uses of Reminiscence: New Ways of Working With Older Adults [Special issue]. *Journal of Gerontological Social Work, 7(1/2).*

Katz, Susan L. (1988). Photocollage as a Therapeutic Modality for Working With Groups, *Social Work with Groups, 10(4),* pp. 83-90.

Koch, Kenneth. (1970). *Wishes, Lies, and Dreams: Teaching Children to Write Poetry.* New York: Harper and Row.

Koch, Kenneth. (1977). *I Never Told Anybody.* New York: Random House.

Kreidler, William J. (1984). *Creative Conflict Resolution: More Than 200 Activities for Keeping Peace in the Classroom.* Glenview, IL: Scott, Foresman.

Lynn, Maxine, & Nisivoccia, Danielle. (1995). Activity-Oriented Group Work with the Mentally Ill: Enhancing Socialization. *Social Work with Groups, 18(2/3),* 95-106.

Malekoff, Andrew. (1997). *Group Work with Adolescents: Principles and Practice* (pp. 146-165). New York: Guilford.

Middleman, Ruth. (1980). The Use of Program: Review and Update. *Social Work with Groups, 3(3),* 5-23.

Middleman, Ruth. (1982). *The Non-Verbal Method in Working with Groups: The Use of Activity in Teaching, Counseling and Therapy.* Hebron, CT: Practitioners' Press. Originally published 1968, New York: Association Press.

Middleman, Ruth R. (Ed.). (1983). Activities and Action in Group Work [Special issue]. *Social Work with Groups,* 6(1).

Northen, Helen. (1988). *Social Work with Groups* (2nd ed., pp. 78-97). New York: Columbia University Press.

Novelly, Maria C. (1985). *Theater Games for Young Performers.* Colorado Springs, CO: Meriwether.

Pollio, David E. (1995). Hoops Group: Group Work with Young 'Street' Men. *Social Work with Groups, 18(2/3),* 107-122.

Potocky, Miriam. (1993). An Art Therapy Group for Clients with Chronic Schizophrenia. *Social Work with Groups, 16*(3), 73-82.

Redl, Fritz, & Wineman, David. (1952). Programming as a Full-Fledged Therapeutic Tool.. In Fritz Redl & Norman D. Wineman (Eds.), *Controls from within: Techniques for the Treatment of the Aggressive Child* (pp. 85-152). Glencoe, IL: Free Press.

Rice, Wayne, & Yaconelli, Mike. (1986). *Play It (Great Games for Groups)*. Grand Rapids, MI: Zondervan.

Ross, Andrew L., & Bernstein, Norman D. (1976). A Framework for the Therapeutic Use of Group Activities. *Child Welfare, 55*(9), 627-640.

Schnekenburger, Erica. (1995). Waking the Heart Up: A Writing Group's Story. *Social Work with Groups, 18*(4), 19-40.

Shulman, Lawrence. (1971). Program in Group Work: Another Look. In William Schwartz & Serapio Zalba (Eds.), *The Practice of Group Work* (pp. 221-240). New York: Columbia University Press.

Shulman, Lawrence. (1992). *The Skills of Helping Individuals, Families and Groups* (pp. 561-568). Itasca, IL: Peacock.

Spolin, Viola. (1986). *Theater Games for the Classroom: A Teacher's Handbook*. Evanston, IL: Northwestern University Press.

Subramanian, Karen, Hernandez, Sylvia, & Martinez, Angie. (1995). Psychoeducational Group Work for Low-Income Latina Mothers with HIV Infection. *Social Work with Groups, 18*(2/3), 53-64.

Vinter, Robert D. (1974). Program Activities: An Analysis of Their Effects on Participant Behavior. In Paul Glasser, Rosemary Sarri, & Robert Vinter (Eds.), *Individual Change through Small Groups* (pp. 233-243). New York: Free.

Waite, Lesley Meirovitz. (1993). Drama Therapy in Small Groups with the Developmentally Disabled. *Social Work with Groups, 16*(4), 95-108.

Whittaker, James K. (1974). Program Activities: Their Selection and Use in a Therapeutic Milieu. In Paul Glasser, Rosemary Sarri, & Robert Vinter (Eds.), *Individual Change through Small Groups* (pp. 244-257). New York: Free Press.

Whittaker, James K. (1976). Differential Use of Program Activities in Child Treatment Groups. *Child Welfare, 55*(7), 459-467.

Wilson, Gertrude, & Ryland, Gladys. (1949). *Social Group Work Practice* (pp. 197-342). Boston: Houghton-Mifflin.

APPENDIX D

ASSIGNMENTS

It is useful for students to be working with a group while they take the course, although this is not a requirement for participation in the course. If students do not have groups, the course will prepare them for effective work at a later time.

Two assignments are suggested for the course. The mid-term assignment is a Group Work Log. The purpose of the log is to encourage students to integrate their work in class and field with their reading and to help them make connections between self, reading, and experience. In the log, students are asked to share ongoing thoughts about matters related to work with groups, to explore and struggle with ideas, issues, and problems that are of interest or that are unclear to them. Students are asked to write on only one side of the page, leaving the other side for instructor comments. Such a format allows the instructor to enter into a dialogue with each student in the class. The log is labor intensive for the instructor, but it can be highly useful educationally for students.

We distribute a handout with the following instructions.

Group Work Log

Please set down your ongoing reactions to course readings, class discussion, and field experiences, or to other experiences that relate to work with groups. Expressing your thoughts in writing will help you to develop your ideas and perceptions and extend your understanding of often conflicting ideas—including those which contradict or confirm your own ideas and experiences in the field. Here are some suggestions and guidelines for the log:

- Evaluate the perspectives of others, or your own.
- Formulate your own questions and ideas about classroom or field work content and express them even when you can only be tentative and speculative.
- Try to make connections between the abstract and concrete— between theories, concepts, and ideas and the ways in which they are played out in your experience.

- When you start an entry with your own experiences, consider testing them out against some relevant reading taken from the bibliography. When your entry is prompted by reading, react critically and try to relate it to your own experiences, questions, other ideas, etc.
- Try to move beyond your first reactions. Stay with the flow of your ideas, expressing them as simply and directly as you can. Permit yourself to speculate and to make mistakes.
- Write your entries on a regular basis throughout the semester and date each entry.
- Type as clearly as possible and on one side of the page.
- Write about the differences (or similarities) in the group work approach to other practice methods.

*   *   *

There are two options for the final assignment. Option 1, Group Description, is for students who are not working with groups. Option 2, Group Analysis, is for students who are working with a group (even if the group has met for only two or three times). We distribute the following two handouts as appropriate.

Group Description

Describe a group that you would like to form and that you think is needed in your agency.

- What are the *needs* that this group would aim to meet?
- What is the *purpose* of the group? (Be careful not to confuse purpose and content here!)
- What would be the group's *composition?* Who would be the members? What are the important areas of commonality and difference that you anticipate among them?
- How would the group be *structured?* What is your reasoning for this structure?
- What is the anticipated *content* of group meetings?
- What would be the nature and content of your *pre-group contact* with potential group members? How would you go about recruitment for the group?
- In what ways would *agency context* affect your efforts to form this group? With whom at the agency would you need to talk

or collaborate? What are possible obstacles in the agency to the formation of this group and how would you go about overcoming them?

- What do you think would be the greatest obstacles in getting this group off the ground? How would you overcome them?
- What are some anticipated difficulties in working with this group? Discuss them.

*   *   *

Group Analysis

The group analysis aims to help workers look systematically at their groups in a way that will aid current understanding and guide future action. The following outline should serve as a guide for analysis. Not all items covered are necessarily applicable to all groups. The outline should not constrict the worker, but serve as an instrument to help in assessing relevant facts.

I. Need
   A. What are the needs, problems, or conditions that this group aims to meet as perceived by group members, worker(s), agency, and other relevant persons?
   B. What commonalities in group members' lives represent potential shared needs?
   C. What are the relevant social, cultural, and racial factors (e.g., values, economic conditions, attitudes) in the group members' environment? How are these expressed by group members and what implications have they had for group activity?
   D. How do social systems affect some or all members (e.g., school, family, agencies, institutions)?
   E. What are the developmental needs of the group members? How are these expressed by the group members and what implications have they had for group activity?

II. Purpose
   A. What is the group purpose as perceived by group members, worker(s), and agency? Has this purpose changed since the group was formed and, if so, in what ways?
   B. What are the goals for each group member as perceived by himself or herself and by the worker(s)?

III. Composition
  A. How many members does the group have? What is the average attendance at group meetings? Have there been discernible shifts in attendance during the period covered?
  B. What are the significant descriptive characteristics of the group members (e.g., age, sex, race, ethnicity, grade in school, family background, physical characteristics, educational background, occupational background, cultural background, socioeconomic level, previous group experience)? Along which of these variables is there heterogeneity or homogeneity? How do these affect group interaction?
  C. What are the significant behavioral characteristics of group members (e.g., interactional style, capacity to use the group experience, relate to and communicate with others, motivation and capacity to achieve the purpose of the group and individual goals and objectives)? Along which of these variables is there heterogeneity or homogeneity? How do these affect group interaction?
  D. Are there individual members who need special attention from the group? Describe.
  E. How many workers does the group have? What are the significant characteristics of the worker(s) (e.g., sex, race, age, ethnicity, educational background, style of work)?

IV. Structure
  A. What is the frequency and time of group meetings? What is the duration of each meeting? How long has the group met and how long is it expected to continue?
  B. Where does the group meet? What are the physical arrangements in the meeting room? How do members get to meetings? Are refreshments served and, if so, who provides them?
  C. Is there a budget for the group? What is the source of funding? If relevant, what is the nature of fees?
  D. What arrangements have been made regarding confidentiality? intra- and inter-agency coordination and collaboration? Give examples of such coordination/collaboration.

V. Content
  A. What takes place at group meetings? Are themes evident in the group content? What has the group done in the way of discussion and/or activities that reflects shared needs

and interests? To what extent do aspects of group discussion and activity meet or not meet the needs of particular individuals and the group as a whole? How is group content determined?

B. What are the significant norms in the group? Have these changed over time?

C. What is the nature of influence, leadership (formal and informal), and followership in the group? Has this changed over time?

D. Are there subgroups? If so, what impact do they have?

E. Are there discernible patterns of interaction or absence of interaction between members? Identify them. Have these changed over time? To what degree do members acknowledge or recognize these patterns of interaction?

F. What is the present quality of the relationship between the worker and group members?

G. Do members play particular roles in the group? If so, identify them. Have these changed over time?

H. Is there any pattern to how decisions are made in the group? How effective is the group's manner of decision making?

I. Is there evidence of mutual aid and/or conflict in the group?

J. What problems and issues does the worker see within the group as a whole? with individual members? To what extent has the group been successful in meeting the special needs of individuals?

K. To what extent has the group been successful in achieving its purpose?

*   *   *

The reader may wish to read more about the Group Work Log and the Group Analysis. These assignments, and two others, the Record of Service and the Approach to Practice, are discussed in: George Getzel, Roselle Kurland, and Robert Salmon (1987), "Teaching and Learning the Practice of Social Group Work: Four Curriculum Tools," found in Joseph Lassner, Kathleen Powell, and Elaine Finnegan (editors), *Social Group Work: Competence and Values in Practice* (Binghamton, NY: Haworth, pp. 35-50).

APPENDIX E
PROCESS RECORDING IN GROUP WORK

Process recording—a chronological recounting of what took place in a group session—is a valuable learning tool for students. It embraces development of the students' skills in work with groups, especially students' awareness and understanding of their roles, interventions, and trends in their practice.

In a process recording, the student sets down *as best as she or he can remember* exactly what occurred in a group session from beginning to end. Both verbal and non-verbal behavior need to be described systematically and as fully as possible. The quality of participation and interaction among group members should be reflected, as should *lack* of participation. In process recording, 100% accuracy is impossible and is not really the aim. Rather, one strives to describe what took place in a group meeting as fully and as best as one can recollect.

Writing process records is time consuming and not easy, especially at first. The more one does it, however, the better (and quicker!) one becomes at it. These efforts benefit students in three ways. First, process recording is an important tool for use in supervision, making it possible for student and supervisor together to look at the student's interventions. Discussion of a student's interventions is an important foundation for the development of professional practice skill. Supervisory discussion of one's work is helped to come alive when process is used as a base.

Second, writing process records increases a student's powers of observation in a group. As the student continues to write process records, she or he becomes increasingly adept at "seeing" what is taking place in the group, noting the complex processes of interaction and behavior in group sessions.

Third, the activity of writing process records sparks many "a-ha" moments for students—experiences of increased clarity and awareness of things that occurred in group and/or patterns and meanings of behavior that were not picked up as they happened.

Many different formats for process recording are possible. Identifying information (e.g., the date of the meeting, members present, members absent, new members, group name/type, number of the group session, length of session) can be included at the start. Pre-meeting contacts with individuals or subgroups can be recorded as well as collateral contacts with significant individuals from other systems (e.g., family, agency, community, etc.) where relevant.

Student thoughts and reactions should be kept separate from the description of what took place in the group. This can be done by using a two-column approach, with a chronological account of events falling in one column and student reactions/thoughts in the other. This format also gives the field instructor a chance to comment on the student's work and observations. An alternative method is to set the student's reactions/thoughts apart, using parentheses throughout the text.

Finally, it is a good idea to include a final paragraph of after-meeting interpretations and reactions, spelling out possible areas for follow-up before the next meeting and for pursuit during the next meeting.

APPENDIX F
A MODEL OF PLANNING FOR SOCIAL WORK WITH GROUPS

Planning for social work with groups—i.e., the thinking and preparation done by the social worker prior to the first group meeting—is an important and often neglected area of practice. Thorough and thoughtful pre-group planning is essential to the success of social work with groups.

The following model of planning for social work with groups is meant to direct and guide the social work practitioner planning to serve clients in a group. The model contains eight components of planning that a worker needs to consider: Social Context, Agency Context, Need, Purpose, Composition, Structure, Content, and Pre-Group Contact. The definition of each component and the factors to be considered under it are given, and interrelationships among the components are presented, one for groups in which membership is not predetermined, the other for groups in which membership is predetermined. In using the model, the worker needs to keep in mind four key points.

First, a worker needs to think concurrently about the eight components while planning proceeds. The eight components of the model are interdependent and overlapping, so decisions made in regard to one component will affect decisions about the others.

Second, the model is meant to guide the worker's thinking throughout the planning stage. It presents areas for worker consideration, decision, and action, but it is not meant as a checklist. In fact, it is unlikely that the worker will ever be able to resolve completely the many issues that each component of the model raises.

Third, the model does not attempt to present material to justify one decision over another. Rather, it will help the worker see areas for planning in which there is uncertainty. If, for instance, use of the model highlights the fact that group size is a key factor in planning for a group, the worker could then seek relevant literature addressing that particular factor or area.

Fourth, the model needs to be used with flexibility. In different groups, different factors in the model will assume different degrees of priority and importance. Not every factor will be of equal importance. Such differences are determined by the situation confronting the worker and by the worker's own theoretical approach to practice. The worker's own judgment and practice approach mean that use of the model needs to be individualized.

Social Context

Social Context refers to influences from the larger social and political environment that affect the delivery of services to clients. Areas to consider include:

* Political environment and its impact on clients and attitudes toward service;
* Laws, regulations, and policies that have an impact upon the nature of service;
* Cultural attitudes toward group participation;
* Geographic, institutional, or organizational community in which the agency exists;
* Profession's responses to the changing needs of clients and its evolving techniques.

Agency Context

Agency Context refers to the conditions existing in the agency or host setting that may have an impact on worker actions and on the group that is being formed.

* Purpose of agency/host setting;
* Agency's/host setting's philosophy and attitudes toward work with groups;
* History of agency's/host setting's experiences in work with groups;
* General needs, problems, or conditions of target population as perceived by agency/host setting;
* Specific needs, problems, or conditions of potential group members as perceived by agency/host setting;
* Tentative conception of group purpose as perceived by agency/host setting;
* Arrangements and preparation for intra-agency coordination and collaboration (both horizontal and vertical);
* Resources that agency/host setting will commit to the group (e.g., staff, time, funds, space, program aids);
* Relationship of agency/host setting to community.

Figure 1. Two Pre-Group Planning Models.

Pre-Group Planning Model
(for use when group composition *is not* predetermined)

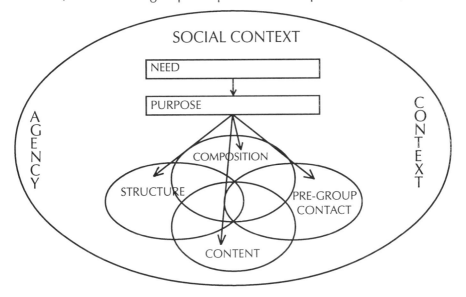

Pre-Group Planning Model
(for use when group composition *is* predetermined)

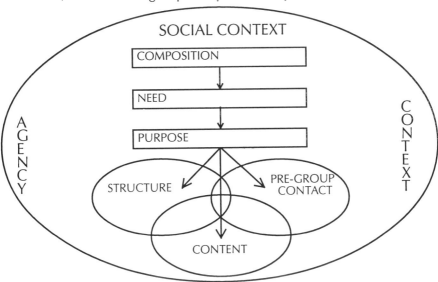

Need

Need refers to individual and social wants, drives, problems, issues, and/or areas of concern that can be expected to exist universally for people in the target population as they function socially and, more specifically, that exist among persons in the particular target population the worker has in mind as potential members of the group she or he is planning.

- General needs, problems, or conditions as perceived by clients/potential members, workers, other relevant persons;
- Specific needs as perceived by potential members, workers, other relevant persons;
- Social and cultural factors (values, economic conditions, attitudes) in the environment of potential group members;
- Developmental needs of potential group members;
- Ability to meet needs, problems, or conditions through the group modality;
- Commonalities and differences regarding the perception of need by members, workers, agency/host setting, and other relevant persons.

Purpose

Purpose refers to the ends toward which the group is formed. It encompasses both the ends and the objectives that the group will pursue collectively (the group purpose) and the hopes, expectations, and objectives that each member holds for the group (individual goals).

- Goals, aims, objectives of potential group members as perceived by themselves and by workers;
- Goals, aims, objectives of workers as perceived by themselves and by potential group members;
- Tentative conception of group purpose as perceived by potential members and by workers;
- Function of the group as perceived by workers (e.g., counseling, development, activity, social action);
- Commonalities and differences regarding the perception of purpose and goals by members, workers, and agency/host setting;

- Evaluation method by which ongoing feedback from members will be encouraged and achievement of purpose will be appraised.

Composition

Composition refers to the number and characteristics of both members and workers who will participate in the group.

- Number of group members;
- Open or closed group—if open, process by which new members will be added;
- Number of workers and their characteristics (e.g., sex, ethnicity, theoretical approach to work with groups, level of skill, personal style, values, and beliefs);
- Descriptive characteristics of members—degree of homogeneity/heterogeneity regarding age, grade in school, sex, racial/ethnic background, language, educational background, occupational background, religious background, cultural background, socioeconomic level, or previous group experience;
- Behavioral characteristics of members—degree of homogeneity/heterogeneity regarding interactional style, stage of psychosocial development, needs, interests, capacity to use the group experience, capacity to relate to and communicate with others, or motivation and capacity to achieve the purpose of the group and their own goals and objectives;
- Significant commonalities and differences among members in regard to descriptive and behavioral characteristics.

Structure

Structure refers to the concrete arrangements that workers make to facilitate the conduct of the group.

- Temporal arrangements—duration of each meeting, duration of the total work, frequency of meetings, time of meetings;
- Physical arrangements—meeting place, size of meeting room, physical arrangements in the meeting room, how members will get to meetings;
- Nature of fees;

- Arrangements regarding confidentiality;
- Arrangements regarding interagency coordination and collaboration.

Content

Content refers to the means that will be used to achieve the group's purpose. It encompasses what is done in the group, how it is done, and why it is done.

- Tentative conception of content of group meetings (e.g., use of discussion, didactic material, other program media);
- Ability of content to facilitate interaction among group members;
- Method of planning group content;
- Supplies and/or equipment needed;
- Content of and preparation for the first group meeting.

Pre-Group Contact

Pre-Group Contact refers to the securing of appropriate members for the group being planned and to their preparation for participation in the group.

- Recruitment of and outreach to potential group members;
- Intake;
- Screening (determination of the client's suitability for the group);
- Assessment/diagnosis of members' strengths, problems, concerns, common life situations;
- Orientation to the group and preparation of the members for the first group meeting;
- Person who will prepare the members for the first group meeting;
- Person who will make pre-group contact;
- Timing of pre-group contact in relation to first group meeting;
- Place of pre-group contact;
- Contact with referral sources, relevant others.

APPENDIX G: STAGES OF GROUP DEVELOPMENT—BEGINNING

Where the Members Are	What Needs to Happen	Role of the Worker
Anxious about the unknown	Orientation:	• Help effect what needs to happen.
Trustful *vs.* distrustful	• worker to group	• Respond when members look to worker for direction, structure, approval, and help.
Approach *vs.* avoidance	• members to situation	
Approach:	• members to worker	• Be more active—group members are more dependent on worker at this point.
• want relationship with worker and other members	• members to other members	
• want to accomplish purpose	• members to plans for group	• Help each member enter the group, allay anxiety, help members communicate and explore, yet keep some distance.
• want to reveal themselves	• members to time, place, frequency, content of meetings	
• desire closeness	A group must form, and ways the group will work become established:	
• want acceptance	• norms	• Acknowledge everyone's anxious feelings, express confidence in group's potential to accomplish purpose.
Avoidance:	• values	
• fear of the unknown	• patterns of communication	
• fear of not being accepted	Purpose of group needs to be made explicit—discussed, agreed upon, accepted. Even if purpose was discussed with each member individually, this needs to be done with everyone so it becomes a reference point (important later on).	• Help members examine and discuss purpose, reach agreement.
• fear of not succeeding		
• fear of being hurt		• Make connections among the members, help them see what they have in common.
• fear of being vulnerable		
• fear of getting involved		
• fear of no confidentiality		
Wary	Commonalities need to be established and recognized as a basis for cohesiveness.	• Help establish group norms—achieved largely through what the worker does, verbally and non-verbally.
Exploring		
Noncommittal		
Giving themselves a chance to draw back		
Keeping their distance		

APPENDIX H

THE PROBLEM-SOLVING PROCESS OF JOHN DEWEY

Step 1: There occurs "an indeterminate situation," a situation in which there is some rupture, great or small, to the smooth on-flowing of life's affairs.

Step 2: There then occurs a refinement of the difficulty into a more particular problematic form; steps are taken by the individual (group) to diagnose the situation, to see more precisely what the problem is.

Step 3: The individual (group) sets out in search of every conceivable potential solution to the problem; the imagination is permitted to run free; any guess, any hunch, any intuition is admissible.

Step 4: Project these possible solutions in the mind so as to consider the consequences each would be likely to lead to. We think through what would happen if we adopted one or another plan of action.

Step 5: Testing. In actual experience or in imagination, do the conjectured consequences actually occur? Test out each solution individually, act on each proposal *as if* it were the answer. Act out the solutions so as to experience the consequences to which they lead. Then evaluate and judge, reach a "conclusion."

Appendix I: Stages of Group Development–Middle

Where the Members Are	What Needs to Happen	Role of the Worker
At beginning of middle stage, members are still: <ul><li>exploring and testing the situation;</li><li>seeing where they fit;</li><li>sizing up each other;</li><li>struggling for power;</li><li>competing for leadership;</li><li>finding their roles;</li><li>determining their status.</li></ul> By the end of middle stage, they: <ul><li>have found their place in the group;</li><li>have found others they like (subgroups may form);</li><li>feel more accepted and understood;</li><li>better accept and understand other members;</li><li>see themselves and other members as distinct individuals;</li><li>recognize similarities and differences and see them as useful</li><li>acknowledge each other's uniqueness;</li><li>see their own contribution;</li><li>feel some affection for and desire to share with other members.</li></ul> Members: <ul><li>seek to understand perceptions of the group that the worker and other members have;</li></ul>	Group culture, style, way of doing things, and norms of behavior need to develop, be recognized, understood, and accepted. Same for norms that define the way conflict and differences are expressed, managed, and resolved. Norms that encourage experimentation, flexibility, and responsibility for supporting and stimulating each other need to be fostered. Patterns of social interaction and communication need to develop. Structure of interpersonal relationships emerges, determining status, ranking, leadership, and roles. A realistic group purpose needs to be reclarified and redefined. Members' own needs and goals must be understood in relation to that purpose and to the needs of other members. Harmony needed between member and worker perceptions of group.	<ul><li>Help effect what needs to happen.</li><li>Support the patterns, play an increasingly less central role, maximize group leadership and functioning.</li><li>Evaluate what is going on: - where the group is at; - how it is moving; - what are the stresses and strains.</li><li>Assess each member: attitudes, relationships, behavior, motivation, goals, how person fares in group.</li><li>Help group reclarify goals and purpose, encourage members' questioning, engage members in decisions and discussion process.</li><li>Continue encouraging development of positive group norms.</li><li>Recognize the commonalities: - among members' goals; - ways of goal accommodation; - interrelated member concerns.</li><li>Recognize the differences: among members, between worker and members.</li><li>Help members get to know each other, see how they can help each other; help identify common interests, concerns, and feelings.</li></ul>

- begin to understand the meaning of the group for them;
- begin to clarify their own goals;
- see that their goals can be met within the group.

Members test the worker: whether worker cares about and accepts them, how worker will use authority, whether worker will protect them. Members begin to understand and accept worker's role, become less dependent on worker, develop more reliance on each other, begin to see worker as unique person.

As they become more self-assured and comfortable, members:
- begin to express themselves more share more of themselves—their experiences, feelings, opinions.
- are willing to risk exposure of themselves and their ideas more.

Discussion becomes less scattered, more focused. Members can do more sustained work on problems and help each other more. As they experience success, members are more willing to bring in problems, to look at themselves. They begin to attach prestige to members' efforts to express themselves and work on problems. Members recognize more similarities/differences. As the group becomes more important to their lives, members view group experience as unique.

Members need to test the worker and other members and come to trust that they can express their feelings and bring problems into the group without being rejected or punished.

Members need to come to respect the similarities and differences among themselves.

Stabilization of membership needs to occur. People need to get involved, committed to the group, its purpose, other members, the worker.

Cohesiveness needs to develop.

The group needs to be seen as a place where members can really work on problems—exchange, argue, confront, try out, really share.

- Allow members to test worker and group rules, but maintain limits; do not let people hurt (demolish) each other.
- Promote flexibility in roles so members can try out and modify ways of contributing to the group and relating to others. Worker may need to confront members directly if they tend to stereotype others.
- Work to improve group communication. Point out when people aren't hearing or listening to each other, or that it is OK to get angry. Encourage members to support or question the comments and behavior of others and to bring things to the group.
- Step in and regulate conflict if it gets too threatening. (Conflict and disagreement are expected now.)
- Confront members about irrational thinking, unacceptable behavior.
- Work with members individually, as needed—to encourage them to express themselves in the group, to increase their understanding of something that happened in the group, or, after much conflict, to help member understand the tendency to want to drop out (run away, avoid a difficult situation).

Appendix J: Stages of Group Development—Ending

Where the Members Are	What Needs to Happen	Role of the Worker
Members talk more about successful efforts to try new things or change their patterns of behavior outside the group. Communication is free and easy.	Ending needs to be discussed.	• Help effect what needs to happen.
	Gains that have been made need to be stabilized.	• Prepare members for termination.
Members begin to move apart—find satisfaction in relationships outside the group (may break ties with members, causing group cohesiveness to weaken) and / or new activities.	Members need to be helped to leave the relationship with the worker, with each other, with the group.	• Assess desirability and readiness for termination. Can members continue to improve outside the group?
		• Assess progress toward achievement of goals.
Members talk about changes that have taken place in themselves and in the group. They review experiences, reminisce, evaluate, show desire to repeat earlier experiences (to show they can do better now).	This group experience, if it made a significant impact on the members, needs to become a frame of reference for the members in approaching new groups and other situations.	• Help members stabilize their gains.
		• Inform members of reality of termination (need for ending discussed well in advance).
	Service to the group needs to be discontinued.	• Anticipate responses of individuals to ending. Set goals for period of time that remains before the end.
Most members view termination with ambivalence and anxiety—an acknowledgment of improvement, while still they fear losing support of worker and group.		• Plan timing and content to maximize remaining sessions.
		• Help members express their ambivalence about ending.
Group experience may have been so good and so gratifying that people may want to continue.		• Help evaluation of the group experience.
		• Support members who have not made as much progress as hoped, or as other members have made.

Many reactions possible:

- Denial—of termination and of the possible meaning of the group experience.
- Regression—return to earlier patterns of behavior, inability to cope with relationships and tasks previously mastered; behave as in earlier stages; negative symptoms may recur as if to show, "We're not better; we still need the group and the worker."
- Flight—miss meetings, quit before the official end; show hostility toward worker and other members (e.g., "I'll leave you before you leave me").
- Constructive flight—move to new groups, other relationships, etc.

- Share observations of progress and confidence in members' abilities to get along without worker and group.
- Support members' efforts to move away from group, to develop new relationships outside the group, to find other resources.
- Indicate nature of any continuing relationship with group or with individuals. Be available for help on an individual basis as needed.
- Communicate with others (staff, family members) who may need to be involved.
- Help members tie their group experience more directly to subsequent life experiences.
- Be aware of own feelings of ambivalence about ending. Worker may be pleased about progress but feel a sense of loss and regret not having been more helpful to more members. Worker may have tendency to try to get everything in at the last minute.

NOTES

NOTES

NOTES

NOTES

NOTES

NOTES